CAMBRIDGE LIBRARY COLLECTION

Books of enduring scholarly value

History

The books reissued in this series include accounts of historical events and movements by eye-witnesses and contemporaries, as well as landmark studies that assembled significant source materials or developed new historiographical methods. The series includes work in social, political and military history on a wide range of periods and regions, giving modern scholars ready access to influential publications of the past.

The English Navy in the Revolution of 1688

First published in 1928, this was one of the first in-depth studies to investigate why the English navy was unable to prevent William of Orange's invasion in 1688. Edward B. Powley argues that a combination of bad strategic choices as well as adverse weather, William's so-called 'Protestant wind', resulted in the Navy failing to stop the Dutch Fleet landing, and ultimately enabled William to take possession of the country and crown. In a detailed chronological narrative of naval events between the spring of 1687 and February 1689, Powley charts the key decisions as documented in the archival record, focusing particularly on the Admiral of the Fleet, Lord Dartmouth's surviving papers and what they reveal about the input of King James II to naval affairs.

T0371077

Cambridge University Press has long been a pioneer in the reissuing of out-of-print titles from its own backlist, producing digital reprints of books that are still sought after by scholars and students but could not be reprinted economically using traditional technology. The Cambridge Library Collection extends this activity to a wider range of books which are still of importance to researchers and professionals, either for the source material they contain, or as landmarks in the history of their academic discipline.

Drawing from the world-renowned collections in the Cambridge University Library, and guided by the advice of experts in each subject area, Cambridge University Press is using state-of-the-art scanning machines in its own Printing House to capture the content of each book selected for inclusion. The files are processed to give a consistently clear, crisp image, and the books finished to the high quality standard for which the Press is recognised around the world. The latest print-on-demand technology ensures that the books will remain available indefinitely, and that orders for single or multiple copies can quickly be supplied.

The Cambridge Library Collection will bring back to life books of enduring scholarly value (including out-of-copyright works originally issued by other publishers) across a wide range of disciplines in the humanities and social sciences and in science and technology.

The English Navy in the Revolution of 1688

EDWARD BARZILLAI POWLEY

CAMBRIDGE
UNIVERSITY PRESS

CAMBRIDGE UNIVERSITY PRESS

Cambridge, New York, Melbourne, Madrid, Cape Town, Singapore,
São Paolo, Delhi, Dubai, Tokyo

Published in the United States of America by Cambridge University Press, New York

www.cambridge.org
Information on this title: www.cambridge.org/9781108013390

This edition first published 1928
This digitally printed version 2010

ISBN 978-1-108-01339-0 Paperback

THE ENGLISH NAVY
IN THE REVOLUTION
OF 1688

Cambridge University Press
Fetter Lane, London
▼
New York
Bombay, Calcutta, Madras
Toronto
Macmillan
▼
Tokyo
Maruzen-Kabushiki-Kaisha

THE ENGLISH NAVY IN THE REVOLUTION OF 1688

By

EDWARD B. POWLEY

Of Balliol College, Oxford, and King's College, London;
Assistant Master, Merchant Taylors' School, Great Crosby;
Temporarily R.N.

FOREWORD BY

Admiral of the Fleet

THE EARL JELLICOE

G.C.B., O.M., G.C.V.O., Hon. D.C.L. Oxford,
Hon. L.L.D. Cambridge

CAMBRIDGE
AT THE UNIVERSITY PRESS
MCMXXVIII

To
THE MEMORY
of
W · H · & H · LEE W ·
THIS RESEARCH IS
DEDICATED

PREFACE

THE part played by the Royal Navy in the Revolution of 1688 was obviously important; but no proper investigation of the subject has been made by students of Naval History. It is hoped that this full presentation of the facts and the findings here reached will be of value. Wrong notions of the preparations of James II and the Secretary Pepys should not prevail; the recognition of the professional merits of Admiral Lord Dartmouth is overdue; historians and their readers must grow accustomed to think of the *invasion* of William of Orange as a colossal gamble—for such it was. Incidentally it may be remarked that some of the circumstances of the surrender of the English fleet to William are quite picturesque; and certain of the details of the frustration of James's attempt to spirit the baby Prince of Wales out of Portsmouth into France are amusing. A curious unsolved problem emerges in connection with James's own flight in France.

An exhaustive search of the English authorities has been made. Most of the materials on the Dutch side perished, some years since, by fire at the Hague. Happily the historian de Jonge had already studied them; and his work has availed, with other accessible data, to check and supplement, as far as necessary, the story revealed by the English sources. James II received information from, but refused the assistance of, Louis XIV, during the crisis. It is believed that the essential facts of the correspondence between the French and English courts have been gathered from D'Avaux, Mazure and Ranke into this narrative.

I wish to express my thanks to Sir Charles H. Firth for the help he so readily tendered to me as a student. In Mr G. N. Clark, Fellow of Oriel College, I found, such is his expert knowledge of Dutch history, an invaluable adviser; and his concern for the completion of my work I recall with gratitude. Mr L. G. Carr Laughton, of the Admiralty Library, to whom I have long owed a debt of inspiration, has read my manuscript with critical care. The Index is the work of a reader at the University Press, and I tender acknowledgement to him. Lastly, I count myself happy that the Earl Jellicoe, greatest of living admirals, commends, by his Foreword, this research to the historian and general reader. For that compliment and kindness I accord him my sincere thanks.

EDWARD B. POWLEY

AUTHORS' CLUB
January 1928

CONTENTS

FOREWORD

IN this interesting volume the author presents us with a clear narrative of the proceedings of the English Fleet just prior to, and during the Revolution of 1688. He investigates closely the reasons for the failure of the Fleet to prevent the successful landing of the Prince of Orange and indicates the extent to which that failure was due to the choice of the original base anchorage selected for the Fleet off the Gunfleet Buoy as well as to what can only be termed most unfortunate weather conditions. Incidentally the reader will learn the extent to which the proposals for Fleet movements were submitted by the Admiral, Lord Dartmouth, to the King or were directed by his Majesty. As a result of this work a critical gap in our Naval History is filled in and the most interesting part of the career of that too long neglected sailor, Lord Dartmouth, is effectively brought to light. Both for his place in the evolution of naval strategy and for his conduct as an English gentleman, placed by circumstances over which he had no control in an impossible position, Lord Dartmouth is shown to deserve the closest study.

The preparation of this volume has involved much research. And Mr Powley will certainly earn the gratitude of all his readers for the thoroughness with which he has fulfilled his task.

JELLICOE
Admiral of the Fleet

CHAPTER I

The Failure of Diplomacy
Spring 1687 to October 2nd, 1688 [1]

IT is well known that, at the close of the spring of 1687, the Dutch emissary, Everard Van Dyckvelt, having completed a brief, special mission[2] from the court of William, Prince of Orange, Stadholder of the United Provinces, to the court of James II, the father of William's consort Mary, heiress-presumptive to the English throne, returned to his master at the Hague; and the high significance attaching to the return of the ambassador from a mission which, from a purely diplomatic point of view, had been quite unnecessarily undertaken, and which has rightly been called an embassy "not to the government but to the opposition",[3] has always been plain to students of Anglo-Dutch diplomacy of the months just preceding the Revolution of 1688. Indeed Mazure, the French historian of our Revolution, has declared with force and simplicity: "Le retour de Dyckvelt décida la fortune de Jacques II en fixant les résolutions du prince d'Orange".[4] Broadly, the statement is true. It was immediately after this embassy that the opposed policies of London and the Hague hardened into an irreconcileable opposition. The conclusion of the embassy is therefore

---

[1] So far as this opening chapter is a matter of general and diplomatic history, it is based on the narratives of Burnet, Kennet, Echard, Rapin-Thoyras, Ralph, Oldmixon, Dalrymple, Mackintosh, Macaulay, Lingard, Ranke, Mazure, etc., supplemented, here and there, from the *Dictionary of National Biography*. But the general impression these authorities yield has been tested closely against certain accessible original materials—notably those printed in the Appendix of Dalrymple, the *Memoirs of James II* (for the worth of which see Ranke's valuable appendix) and *The Negotiations of the Count d'Avaux*. In turn, part of Dalrymple's Appendix has been tested against the (uncalendared) State Papers Domestic (King William's Chest) in the Public Record Office.

[2] He had not displaced Van Citters, the permanent Dutch representative in London, who filled a non-spectacular, but none the less useful, rôle at this time.

[3] Macaulay, II, p. 245.   [4] Mazure, II, p. 256.

that appropriate place at which, for the purpose of such a work
as the present, to attempt to capture the aims and to gauge the
character of the baffled diplomacy which, in so short a space,
was to provide for Europe the spectacle of a prince intervening
by force in the domestic concerns of his father-in-law, prose-
cuting a design quite indistinguishable from an overt act of war.

An observer, far less capable than the Prince's shrewd emissary Dyckvelt, could not, in the England of early 1687, have
failed to observe the effect of the King's domestic policy which
had openly set itself the task of nullifying, by use of the royal
prerogative, the action of the "Tests"; and Dyckvelt, who
seems to have added to native shrewdness the gift of inspiring
the confidence of others, had used the advantages of a privileged position to estimate the strength of the growing opposition
to the King's policy, had employed his opportunities to gather
from representative leaders their views of the developing
situation, nay, had gone further and encouraged, as far as, and
perhaps a little further than, diplomatic discretion allowed,
those things in the conduct of the English opposition of which
he knew his master approved. The visible evidence of the confidence he had inspired lay in certain letters he had taken with
him to Holland, compromising communications from the
leaders of those who had begun already to look to William and
Mary in the hope of a deliverance to come. For example, in
one such letter to the Prince, the Tory Nottingham declared,
as he spoke of the factors of discontent, "he" (Dyckvelt) "has
so fully informed himself of them that he can give you a very
exact account of them: and of one thing especially he may
assure you, and that is the universal concurrence of all Protestants in paying the utmost respect and duty to your Highness
for you are the person on whom they found their hopes, as
having already seen you a refuge to the miserable and a most
eminent defender of their religion". Likewise, Danby expressed, in a similar missive, the opinion that, could a personal
conference be arranged, "some overtures might be made which
would be of some use" to the Prince's service.[1] Dyckvelt had
also, of course, borne with him a letter from King James. To

---

[1] Dalrymple, App. pp. 183, 194, May 28 and 30 respectively.

his son-in-law James wrote: "I have spoken to him"—Dyck-velt, that is—"of your private concerns of which he will give you an account as also of the public affairs here, and have spoken very (*sic*) to him of them, and told him (what I think) I have reason to expect from you for the good of the monarchy as well as our family".[1] Plainly the envoy's gathered impressions, the confidences he bore, his official unfolding of the royal will and sentiment of James called for the serious attention which they at once received.

Now no one will deny that the husband of the heiress-in-tail and the heiress herself-in-tail to a great estate may very properly watch with concern the administration of that property. To discredit the genuine sympathy of William and Mary at this time with the cause of English Protestantism and a very necessary, if less genuine, respect for her liberty would be unwarrantable; on the other hand, to believe that the concern of William was merely for a right settlement of the affairs of a country which, one day, he might be called upon through, or with, Mary to govern, is, in the light of the known international relations of the United Provinces, of which he was Stadholder, entirely impossible. He was seeking constantly to checkmate the French king. England by immediate alliance could have helped exceedingly his project; and, in any case, James's benevolence was necessary to the success of his design. Contrasted with that design nothing else mattered. England was important in her relation to his life scheme.

The Prince weighed his information. He answered James. He thanked His Majesty for his goodness in wishing to take care of his particular interest; but, while he disclaimed sympathy with persecution, he could not concur in what His Majesty asked of him in respect of the Tests. His letter (June 17/7)[2] really marks a crisis in the relation of the courts. Thereupon James complained to William of Dyckvelt's conduct during the embassy.[3] Such an answer concerning the Tests implies that the return of Dyckvelt had convinced William that no alliance

---

[1] Dalrymple, App. p. 192, May 18.   [2] *Ibid.* p. 184.
[3] *Ibid.* p. 185, June 16. For parallel evidence see d'Avaux, IV, p. 118 (June 12).

could be obtained from an England ruled by King James, though it had left him undisturbed in a sense of his admitted family interest in English affairs. But the crucial importance of Dyckvelt's work was not reflected in the royal letter. William had been shown that religious sympathy and political foresight alike demanded that he should guardedly countenance the English opposition; above all, it familiarised him with the suggestion that armed 'intervention might place the resources of England under his sway.[1]

But, almost certainly, no proposal of alliance could with success have been made, even had William answered otherwise about the Tests. Neutrality in the impending struggle suggested no dangers to James. The work which would fall on the redoubtable French armies would be great—great in proportion to the ambition of Louis's designs; as for the French navy, however fine or new its ships might be, James probably shared of it the unflattering opinion which his sailors had formed in the Third Dutch War; the Dutch might reasonably be expected to check any dangerous bid for power at sea should the French King care to make it. An ill wind to the Provinces might blow England good. Thrice in three decades the English nation had striven to destroy the ocean-borne trade of Holland (till Protestantism had stopped him, James had played a sailor's part); and, if a policy of neutrality would allow English merchants to profit by the harassing of Dutch trade, then, James may well have considered, so much the better for the national interests. If thus he argued—and his past career is the justification for the hypothesis—then, judging from some of the difficulties which faced his successor in 1701, he may be credited with correctly interpreting the national sentiment as far as it could be cleared of religious feeling and, equally, freed of the fear of tyranny. Admittedly James did not hold that estimate steadily before his eyes and, in not doing so, allowed Louis XIV to act on the congenial assumption that "good correspondence"—to use the current diplomatic term—with James could be cultivated

---

[1] Burnet credits Charles Mordaunt (third Earl of Peterborough) with making the proposal in 1686, and says that the Prince thought it "too romantic ...to build upon it" (p. 762).

through an obviously interested patronage. A Catholicism which would not listen to the voice of Rome, an inherent love of authority, both seeking with an uncertain touch means to their ends, sufficiently account for the wavering attitude of James which later events declare.[1]

That summer (1687) James returned to his self-appointed religious task.[2] All that he forthwith did reacted to create a breach between his court and that of the Hague, and a great body of his people endured his paraded religion and concomitant arbitrary rule only because they turned towards Mary and her husband with an orientation which made a bond between a people and a court, though scarcely between a people and a people.

In November the pique which the attitude of his subjects had inspired in James must have deepened into resentment at the broadcast circulation of Pensionary Fagel's letter; for the letter revealed the Prince and Princess interfering, however deferentially, in the domestic affairs of England and publicly encouraging the passive recalcitrancy of James's people. One may speculate as to the probability that William knew at or about that time, anything of a plan to tamper with the birthright of Mary by annulling the Irish Act of Settlement,[3] or wonder whether he was aware of the offer of Louis to provide James with troops "pour opprimer ses ennemis et se faire obéir de ses sujets"[4] or of the concluded arrangement that Louis should pay

---

[1] For James's attitude see: *Memoirs of James II*, II, pp. 177 *et seq.*; also Mackintosh, pp. 373 *et seq.* and Seeley, *Growth of British Policy*, II. Mackintosh quotes a remark by James to Van Citters: "Vassal! Vassal de France! ...Sir, if Parliament enabled me, I would bring this Kingdom to a height of consideration, abroad and at home, never reached under any of my predecessors" (Van Citters, Aug. 27, 1686); Seeley relies much upon the *Memoirs*. Of the relations of James and Louis at an early stage, he writes (p. 285), "meanwhile there was no conspiracy but only a kind of general agreement, the habitual sympathy of relatives".

[2] D'Avaux alleges that, in "a letter written the second of February from London by a Jesuit of Liège which happened to be intercepted", the Jesuit makes the King say "if he had known he had been a priest he would sooner have drawn back than suffered him to kiss his hand upon his knees: that he afterwards told him he was resolved to convert England or die a martyr... he looked upon himself as a true son of the Society". D'Avaux, IV, p. 122.

[3] Dalrymple, App. p. 262; Barillon to Louis, Oct. 16, 1687.

[4] *Ibid.* p. 263; Barillon to Louis, Nov. 10, 1687.

for the upkeep of some, at least, of the six English regiments then in Dutch pay, and which it was intended shortly to withdraw to England.[1] To decide that he knew of these matters would require a minute study of diplomatic materials and much shrewd guessing. In particular it would involve judgement upon Sunderland, whom the clever lampoon can scarcely be said to have libelled.

> That Proteus ever acting in disguise,
> That finished statesman intricately wise,
> A second Machiavel, who soared above
> The little ties of gratitude and love.[2]

Sunderland had certainly been of service to William on an earlier occasion.[3] Bevil Skelton, James's representative in Paris, suspected him. Barillon, Louis's ambassador in London, was at that moment bidden to observe him closely. But Barillon saw no cause to distrust him[4] and his purse continued to bulge with French gratifications.[5] Suspicion would indeed lead one to fling a wide net. Sunderland's "dearest partner in greatness" —the Lady Anne—and James's envoy at the Hague, Skelton's successor, the Marquess d'Albeville (to give the "intriguing, pushing Irishman named White" his somehow acquired Austrian title),[6] would hardly escape the toils.[7]

The first move for the recall of the regiments was taken by James in January 1687/8.[8] When the full demands were made, William certainly hindered the return of all save the officers; and the affair entered upon the stage of proclamation and protest from which James was to obtain little satisfaction.[9]

In tracing thus far onward from the spring of 1687 the course of Anglo-Dutch diplomacy, the rival sets of interests—those of

---

[1] Dalrymple, App. p. 263; Barillon to Louis, Dec. 8, 1687, and preceding letters.
[2] Quoted in D.N.B. article, "Spencer, Robert; second Earl of Sunderland", from "Faction Displayed", State Poems 1716, IV, p. 90.
[3] In 1680. See article cited, note 2.
[4] Dalrymple, App. p. 271; Barillon to Louis, Jan. 5, 1688.
[5] Ibid. p. 280; Barillon to Louis, July 26, 1688.
[6] Macaulay, II, 47. He was also an English baronet; ibid. pp. 242-3.
[7] See article cited, note 2.
[8] Dalrymple, App. p. 265; James to William, Jan. 17, 1688.
[9] London Gazette, Mar. 15-19, 1687/8; Ap. 5-9, 1688; Dalrymple, App. pp. 266 et seq.

William in respect to James, and of James in respect to William
—have been suggested and thrown somewhat into contrast.
Till January 1687/8 James's interests stood thus: A design to
secure William's support for his domestic policy—which was
the abolition of the Tests and the use, as far as he needed, of
arbitrary rule—because the policy was, in an intelligible sense,
a family affair and it was galling to James to reflect that his
policy would not survive him. It was remarked that the latent
hostility to Dutch trade was, for a time, suppressed. On the
other hand, William's interests may be summarised as: A concern of the husband of the heiress-in-tail in the administration
of a great estate; a desire to show conscientious sympathy with
the cause of English Protestantism and a wish in some way to
unite England and the Provinces of his Stadholdership against
France. It has been strongly suggested that diplomacy, having
reached an *impasse*, could hope to achieve nothing beyond the
avoidance of a collision between those rival aims; but it has not,
however, been suggested that the breaking-point had quite
been reached. Indeed, one great consideration from the Prince's
point of view (a consideration not so far stressed in this survey)
dictated calculated inaction; for fate had, after all, loaded the
dice in his favour. The accession of Mary was, in the fulness of
time, reasonably certain; and that event would both yield aid
to the English Protestants and give the desired pooling of Dutch
and English resources against Louis as its firstfruits. William
could afford to wait. Chance might indeed crown him without
his stir.

On a sudden, however, as the month of January wore on,
momentous gossipings flew abroad and it became impossible
to doubt the rumours that Mary of Modena was with child.[1]
Prospectively the interests of James were totally changed;
prospectively William's support for the kingly domestic policy
no longer remained a necessity; even the rivalry to Dutch trade
might be more or less suffered to revive. As against William,
James could expect in a little while to be so happily placed as to
have no interest which he need strive at all actively to compass.

[1] Dalrymple, App. p. 273; Barillon to Louis, Jan. 5, 1688; Mackintosh,
p. 202.

On the other hand, the interests of William remained, in part, unchanged, in part, in all human likelihood, drastically altered. The desire to help the cause of English Protestantism persisted; the legal concern of the husband in the wife's once certain fortune was, there could be little doubt, to be taken away. As for the wish for an Anglo-Dutch alliance, that, it seemed, must become a proven vanity and therein a great hope count mockingly for naught.

It is by no means difficult to imagine how, in the suddenly altered circumstances, it was very hard, even for the phlegmatic William, to accept this impending disappointment of Mary's hopes and of his hopes in Mary. The temptation to clutch at the view that Mary remained still a need to the Protestantism of England doubtless presented a strong appeal to a Prince who could see through diplomacy no chance of satisfying his good-will towards the Protestant party in England or to effect the alliance on which his anti-French design, his constantly nursed ambition, depended. What indeed was there left to him as an alternative to the surrender to brooding disappointment over a thwarted religious and family interest and a wrecked international aim? The single possible answer would stealthily re-suggest itself. If this English opposition, a leaven the strength of which Dyckvelt had laboured so carefully to ascertain, would go to the point of incipient rebellion, if there should be found to exist some downright evidence of sedition in that royal but none the less Protestant service, the navy of England, if (to William, the soldier, a possibly yet more appealing contingency) unequivocal assurances could be obtained that much gentry would pledge themselves to await only the display of his banner upon English soil to rise and to risk everything for their cause, such circum-stances would admittedly rank as by no means negligible arguments to urge towards the pursuit of the daring, if unattrac-tive course, the success of which would compass all that stood common to William's cause, as he still conceived it, and the Protestant constitutional desires of the English opposition. It is safe to conclude that it was at this time that the Prince, with a mind that can scarce have been attracted by so adventurous and plainly hazardous a notion as "intervention", finally habituated himself to the uncomfortable idea and forced himself to face the broad terms of the problem in warfare which would confront him, should he once settle upon the intervention design.

For several months the French Ambassador at the Hague, the Comte d'Avaux, had watched narrowly the signs of the Dutch naval activity. In the Prince's interference with the customs duties d'Avaux had suspected, as early as August 1687, unrevealed ends, and had reported "He has this affair very much at heart for it may facilitate some of his designs and especially the maintenance of good seamen".[1] A month later, the Frenchman had noted "The province of Holland was still employed in regulating the affairs relating to the farm of the duties of import and export, which have been levied with such rigour, after the liberty which the merchants had hitherto enjoyed of not paying them, that in the month of August, which is just elapsed, the receipt was augmented in Rotterdam six times more than usual and at Amsterdam ten times".[2] In November the ambassador had further declared that saltpetre and the best masts were unattainable in Dutch markets.[3] D'Avaux's early observations in the month of January 1687/8 to the effect that the receivers of customs were required to give their March estimates, that the income was allocated to Admiralty supply, that from the Colleges of Admiralty[4] had been requisitioned many 30–50 gunned ships (Maes-Rotterdam 4, Amsterdam 12, Zealand 2, Friesland 2, N. Holland 0), that William desired to avoid direct appeal to the Provinces, were of really important character.[5]

It is appropriate to observe that at the close of the year the Earl of Peterborough was put in command of a small Dutch squadron in the West Indies. "The object of this commission," says an authority, "has not been explained, though it has been suggested that it was 'to try the temper of the English colonies and their attachment to the reigning sovereign.' It is probable

---

[1] D'Avaux, IV, Aug. 7, 1687.   [2] Ibid. Sept. 25, 1687.
[3] Ibid. Nov. 6, 1687.
[4] Five separate Boards of Admiralty provided and equipped the warships of the Provinces; see p. 172.
[5] D'Avaux, IV, Jan. 1, 2, 1688.

that Mordaunt was instructed to sound Narbrough, who was in command of the English squadron, at that time engaged in an attempt to recover treasure from a Spanish wreck. The actual pretext was an intention 'to fish' for the treasure; but 'they were wholly unprovided to work the wreck', and after a few days, during which the two commanders met on friendly terms, Mordaunt's Dutch squadron took its departure and returned to Europe".[1] Peterborough remained with the Prince.

Now, had William, in the January of 1687/8, possessed adequate means for intervention—ready naval forces, transports and waiting soldiers—can it be said that he probably would have taken the daring course and tempted fortune? The question is useful as bringing to light an all-important consideration. William could not act as if his English interests alone counted. If a Franco-Dutch war, then already seen to be imminent, began at once by an attack of France upon the Provinces, the Stadholder would be fixed to Dutch soil and an English intervention scheme, which, in any case, a Dutchman might have stigmatised as a quixotic crusade, would become utterly unreasonable. But William had no sufficient forces available; and it is not likely that one so self-possessed, would, at that stage, have been stampeded into unreasoned precipitancy. The child was not yet born. Nor is it likely that the particular problem in warfare which the scheme of intervention had set before the Prince had been solved (if indeed it ever could be) to anything like his or his advisers' satisfaction. It was, however, only natural that henceforth William should anticipate the possible needs of an intervention policy. So he is found concentrating upon the task of preparing armaments and improving alliances which subserved the specific end. To ensure that any move by France should not quash the probable scheme, he went warily and kept up diplomatic appearances. The fact that Van Citters had apparently demanded 20 ships of England to help clear the Channel of Algerines is noted by d'Avaux for

---

[1] Laughton, *D.N.B.* article "Mordaunt, Charles, third Earl of Peterborough", using Charnock, *Biog. Nav.* III, p. 316, and Dartmouth MSS XI, 5, p. 136.

August 1687.[1] The 'scourge of Christendom' was real enough to make any determination by a maritime power such as the Provinces to take action against the corsairs a wholly accountable undertaking. A French historian states that, under article 20 of treatises repeated in the Treaty of 1687, England was bound to provide 20 ships for co-operation against the Algerines and that, when Van Citters asked James for his help, it is said that James railed at the idea of the puissant Provinces needing his assistance![2] Clearly, however, the Algerine project might serve to William as a useful pretext and blind.

Louis was, from the first, convinced that the armament was being prepared against James; and, from late February to the end of May, France was constantly urging James to join in support of Denmark in the quarrel with the duchy of Schleswig. Twenty-five ships were to be used for the purpose.[3] Such suspicion or knowledge of these negotiations as William may have gathered must have added to his annoyance; though it is fair to retort that James had cause to watch narrowly any measure of Dutch alliance with Sweden.[4] Whatever the extent of the Prince's intelligences (and he had one important visitor in the person of Russell[5]) he could not fail to learn of the bustle in the English dockyards which became noticeable in May and June;[6] and he could pretend to precautionary emulation if the excuse were needed. James was probably ill at ease as to his son-in-law's intentions in general. If he had no need to seek actively the satisfaction of any interest as against his son-in-law, he was not thereby necessarily rendered blind to the fact that William showed a somewhat unusual naval activity—"he knew there were those in Holland who gave themselves some hopes of seeing English Lords at the head of some of their squadrons; but he would take care to prevent it".[7] Words of

---

[1] D'Avaux, IV, p. 130.   [2] Mazure, II, p. 261.   [3] Dalrymple, App. p. 280.
[4] Sweden was a great supplier of naval stores to England.
[5] Edward Russell (1653–1727), Earl of Orford.
[6] Article "Naval Preparations of James II in 1688" by J. R. Tanner, *Eng. Hist. Review*, 1893. This article is based on "Admiralty Letters" in the Pepysian Library at Magdalene College, Cambridge. These appear to be Secretary's Letters which should have found their way into the Public Record Office (Adm. Letters, XIV, 142–167, 176–7, 180, 186).
[7] Dalrymple, App. p. 271.

that sort, reported as spoken to Lord Danby's son in March, are not without omen. None the less, James's letters to the Prince, all through the spring, showed, except in their concluding formula, no trace of acerbity.[1]

The understanding quietly arrived at in April between the Great Elector Frederick William of Brandenburg and the Prince was to prove especially useful to William—providing soldiery and placing at his service the leadership of the great Marshal Schomberg.

By this time the heavy duties were jeopardising Dutch trade.[2]

It is common knowledge that, in England, the month of May closed memorably. The Church of England, led by an archbishop and six bishops, revolted at the demand for the public reading of a second Indulgence. On June 10th the Queen was delivered of a man child; and the rest of the month was a crescendo of excitement leading up to the wild demonstrations which, upon the 30th, greeted the acquittal of the seven bishops whom James had proceeded against in the Court of King's Bench. On that day the celebrated invitation bearing the seven names was sent to William[3]—an invitation which he expected and the receipt of which, it seems clear, he had made a condition of intervention.

It is often said that the invitation was conveyed to Holland by Admiral Herbert disguised as a common sailor. The invitation itself contains the words "we have desired Mr H. to consult you about all such matters" (i.e. arms, ammunition, etc.) and it is known that Herbert reached Holland in July at a time when D'Avaux declared "the naval armament was ... pushed on with more vigour than ever".[4] Arthur

---

[1] Cp. Dalrymple, App. p. 290, Jan. 10, 1688: "I can say no more, than that you shall find me as kind as you can desire..."; and App. p. 290, Ap. 3: "you shall find me as kind as you can expect.... For my sonne the Prince of Orange".

[2] Of Portuguese ships D'Avaux declared that 15 only, in place of 60 of the previous year, called at ports in the Provinces (D'Avaux, IV, p. 166, Ap. 15). He depicted trade with France as at a standstill (p. 167, Ap. 29).

[3] Dalrymple, App. p. 228, June 30.

[4] D'Avaux, IV, p. 181, for quotation. For circumstances and date see same and following page of D'Avaux: "On that very day (last Friday) Vice-Admiral Herbert arrived from Holland. He had been expressly forbid by the King his master to leave the Kingdom; so that in order to facilitate his escape he

Herbert,[1] the son of Sir Edward Herbert, was 41 years of age. At 19 he had gone to sea and, like other sailors of a period of Dutch wars and Algerine piracy, had found opportunities for deserving service. In his case it was rather more than usually varied. In 1678 he joined Narbrough in the Straits and served as his vice-admiral, his advent on the station made noteworthy by a sharp brush with an Algerine, which surrendered as Rear-Admiral Strickland came up. In this fight Herbert was, for a second time, wounded, losing by accident an eye. Narbrough left the command in his hands in 1679; he fought and negotiated as occasion arose; and at Tangiers in 1683 gave hostages to the scandal-mongers by having a house ashore and keeping a harem.[2] When Dartmouth arrived to evacuate Tangiers in 1683, Herbert sailed for England. Favours were granted him. He became Rear-Admiral of England and Master of the Robes; and Colonel of a regiment of foot.[3] He sat in Parliament. March 1686/7 saw his downfall because, like others, he refused to facilitate the repeal of the Tests. He had lost £4000 a year and his Wardrobe accounts were being subjected to a close scrutiny, at the time when an invitation from William, conveyed to him by Russell, left him without words suitable to the sense of his Highness's goodness in the midst of his misfortunes.[4] It mattered little to William that this ill-favoured, acrid-tempered admiral who, no more than Churchill, could be expected to "live the life of a saint",[5] but who, like him, had some respect for the Protestant faith, should

disguised himself in the habit of a sailor. As soon as he came ashore he went to wait on the Prince..." (July 20). Also: "There had been a vessel continually passing between the shores. He came in it". Cp. Burnet, p. 761.

[1] *D.N.B.* article "Herbert, Arthur, Earl of Torrington".

[2] Probably true. One particular letter in B.M. MSS, Egerton 2621, a long way from creditable to its writer Russell or its receiver Herbert, would make credence easy. On this MS, under the title "Correspondence of Admiral Herbert during the Revolution" appeared an article in the *Eng. Hist. Review*, 1886, by E. M. Thompson.

[3] *Memoirs of James II*, II, p. 204. See also Dalton's *Army Lists*, II, Introduction, for comments on the army commissions of many of the chief naval officers mentioned in these pages.

[4] Dalrymple, App. p. 225; Herbert to Prince, May 24. There is extant a letter in which the Prince briefly expressed confidence in the Admiral (B.M. MSS, Egerton 2621, June 27).

[5] Dalrymple, App. p. 190; Churchill to Prince, May 17, 1687.

make Burnet "often reflect on the providence of God, that makes some men instruments in great things to which they themselves have no sort of affection or disposition".[1] It was more to the point that the King was "most extremely angry with him"[2] and that he was the darling of the British seamen. To the Prince, such a man was in himself a host, and the document he brought an earnest of success. Reading it, William felt that he could count at last on a widespread rising in which men of opposed political and religious camps, Tories no less than Whigs, Churchmen side by side with Nonconformists, would be found under the standard of revolt; that England had become a country whose inhabitants, though not divided into parties dwelling in geographical bounds, were yet, for the more part, his friends. Apart from the evidence of the working of disaffection in the English army, of which the paper spoke, he had clear knowledge of sedition in the navy of the King. Discounting for exaggeration of his prospects he could believe it credible that force used judiciously might carry the day. He hastened his designs; transports and soldiers, arms, provisions were needed in unobtrusive readiness and the scheme and details of operations had at length (however annoying the difficulties of the particular problem in warfare which the intervention scheme had propounded) to be squarely faced and boldly decided. Most difficult of all necessities, diplomatic appearances had to be maintained. For, should the scheme be plainly discovered, it might, as Sidney feared, go hard with the leaders of the English revolt;[3] the King of England, alarmed, would certainly mature defence and possibly aggression; and either course might, in practice, mean the making by James of common cause with the French King.

But William, who could rely upon the debonair assurance of Zulestein, sent a second time to England, and on the sure

---

[1] Burnet, p. 762. Cp. his attitude to Churchill. For other evidence of Burnet's attitude to Herbert see B.M. MSS, Egerton 2621.

[2] Dalrymple, App. p. 237; Russell to Prince, July 28.

[3] "It is most certain that if it be made public above a fortnight before it is put in execution all your particular friends will be clapped up, which will terrify others, or at least make them not know what to do, and will, in all probability ruin the whole design" (Dalrymple, App. p. 231, June 30).

appeal of Fagel's pen, was also, with a remarkable honesty and circumspection, served by the necessarily widening circle of those who knew his secret. Yet great difficulties stood in the way. How long the French-Dutch conflict would wait, William had no power to tell. As has been observed, if war broke out, the whole design would be impossible.

As early as June 7th,[1] Louis, who had been kept well informed by his ambassador, had transmitted a warning to James to watch narrowly the Dutch preparations and had offered to join 16 ships to the English fleet. Barillon, Louis's ambassador, reported on the 10th that James had accepted the offer and said Sunderland proposed the report be made public;[2] on the 14th he stated that James had changed his mind, not believing himself in any danger.[3] James, all other considerations apart, probably considered aid unnecessary. The close of May had seen the first moves for a concentration in the Downs.[4] On the 14th of June it was reported from Deal that: "Sir Roger Strickland Rear-Admiral of England rides present admiral in the Downs of a squadron of more than 20 nimble Friggots and Fireships well appointed and daily expected to be joined by others of yet greater force from the river of the Thames".[5] He wore his flag on the 'Mary'.[6] The order which James's Secretary of the Admiralty had drafted, in compliance with the Order in Council[7] that the birth of the Prince should be celebrated in the fleet, had reached the Downs before the 15th when, "particularly by the long and loud discharges of their guns",[8] the ships celebrated the event. (It may be noticed, *en passant*, that an important Order in Council of the 22nd instant regularised, in an elaborate schedule, the whole etiquette of salutes between English warships, conserving a great deal of

---

[1] Dalrymple, App. p. 282; Louis to Barillon.
[2] *Ibid.* p. 282; Barillon to Louis.   [3] *Ibid.*
[4] *London Gazette*, May 28–31, May 31–June 4.
[5] *Ibid.* June 14–18. The date of Strickland's commission is uncertain. There is a record of a court martial held by virtue of that commission on April 23rd on board the 'Bristol'. A fire on the 'Lark' resulted in the whipping of the carpenter's servant "for his negligence and terror to others" (Admiralty Papers in P.R.O.; Courts Martial, Ad. 1, 5253).
[6] Charnock, *Biog. Nav.* 1, p. 180.
[7] Admiralty Papers in P.R.O.; Orders in Council, Ad. 1, 5139.
[8] *London Gazette*, June 14–18.

good powder by establishing the principle of "no salutes of guns except in foreign ports"; thereafter at sea and in home ports, the sailors' noise-making propensity was to be satisfied by cheering.)[1] Strickland was instructed to await, in the Downs, further orders.[2]

Sir Roger,[3] who came of a Lancashire family, was 48 years of age and had followed the sea since he was 21. He had distinguished himself in the battle of Solebay, 1672, and his conduct in the great fights of 1673 had won him a well-deserved knighthood. He had first hoisted a rear-admiral's flag under Narbrough in the Mediterranean in 1677. Next year he was in company there with Vice-Admiral Herbert; but, not long after, returned to England and was more or less out of sea-employ till James ascended the throne. While ashore he had sat in Parliament and acted as a deputy governor of Southsea. He had commanded a squadron off Algiers in 1686; he was Vice-Admiral to Grafton in 1687. The dignities of Rear-Admiral of England and Admiral of the Blue were conferred in the October just past, and his appointment to this command was not unnatural. There can be little doubt he was a Catholic; but the extent to which his religion had told in his favour might easily be over-estimated.

Yet further directions reached the Admiral, bearing date June 18th, and providing that he should send "2 small nimble frigots to cruise 6 or 8 days about the back of the Goodwin Sand and 2 of the like sort about Orfordness: and as they returned to be sent back again or others in their room for to look out and endeavour to speak with all ships passing those ways, and give what intelligence they coud of the number, force, and motion of the ships of any foreign prince or state, and other occurences fit for his Majesties knowledge, which he was to communicate by the quickest conveyances, by the hands of the

---

[1] See note 7, p. 15.

[2] *Memoirs relating to the Lord Torrington*, edited by Sir J. K. Laughton for Camden Society, 1899. The original is a MS in the British Museum (Add. 31,958), author unknown. See a special Note at end of this work for criticism of the relation of this document to Josiah Burchett's *Transactions at Sea* 1688–1697.

[3] *D.B.N.* article "Strickland, Sir Roger"; Burnet, p. 755.

Secretary of the Admiralty"; for, adds our informant, "a fleet at this time fitting out in Holland had alarmed the Court, and so these scouts were sent over to observe the States' motions ".[1] New orders of July 2nd caused Strickland, after a council of war, to weigh anchor on the afternoon of the 5th, and stand northward, leaving two ships in the Downs and the frigates upon their appointed service. With some score ships he cruised to Solebay, then put in at the Nore. The King-Lord High Admiral was not lax of duty. He, "with the Prince of Denmark went down the river there, to view and consult with the flags and other officers, what was most advisable to be done to intercept the Prince of Orange, whose designs were now known, but not in what part of the kingdom he intended to land. The King went on board most of the ships in the fleet, not only to view their condition but likewise to ingratiate himself with the officers and seamen, behaving with great affability and taking notice of every perticular officer".[2] A further ten days' cruise off Suffolk followed. On the last day of the month Strickland was back in the Downs.[3]

Louis, in the meantime, had taken the refusal of James in good part, declaring, none the less, that he would keep his ships in readiness; their retention alone would, he thought, check the temerity of the Prince's undertaking.[4] He had no cause to change his notions of the impending danger; for, hereabouts, he was informed by d'Avaux: "The Pensionary Fagel having found that there was a sufficient fund in the offices of the Admiralty for the pay of the seamen, it was resolved to raise 6000 ",[5] and the frequency of d'Avaux's communications may be gathered from an August comment—"I gave an account four times in a week of the state of the fleet".[6]

The first week in August passed quietly; but Barillon complained to Louis that d'Albeville's reports were by no means circumstantial.[7] By the 9th,[8] it was known in England that a

---

[1] *Memoirs...Torrington*, p. 18.   [2] *Ibid*. pp. 18–19.
[3] *Ibid*. p. 19; *London Gazette*, July 30–Aug. 2.
[4] Dalrymple, App. p. 282; Louis to Barillon, July 24, 1688.
[5] D'Avaux, IV, July 27.   [6] *Ibid*. Aug. 24.
[7] Dalrymple, App. p. 282; Barillon to Louis, Aug. 2, 1688.
[8] On August 9th at a court martial held by the King's orders, aboard

Dutch squadron had been detached northward to meet the home-coming Dutch East Indies ships.[1] William, recalling the attack of Sir Robert Holmes on the Smyrna-Lisbon convoy of 1671-2, with which quasi-piratical escapade the Third Dutch War had begun without ceremonious declarations, thought it better to divert the argosies by the Hebrides and Orkneys (a precaution the Dutch wars had taught) rather than to expose their freights in the Channel, or alternatively, to send warships to meet them in the Channel at a time when, above all others, provocative demonstration had to be avoided. On the 12th, Louis wrote to Barillon to advise James to set himself in readiness "par terre et par mer";[2] on the 16th Strickland's fleet was prevented from sailing westward;[3] and "the present conjunction of Affair with respect to ye Preparations wch are making by our neighbours the Dutch" caused, upon the 20th, the stoppage of all leave.[4] Next day a yacht (Captain Cotton) was sent specially to reconnoitre the Dutch coast;[5] and two men-of-war, engaged upon the transport of soldiers to the Channel Isles, dropped their task for more important business and headed for the Downs.[6] The Navy Board received injunctions to fit out a substantial number of additional vessels; this work, wrote Pepys on the 22nd, "all to be dispatched as for life and Death";[7] and perhaps the admonition was needed, for Sir Wm Booth and Sir John Berry, Commissioners of the Navy, had, according to Luttrell, been humouring a "difference" which had brought upon them a suspension from duty.[8] New orders were drafted for Strickland on the 22nd.[9] For reasons which will later become apparent, it is necessary to indicate somewhat fully their character and to trace the deliberations to which they led. Allowing freedom of action to rest at the discretion of the Ad-

the 'Mary' in the Downs, a corporal, for mortally wounding a steward in the preceding February at Port Royal, Jamaica, was sentenced to be hanged. The Judge Advocate was Henry Croome and 24 officers were present (Admiralty Papers, P.R.O. Courts Martial, Ad. I, 5253).

[1] London Gazette, Aug. 9-12.
[2] Dalrymple, App. p. 283; Louis to Barillon, Aug. 12, 1688.
[3] See article referred to in note 6, p. 11. Quotation from Adm. Letter, XIV, 350, there used.   [4] Ibid. 358.
[5] Ibid. 366.   [6] Ibid. 366.   [7] Ibid. 368.
[8] Luttrell's Relation, July 31.
[9] Burchett, p. 3 (better text), Memoirs...Torrington, p. 19.

miral, advised by his captains, the Instructions yet made definite suggestions as to the disposition of the ships. Scouting off Orfordness and the Downs was still to be provided for; if the emergency for dealing with the vessels of the States, whose destination might be northward, into the River, into the Downs or the Channel, arose, Sir Roger was advised to put to sea from the Downs which, it is assumed, would remain his base, either by the North or South Foreland, to endeavour to get between them and their home, to watch them, and, if necessary, to fall upon them. At that time 26 ships were with Sir Roger—a third rate, sixteen fourth rates and the rest smaller—35 were to be fitted out to join him—another half-score third rates and as many fourth rates.[1] No time was lost by the Admiral in communicating his instructions to the "most experienced officers of his squadron... who were of opinion with himself that they ought, when victualed, to sail to the Buoy of the Gunfleet, on this side of Harwich, since they might sooner gain intelligence there of the motions of the Dutch than by staying in the Downs; for with westerly winds it might be five or six days before the scouts off of Orfordness coud ply it up; whereas the squadron might sooner put to sea from the Gunfleet upon notice that the Dutch were come out". The King was acquainted with this opinion and immediately intimated his disapproval on the ground that "the Gunfleet was not only at that time of the year a very ill road; but that if the wind came easterly, he woud be liable to be driven by the Dutch up the river, which of all things was to be avoided". The Admiral was instructed to leave the Downs on the first easterly wind. He was told to take station between "the North Sands Head and the Kentish Knock; there to continue under sail the day time, and to anchor in the night, if it was fair weather, and if it shoud over blow, and the Dutch not appear, then to go by the back of the Goodwin, to Bulloign Bay, there to ride so long as it shoud over blow" Of these further instructions we learn that they were "founded upon a solemn debate held on that affair the day before, being Sunday, August 26, in his Majesties closet at Windsor, with the following persons specially sumoned from London to attend his Majesty (the

---

[1] Burchett, p. 3 (better text), *Memoirs... Torrington*, p. 19.

Lord Dartmouth and Mr Pepys being present); Sir John
Berry, with 3 Elder Brothers of Trinity House, Capt. Atkinson,
Capt. Mudd, and Capt. Butter, as also Capt. Clements, being
all brought by Sir John Berry".[1]

According to James's "Fighting Instructions"[2] an English
fleet went into battle 'line-ahead'. Only when in that formation could the full weight of all the broadsides be simultaneously
exercised; and ships thus ranged rendered the best mutual
support. The same practice was customary in the Dutch and
French navies. But Strickland's score ships—a third of the
number used in most of the battles of the Dutch wars and by
no means all he would shortly command—would, so ranged,
quite likely, trail over a mile of sea. Obviously a line, one, two
or three miles long, required, against an equally sinuous enemy,
a good deal of sea room for manœuvring. Let the reader turn to
the Chart at the end of this work, and observe that the lie of the
sands subtends from the open sea an angle of 60° at the Gunfleet
Buoy, while the new cruising ground apparently gives, on the
Chart, three times that limit of freedom. That contrast must
not be allowed to lead to rash conclusions. Strickland, surprised
at either post by the Dutch, they being intent on battle decision
or blockade and coming down with an east wind with the tide at
flood, would be likely to fare ill. At the Gunfleet the Admiral
could neither manœuvre nor retire except into still more certain
uselessness; yet his lot, were he taken unawares upon the more
southerly station, might well be similar, inasmuch as the Downs
and the Channel would only serve 'to friend' if the Dutch
formed carelessly enough to permit them to prove so. And as
to the Downs, it is further to be remembered that it would have
been open to the Dutch to use them again as a trap, just as in
similar circumstances they had done in 1639, and had proposed
to do in 1652. Considered as stations from which to initiate
pursuit to the northward, there was nothing to choose between
the newly suggested ground and the Gunfleet, since, with the
wind at east and the tide at flood, northward attack could be

---

[1] *Memoirs...Torrington*, pp. 21 *et seq.*; Burchett, p. 9. Burchett calls him
(probably correctly) Rutter. The three Trinity House captains held no
naval commission.

[2] May be seen in *Fighting Instructions* 1530–1816 (Corbett).

prosecuted from neither. For the start of a southward pursuit however, the Gunfleet imposed a handicap; a wind at east and the tide running at flood ruled out a venture which, probably at any state of wind and tide, could be attempted from the rendezvous off the Kentish coast. In one single respect the Gunfleet scored. The Gunfleet, being more directly opposite to the Dutch base, was far better placed for the quick collection of advices of enemy movement and, consequently, better situated for the undelayed launching of a blow, especially should the Dutch be moving to the northward. It was no exaggeration for Strickland and his captains to hold that it might take five or six days for "the scouts off of Orfordness" to "ply it up" with the wind westerly, which five or six days might well give the Dutch space for an unmolested landing on the north-east coast.

There can be no doubt that upon that particular Sunday just referred to, August 26th, the King was awake to the possibility of attack by William. So thought Barillon,[1] who says James desired French ships to be kept ready at Brest. And, before he left for Windsor, Pepys wrote to his subordinates, Booth and Pett, urging them to assiduous duty "it being ye time in Our whole Lives where in ye can be of most use and importance to him".[2] But on the 30th, Barillon considered James less convinced of the hostile purpose of the Prince's movements.[3] A letter from Pepys, September 3rd, to Captain Killigrew at Gibraltar is to the point: "the king our master has now about 14 or 20 daies been greatly awakened and indeed little less than surprised by a sudden and extraordy preparation in Holland for some immediate enterprize at sea"; but the same letter shows that James had only prepared in readiness for a general contingency and had no fixed conviction as to the objective of the enemy fleet.[4]

At this time it appears that Bonrepos, formerly a high-placed official of the French marine, who has been described by one historian as "a second French plenipotentiary in England"..."who had only received full powers for com-

---

[1] Dalrymple, App. p. 283; Barillon to Louis.
[2] Admiralty Letters in article previously referred to xiv, 370.
[3] Dalrymple, App. p. 283; Barillon to Louis.
[4] Admiralty Letters in article previously referred to xiv, 386.

mercial transactions, but who liked to have a hand in all things ",[1] received recall to Versailles. The despatch (dated Versailles 8 September)[2] which bade him return is, in one respect, of great interest; for, apart from the fact that it shows Louis moving round to the point of view that William's design could not mature that year, it makes plain the all-important circumstance that Louis did not mean to supply ships for immediate junction with the English fleet. He did not intend to do so for the best of all possible reasons. He appears not to have had the necessary vessels available at Brest and was not able to bring round ships from the Mediterranean in order to make up a squadron.

On September 2nd Strickland got advice from one of his scouts that "25 Sail of the Dutch fleet, 16 of them great Ships, were off Georee some of them under Sail, with 3 Flags viz. Admiral Vice and Rear".[3] Such news was at least definite but probably had nothing to do with James's resolve to make diplomatic remonstrances. D'Albeville presented a memorial to the States complaining that "at a season when ordinarily all action especially at sea is laid aside" the preparations of the States were a source of disquiet to England.[4] Louis, however, went much further; he instructed d'Avaux to confront the assembled States General with the declaration that it was evident the scheme afoot was directed against England and that as his master was the ally of James, he could not allow it to develop to James's hurt.[5] What James thought of the interposition may be gathered from the fact that Skelton, who had inspired the *coup de théâtre*, was recalled and sent to the Tower. For William the effrontery of Louis was the best of all possible happenings; it united the States General in an angry determination which allowed the Stadholder to proceed more easily with his half-hidden design. The concern of Louis was seen also in

---

[1] Ranke, IV, pp. 285, 286.
[2] I.e. Aug. 29. O.S. Despatch quoted in *L'Italie en 1671...*, Pierre Clement, p. 337.
[3] Burchett, p. 11.
[4] *Memoirs of James II*, II, p. 178, Sep. 5.
[5] *Ibid.* p. 179, Sep. 9. D'Avaux alleges that the English and French papers were put in almost simultaneously (IV, p. 205). Cp. Burnet, p. 768. Copies in State Papers Domestic (King William's Chest, uncalendared) show d'Albeville's dated the 8th and that of D'Avaux the 9th.

the fact that Bonrepos reached London again by the 9th with advice and offers of assistance of ships, which offers were apparently accepted.[1] Indeed, if a French historian is to be trusted, a treaty was made, for he declares "Bonrepaus arriva le 8 Septembre et cinq jours après un traité fut conclu et signé pour le jonction des vaisseaux de France avec ceux d'Angleterre". By article 6 of this treaty the French squadron was to be brought to the anchorage of Bertheaume at the entrance to Brest; thence, according to circumstance, to rendezvous at Portsmouth or the Dunes (?) while supreme command should rest with the English Admiral.[2] It cannot be credited that the circumstances of Louis had so far changed during the hurried visit of Bonrepos to Versailles as to make possible the speedy realisation of a previously impracticable plan; and Ranke has properly observed that "no understanding was arrived at either as to the number of ships which should take part in the combination nor as to the time of it".[3] On the same day as that on which the agreement is said to have been reached, Barillon reported that "His Britannic Majesty and his most confidential ministers" were not so perturbed at developments in Holland as to believe in invasion.[4] So the month passed on.[5] And as it opened propitiously for William, so it closed in like manner. It has already been observed that, in Dutch eyes, the scheme must necessarily appear unpatriotic if war threatened the frontiers. The insolence of Louis boded ill: the expedition might indeed never be able to sail. But as the action of d'Avaux had made the Dutch authorities not indisposed to see the venture undertaken, were it a practicable plan, so now Louis

[1] Dalrymple, App. p. 284; Barillon to Louis, Sep. 9.
[2] "Dunes" = the Downs. Mazure, III, p. 67.
[3] Ranke, IV, p. 419.
[4] Dalrymple, App. p. 284; Barillon to Louis, Sep. 13.
[5] Mazure asserts that Van Citters demanded a repudiation of France and was met with the retort: "Je n'ai besoin de protecteur et je ne prétends pas être traité à la manière du Cardinal de Furstenberg". Also, Mazure alleges, on the 21st, the States demanded the communication of all treaties concerning France (III, p. 90).
The French naval historians C. de la Roncière, *Historie de la Marine Française*, and G. Lacour Gayet, *La Marine Militaire de la France sous les Règnes de Louis XIII et de Louis XIV* have not reached this period; L. Guérin, *Histoire Maritime de France*, III, does not mention the English Revolution.

rendered the design possible by throwing his troops against the middle Rhine, committing himself to a campaign which guaranteed the immunity of the Provinces (in the then state of William's alliances) from an attack that winter.

Louis has been adversely criticised for lack of foresight; and nothing is easier than to suppose that he might, at the cost of a few thousand men sent to demonstrate against the Provinces, and a show of naval readiness, have tied the transport hawsers to their North Sea quays. Admittedly, as a contemporary expressed it, "The conduct of France at that time with relation to the States was very unaccountable; and proved as favourable to the Prince of Orange's design as if he had directed it";[1] and, whatever course conjecture runs, many moves in the statecraft of Louis at this juncture will remain inexplicable. Among them the choice of a German battle ground is chief. But if that choice is not easily accounted for, excellent reason has been provided to show why Louis did not attempt naval activity against the Provinces. It was simply not in his power to intervene by sea. Possibly the Prince was well advertised of his rival's impotence outside the Mediterranean. In any case, it is not likely that, once the Prince found himself unmolested on the frontier, he wasted much thought over the bare possibility of an unsupported surprise naval attack by France, in his absence, upon his Provinces. Nor, for that matter, does it appear that the possibility of a union of a French squadron with the English fleet ever weighed upon his mind.

England at the end of September was still a house divided against itself. To folly the King had added folly; and he saw fit on the 28th to issue a Royal Proclamation which failed of all effect because the writs for a new Parliament were withdrawn.[2] The imminence of the danger could no longer be doubted. The *Gazette* was full henceforth of detailed news of preparations. But as Lord High Admiral, James had continued to attend to his special duty. About the 19th of the month he visited the Medway "to see himself in what readiness they" (the ships fitting out) "and the fortifications were in; for he was very pressing, upon the advice he had received that the Dutch lay off Goree

---

[1] Burnet, p. 769.   [2] *London Gazette*, Sep. 27–Oct. 1.

ready to sail ".[1] Doubtless there had been the usual difficulties in securing seamen. Strickland had complained and been allowed to take aboard soldiers:[2] but complaints of ill manning are too common to this and the next century to cause surprise or warrant a firm inference. On the 23rd an Order in Council authorised the Admiral, commanders and other appointed officers and heads of the Companies of Watermen and Free Fishermen to collect by pressing—subject to the grant of protection to mariners in outward-bound merchantmen.[3] On the 24th an important change was made. James superseded Strickland, issuing a commission to Lord Dartmouth to be "Admiral and chief Commander of His Majesty's Ships in the narrow seas for the present expedition ".[4] With it was issued the customary authority for the holding of courts martial; but no sentence of death could be enforced without reference to the Lord High Admiral.[5]

George Legge,[6] eldest son of plain William Legge the well-known royalist, had reached the age of 40. He had, as a young man of 17, very fresh from Cambridge, seen his first service under Sir Edward Spragge (his cousin) in the Second Dutch War, and though only 20, he had been made captain at its close in 1667. Throughout the Third Dutch War he had fought with

[1] *Memoirs...Torrington*, p. 23.
[2] *Ibid.* p. 20; Burchett, p. 8, and p. 11. See also Admiralty Papers in article previously cited.
[3] Admiralty Papers in P.R.O. Ad. 1, 5139. The Watermen's Company was one of the ancient Companies of the City of London, with which, in 1667, the Lightermen's Company was united. The Watermen's and Lightermen's Company, with limited functions, still exists. The Watermen were liable by Statute (2 and 3 Phil. and Mar.) to impressment; and much of their uncalendared records, which just reach back to this period, are taken up with affairs of impressments. The Free Fishermen are not to be confused with the ancient and opulent Fishmonger's Company of the City of London. The former "was incorporated by Letters Patent of the third of James the Second, Anno 1687, by the Name of the Free Fishermen of London; but have neither Livery, Hall nor Arms, that I can learn", writes Maitland in his *London*, p. 1245, and gives a reference to Griffith's *Conservacy* for "K. Charles' Charter". Reference to the *Conservacy*, pp. 134 fol. shows that the Charter dates to 1634, and that the Company was almost extinct at the date of incorporation. See also *B.M. Catalogue* under "Thames". The whole history of this Company has been left in such an obscure state that writers about London usually say nothing of it.
[4] Dartmouth MSS, XI, 5, p. 261.   [5] *Ibid.*
[6] *D.N.B.* article, "Legge, George, first Baron Dartmouth".

distinction. Civil and military appointments he had also held
—he resigned the governorship of Portsmouth to become, in
1682, Master of the Ordnance, a post he still held. In that year,
"following his father's steps in divers military employments,
especially in sundry sharp and dangerous naval fights, wherein
he did freely hazard his life", he was made a baron. He took
the fleet to Tangier in 1684 and superintended the evacuation
of that place. It has been contended "his experience afloat was
extremely small, he had no pretensions to be a practical seaman".[1]
That is perhaps an extreme statement. His appointment was
dictated by weighty considerations. Sir Roger Strickland was,
as has been observed, a Catholic; and, for a Catholic in command of an English fleet, the times were out of joint. If he had
proceeded to hear Mass in the cabin or to order its celebration
on the quarter-deck, he was certainly asking for trouble. Tradi-
tion would impute some such practices to Strickland; but the
truth is not easy to find. "My old friend Sir Roger hath been
very indiscreet and his behaviour hath been very disobliging
all this summer which I could not at first believe, but he is
sensible himselfe of the generall dislike there is of him",[2] wrote
Dartmouth to the King upon October 22nd. An indiscreet
admiral could not be left in command. If however Dartmouth
lacked the completest qualifications of a sailor he was certainly
no Catholic; and though, perhaps, it would be possible to suggest the names of Protestant captains of experience who might
have taken Strickland's place, yet, in such an hour of peril,
when James could not but have been aware of the danger of
sedition in the ranks of his officers as well as among the common
sailors of his fleet, no appointment could have been wiser than
that of Baron Dartmouth.

Protestant though he was, his loyalty was beyond all question,
and in him the King trusted even as a father in his son;[3] no

[1] *Ibid.*; Corbett, *Fighting Instructions* 1530–1816, p. 169, is much more
favourable.
[2] Dartmouth MSS, XI, 5, p. 261. See also Charnock, *Biog. Nav.* I, p. 180;
and Mackintosh, p. 287. Burnet, p. 755, and *Life of Captain Stephen Martin*
1664–1740, p. 6, are the nearest contemporary evidence. Mr Martin, a young
officer in the 'Montague' was discharged for gibing at Popery; but he was
able to find service with Leake on board the 'Firedrake'.
[3] Echard prints his signature among those on the warrant which consigned

man doubted Dartmouth's integrity; he had great prestige. A possible precedent for such a choice could, perhaps, be discovered; only a hundred years had elapsed since Lord Howard of Effingham had commanded in a not wholly dissimilar crisis. He, being wise, had been guided by Drake and Frobiser. Dartmouth might rely upon the advice of captains of great skill even if of lesser fame. In that age, no hard and fast rule dictated that a commander, either by land or sea, should first be master of his art. The practice of the wars of the Commonwealth and Restoration, and the fact that the young Duke of Grafton thought himself badly treated when his uncle refused to yield to his solicitation for this same commission, show how little cause is there for surprise.[1] It is reported that Dartmouth had, since the time of Monmouth's rebellion, warned the King that William would make such an effort as this which he was now called upon to encounter.[2]

On September 25th Dartmouth appointed Captain Grenville Collins—the most celebrated hydrographer of his day—as Master (i.e. navigating officer) of the 'Resolution', one of the third rates which, fitting out at Blackstakes, was to be his flagship. He hastened by yacht and coach to Chatham "to dispatch his own and other ships which were ordered out". Collins went down the river in the Admiral's yacht, and the magnanimity of Dartmouth, as well, perhaps, as a proper measure of anxiety to get his Master aboard, are reflected in the following entry in Collins's journal: "at Gravesend I was taken with a lameness in all my limbs and was not able to move myself, so was put to bed at the Black Boy. In the morning [September 27th] Lord Dartmouth came to Gravesend from Chatham to go to London. He gave me the honour of a most kind visit, giving the doctor great charge of me, and that I might not want for anything, presented the doctor with a fee and gave me ten pounds to bear the charge of my sickness".[3]

On the 28th Dartmouth transmitted rather than initiated

the bishops to the Tower; III, p. 861; and Oldmixon, p. 732, and Rapin-Thoyras, II, p. 763, follow him.
[1] *D.N.B.* article, "Fitzroy, Henry, first Duke of Grafton".
[2] *Memoirs of James II*, II, p. 177.
[3] "Journal of Captain Grenville Collins", Dartmouth MSS, XV, 1, p. 54.

orders for Strickland's fleet to come to the Buoy of the Nore[1]
and, similarly, next day forwarded instructions to forbear the
search of foreign ships.[2] In coming round, Strickland was
directed to leave two of the cleanest frigates[3] off Orfordness and
"as a Matter of greatest Importance, so to employ all the Scout-
Vessels as that he might have from them, and King James
himself from him, the most frequent, quick and exact Accounts
of their [the Dutch] Proceedings on their own Coast and their
departure thence". This order of recall may possibly somewhat
startle the reader; but he will be better able to understand its
significance when the text and appendix of Dartmouth's Instructions are before him. The matter will be referred to in
the course of a few pages. Dartmouth, coming from London
on the evening of the 29th, sent his boat ashore for Collins.
On October 2nd again coming down from London, doubtless
with his Instructions in his pocket, Dartmouth sent once more
for his Master who then joined him. At midnight or earlier
they reached the 'Resolution', by this time anchored at the
Buoy, and next day they went aboard.[4] It would seem that,
on the same night, Dartmouth sent to Pepys a letter giving a
report as to the state of the fleet with respect to men and
provisions.[5]

The reports of two smack masters hereabouts put the Dutch
strength at 25 sail.[6]

Now Dartmouth's Instructions were as follows:[7]

James R.

Whereas we received undoubted Advice, That a great and sudden
Invasion from Holland, with an Armed Force of Foreigners and
Strangers, will be made speedily in an Hostile manner upon this
Our Kingdom; Our Will and Pleasure is, That all Necessary Orders
being by you issued for the hastening Our Ships and Vessels now
fitting forth out of the Rivers of Thames and Medway, and from
Portsmouth, together with those already at Sea under Command of
Sir Roger Strickland Kt. Vice-Admiral of Our said Fleet, to their
intended Rendezvous at the Buoy of the Nore, (a perfect List of all

[1] Dartmouth MSS, XI, 5, p. 255.   [2] *Ibid.*
[3] Burchett, p. 11.
[4] "Journal of Captain Grenville Collins", Dartmouth MSS, XV, I, p. 55.
[5] Dartmouth MSS, XV, I, p. 59.   [6] *Ibid.*
[7] Burchett, p. 12; *Memoirs...Torrington*, p. 23.

which Ships, Fireships, and other Vessels is here-unto annexed) you
do with all diligence repair on board Our Ship Resolution, Captain
William Davis Commander, or such other of Our Ships as you shall
now, and at any time or times hereafter, think fit to bear Our Flag
(as Admiral) upon, taking upon you the Charge and Conduct of Our
said Fleet, and what other Ships shall at any time hereafter be by Us set
forth for re-inforcing the same. Which Fleet, and every part thereof,
We (out of Our entire reliance upon your approved Loyalty, Valour,
Circumspection, and Experience) do hereby Authorize and Empower
you to lead, and by your Orders to direct and dispose of at all such
Times, and in all Emergencies, as you in your Discretion shall
judge most conducing to Our Honour, and the Security of Our
Dominions, and particularly in the preventing the approach of any
Fleet or Number of Ships of War from Holland upon any of our
Coasts, or their making any Descent upon the same. Towards your
more effectual Execution whereof, We do hereby farther Empower
and Require you, to endeavour by all Hostile Means to sink, burn,
take, and otherwise destroy and disable the said Fleet and Ships
thereof, when and wheresoever you shall meet with, or otherwise
think fit to look out for and attack the same, giving a perfect Account
of your proceedings therein to the Secretary of Our Admiralty for
Our Information: And for so doing, this shall be your Warrant.
Given at Our Court at Whitehall this First of October 1688.

By His Majesty's Command,

S. Pepys.

By analysing Burchett's version of the detailed list attached to
the Instructions the following result may be obtained:

	Fitted out	Fitting out	Total
Third rates	2	10	12
Fourth rates	14	11	25
Fireships	5	13	18[1]
Sixth rates	2	1	3
Yachts	3	—	3
	26*	35†	61

* Strickland bringing in the two third rates and eleven fourth rates, one
sixth rate and three fireships, while leaving one fourth rate and one fireship
off Orfordness and one sixth rate in the Downs. The other fitted-out ships
were at the Nore.

† All at the Nore with the exception of five ships of the line and four
fireships at Portsmouth and Spithead.

[1] The *Memoirs...Torrington* list abstract shows these to be fifth-rates—
which they were (converted). (See Pepys to Dartmouth, Dartmouth MSS, XI,
5, p. 199.)

It will be remembered that the number of ships said to be fitting for Strickland on August 22nd was 35. None of them evidently had got to sea within the month which had, since then, elapsed; but it is necessary to notice that the appointment of Dartmouth did not mean an increase in the size of the projected fleet. Of capital ships third and fourth rates only were listed for employ because, in the winter season, no larger vessels could have kept the sea.[1]

Obviously, by the time the Instructions were issued, the Dutch preparations could no longer be misunderstood; but to what, in the first place (p. 6), was said concerning the putting in train of the Prince's preparations, little, as showing in detail the progress of the equipment, can be added. This narrative, continuing, has indicated, through the comments of D'Avaux, the stealthy certainty of the preparations. The stealth is not to be doubted; the certainty appeared in the completion of the event. None the less, to over-estimate the secrecy of the preparations is irrational. Commissioning ships, the mustering troops "at Nimeghen not very far from the Brandenburger's camp"[2] and the arrangements for a loan "for so chargeable an expedition"[3] were the clear evidence of a great design. And surely the religious fervour, which was, of a truth, the inspiration of the movement, which saw in the Prince "another Joshua ...another good Josiah...another David and a man after God's own heart," the bulwark on the continent against a French Catholicism, against "blood-thirsty Papists" whose deeds, following the Revocation of the Edict of Nantes, were, in a hundred pamphlets, spread with exaggeration broadcast, "very few English hearts capable of conceiving it, our Nation (God be praised) being unacquainted with such abominable practices"[4] —surely such religious fervour need not be assumed to have

---

[1] It is not possible to make the detailed list and the abstract in Burchett agree nor to account for the fact that the abstract, giving inaccurate rate figures, itself correctly adds up to a total tallying with the list total. The analysis on the preceding page is not Burchett's own analysis. Again, between Burchett's list and that given in the *Memoirs...Torrington* list, there is discrepancy. In the *Memoirs* list the 'Assurance' is classified (wrongly) as a third rate; and the number of fireships fitted out is there given as 11 with 7 to follow; Burchett is much more probably right than the *Memoirs...Torrington* in that matter. The totals of Burchett and *Memoirs...Torrington*, however, agree (61).

[2] Whittle's *Diary*, p. 9.   [3] Burnet, p. 778.
[4] Whittle's *Diary*, p. 2.

acted always with trained Jesuit discreetness. It is affirmed however that "Bentinck, Dykvelt, Herbert and Van Hulst were for two months constantly at the Hague giving all necessary orders with so little noise that nothing broke out all that while ",[1] that "Matters went on in Holland with great secrecy till September", and that "Then it was known. . . ".[2] Certainly by that time the scheme could not be veiled. There is no available detailed report of the state of the Dutch preparations just at the time Dartmouth received his orders; but as the September 2nd report of 25 sail and the, month later, smacksmen's estimate of 25 sail[3] are not contradicted by any other considerations, the figure may nearly enough have indicated the number of fighting vessels so far fitted out by the Dutch.

It is with the issue of Lord Dartmouth's Instructions, that the virtual outbreak of war is reached, a war in which the Prince is to seek to satisfy a family and an international interest, a war, in which, at an appropriate time, the English opposition will join to gain its desires, a war in which James stands wholly upon the defensive. It is just worth notice that it does not appear that the "good correspondence" of the courts was ever formally broken.

*   *   *   *   *   *

Before leaving the chapter, two comments must be made. In the first place, no naval historian can neglect to praise the Dutch secrecy and quiet preparations. Secondly, it is necessary to meet a criticism which, in the pages of Macaulay, one finds levelled at the English King. Macaulay gibes at the "stupid security"[4] of James. That must be challenged. It may or may not have been stupid for James to hold the opinion (if indeed he did so) that an invasion which only became practicable at the end of September, through the moving of Louis's troops to the Rhine, would not come to pass. But it seems unreasonable to accuse the King-Lord High Admiral of perpetuating a state of insecurity when, as the narrative shows, he was far from being caught by surprise, and had had, for months, at sea, a fleet

---

[1] Burnet, p. 781.   [2] *Ibid.* p. 766.
[3] See p. 28.   [4] Macaulay, II, p. 451.

which could not have been inferior to the Dutch strength of 25 sail, "16 of them great ships", at which figure, upon September 2nd, the scouts reporting to Strickland had estimated the extent of the enemy's preparations, and which observation reports as late as the beginning of October had served to confirm. James's reliance upon Strickland's fleet, especially in view of the fact that 35 vessels were being fitted out to join the ships at sea, was reasonable and proper. The refusal of French aid was a turning away of unwanted forces. And, in refusing, James acted in line with accepted national policy. One cannot resist the remark that Macaulay seems never to have heard of Strickland! The great historian is too content to write as though all things were done in haste when, at the end of September, Dartmouth assumed the English command. Nothing could be further from the truth.

For an Appendix to this chapter see p. 161

CHAPTER II

Hostilities begun; the Prince's False Start
October 3rd to 29th

WHEN on the morning of October 3rd, the Union was broken at the main of the 'Resolution', 16 sail of fighting ships and 6 fireships lay round about the Buoy of the Nore under Dartmouth's command.[1] Besides the 'Resolution' at least one third rate had got to sea.[2] The Strickland fleet had come in, in obedience to the orders Dartmouth had transmitted.[3] Scouts were abroad. Before the Admiral, already much in the confidence of the King, lay his formal Instructions, speaking, at their outset, of the menace as one of invasion, referring to the ordered concentration for reinforcement at the Buoy of the Nore as to an enjoined task already begun, and commending into the Admiral's hands, in wide discretion, the thwarting of the enemy's purpose.

Opposite, in equal strength, off the Brill, some forty or more leagues across the North Sea, lay the enemy, Lieutenant-Admiral Cornelius Evertsen commanding. Reinforcements were going out to the fleet; preparing transports and store ships crowded the Dutch harbours; the wharves and inland camps were all bustle. The final charge of the expedition had still not been assigned to any admiral; but some definite appointment could not much longer be delayed.

On both sides hostility had become quite overt; and, with the season of the year so far spent, none, on either side, could think of delay as indefinite.

The Prince pressed on his last preparations apace. To the rendezvous of the fighting ships, two or three leagues off the Brill, more warships went out; and while

The men of War were riding at anchor in the forementioned place, waiting for his Highness the Prince of Orange's Orders, what to do,

[1] "Journal of Captain Grenville Collins", Dartmouth MSS XV, I, p. 55.
[2] *Memoirs...Torrington*, p. 23. [3] *Ibid.*

or where to go; sundry hundreds of Merchants Ships, Pinks, Fly-boats, and others were hired for this Service, and many immediately sent to the Fleet; others went for men here and there, according as they received orders; some were to carry Soldiers, others to carry Horses; some hay, others Artillery, or Ammunition, and all sorts of Necessaries convenient for the War: Many Martscutes[1] and flat-bottom'd Boats, which belong to the River only, to transport Goods and People from City to City were hired now to transport the Soldiers from Nimighen unto the Men of War and Merchant-Ships, Pinks and Flyboats riding at anchor, ready to receive them.[2]

That the camp at Nimeguen was thus struck at the very begin-ning of October is quite certain;[3] and it is well established that Hiob de Wildt, Secretary to the Admiralty College of Amster-dam and the most efficient Dutch naval administrator of the time, and Lieutenant-Admiral Bastiaensze Schepers were the agents responsible for the effective embarcation of soldiers, equipment and supplies.[4] The work was not carried out in smooth weather; indeed the weather worsened as the first fortnight of the month wore on. Then "one night the Winds were so very high, and the Air so tempestuous and stormy, shaking the very Houses and People in their Beds" that "the whole Fleet was in great peril: and after this, various false Reports were spread all over the Netherlands"; to the deception and dismay of all save those who "understood better the Holland manner of Ships, and the Art of Navigation".[5] The men of war could and did ride out the intermittent bad weather off the Holland Zeeland coasts, while the smaller craft found refuge in the outfalling rivers behind Schouwen and Over Flakkee where Goeree, Helvoetsluys, Brill and Rotterdam were to friend—Rotterdam especially, the headquarters of the Admiralty of the Maas and a port possessing docks and stores belonging to the East India Company. The facilities which the Company offered were gladly used.[6] William was somewhat exercised during the

[1] "Martscute", *anglice* market-boat. It does not connote a particular type.
[2] Whittle's *Diary*, p. 12.
[3] Burnet, p. 781.
[4] For the former, de Bostaquet, p. 196, and elsewhere. See also *Dutch Alliance*, Clark, pp. 17, 19; for both de Wildt and Bastiaensze Schepers see de Jonge, III, p. 40.
[5] Whittle's *Diary*, p. 14.
[6] de Jonge, III, p. 55.

fortnight for the safety of his main fleet and gathering convoys;[1] but all, great or small, were, with few exceptions, safe still at the fortnight's end; and, though time was taken up in the third week with much necessary refitting, it was a matter for satisfaction that things were no worse. The weather "began to settle" and the "wind blew a fresh Gale day by day"; indeed it had got into the S.E. whereupon it "continued favourable that quarter of the Moon", which is to say that, though it veered a great deal about E., it blew no longer from the dreaded westward. Preparations were "expedited". "Some Regiments were expected down the River, and those being come, everything was sent to the Fleet, as Provision for one month, the Artillery, Magazine, Powder, Ball, Match, Tents, Tent-poles, Stocking-axes, Spades, and all sorts of Utensils convenient in War; and then Hay and Provender for the Horses, Fresh Water, and a hundred things more..."[2] Of course, it was natural to push stores aboard right up to the last moment, but it must not be lost sight of that every day's delay had eaten into the provisions already loaded.[3] At last came the real indication of a readiness for sailing; the horses began to be shipped at Rotterdam. The horse-transports then cast off, and made a junction with all the other ships lying off Helvoetsluys, on Thursday the 18th.[4] Crowds gathered to say their adieux and to wish God-speed to the expedition. The Prince had taken a touching farewell of the States General, two days earlier, when he had protested that he had always served their welfare and that "He took God to witness he went to England with no other intentions, but those he had set out in his declaration".[5] He left with them the Princess Mary.

On paper the expedition appears, at this stage, to have consisted of the following ships:[6]

(a) 13 ships of 60 guns and over, 8 of 50 and over, 11 of 40

---

[1] B.M. MSS, Egerton 2621; Prince to Herbert.
[2] Whittle's *Diary*, p. 15.   [3] Burnet, p. 782.
[4] Huygens's *Journaal*.   [5] Burnet, p. 782.
[6] The facts in this paragraph are, for the more part, collated from de Jonge, either from the text in Book III, pp. 54–5, or from the Appendix I, except as noted below. The date of the Appendix I list of ships, their armaments and commanders, is a little difficult to fix; but that point is not particularly important.

Burnet's idea that the Dutch showed bitterness at Herbert's appointment

and over, 11 of 30 and over, 6 of 20 and over, 10 fireships and
a few miscellaneous war vessels—or 49 ships of war other than
the 10 fireships and miscellaneous war craft.

(b) At least 200 transports.

Most of the warships were supplied by the great Admiralties
of the Maas and Amsterdam. Certainly the whole figure of
great and small was not much in excess of 60. In traditional
manner the warships were divided into three equal squadrons,
each further subdivided into three smaller units. The complete
command passed on the 27/17th to the Englishman Herbert
dignified now as Lieutenant-Admiral-General[1] and Instructions were issued to him. He flew his flag at the main of the
62-gun 'Leyden'. Lieutenant-Admiral Cornelius Evertsen, who
resigned the command, took charge of a squadron and hoisted
his flag at the fore of the 'Cortgene' (50 guns). Lieutenant-
Admiral Van Almonde in the 'Provincie van Utrecht' (62
guns) took command of the other squadron and, possibly, ran
up his flag at the mizzen. The squadrons were called white, red
and blue. Doubtless Herbert's was the red, while Evertsen
commanded the white and Van Almonde the blue. Each
squadron had, after the manner of the time, its vice-admiral
and its 'schout-by-nact' roughly corresponding to an English
Rear-Admiral. Each ship bore the token of its squadron. The
Prince was accommodated in the new frigate 'den Briel' (30

(Burnet, p. 775) is partially controverted by de Jonge. A somewhat obscure
affair is to be mentioned in connection with Herbert's commission. Herbert
had been challenged in a letter written in September on behalf of Lord
Dartmouth by Constable, afterwards Lord Dunbar, ("my Lord Dartmouth
hearing you said very reflecting things of him") to a meeting on the sands at
Ostend. Acceptance of the Prince's commission was in some strange way,
in fact or in pretence, held by Herbert to be connected with the disposal of
the challenge. He showed the letter eventually to the Prince who "bid the
admiral put the letter in his pocket and told him he should meet Lord
Dartmouth at sea" (B.M. MSS, Egerton 2621).

It should be observed that Van Almonde changed from the 'Provincie van
Utrecht' into the 68-gun 'Maagd van Dordrecht' after the stormy weather
of the first fortnight of October (cf. p. 65).

de Jonge's fleet estimate is acceptable. His transport figure, 400, is a paper
estimate. P. J. Blok, *Prins Willem III naar Torbay*, citing Admiraliteitsarchief,
No. 251 (Rijksarchief), agrees, broadly, with de Jonge; totals nearer 200, e.g.
those of Huygens (Nov. 7, N.S.) and of certain engravings, are to be preferred. Burnet, Rapin-Thoyras and Whittle exaggerate.

[1] Lieutenant, that is, to William in the office of Admiral-General.

guns)—J. Van der Esch commander—and with him were Lieutenant-Admiral W. Bastiaensze Schepers and Vice-Admiral Van Stirum and Mr Russell. Contemporary engravings purport to show the exact way in which the transports and squadrons were disposed or in which it was intended they should be disposed, at some time or other, or perhaps, all the while, during the voyage. One in particular[1] shows the transports to the number of 206, in nine unequal groups, each led by a big vessel, the groups and vessels so arranged as to form a square with one group at each corner, one in the middle of each side and one in the centre: 13 big ships, under Van Almonde, in line ahead, sail on the starboard side of the convoy, 13 others, under Evertsen, in line ahead on the port side and yet 13 more, under Herbert, astern in line abreast. In each squadron the flagship of the admiral is in the centre, the flags of the vice-admirals and the schouten-by-nacht being carried equidistantly from the ends of the lines. Farther to starboard, to port and astern are unequal groups of fireships. Ten smaller ships, in line abreast, "lead" the square. In the van, just ahead of the line of 10 small ships, is to be seen the Prince's frigate, while two pilot vessels go in advance of the Prince. Whether a great concourse of sailing vessels, some big, some small, could, in the North Sea, in the prevailing weather, pick up, let alone maintain, such an elaborate formation is very much to be doubted. That the expedition did, on this occasion, at going out, succeed in so sailing is directly contradicted by other evidence.[2]

The expedition moved out on Friday the 19th, took up the Prince at the Put and got to sea next day.[3] But the sailing was ill starred. The wind, which had swept round ominously to the S.W. even before the vessels had weighed, hardened ere

---

[1] By D. Marot, Sutherland Collection. There are many in the collection; this is reproduced in Dr Firth's *Macaulay*, III, p. 1123. It gives names of commanders and gunning of ships. It may therefore be compared with de Jonge's Appendix, and may be used in conjunction with Whittle, for determining the exact disposal of the companies of soldiers and their numbers. See p. 89 for numbers.

[2] See next paragraph; see also Rapin-Thoyras, II, p. 776.

[3] Huygens's *Journaal* for this paragraph and next. Whittle confuses the day on which the Prince sailed, speaking of "Saturday" the "19th".

they were three good leagues clear of the Brill into a gale blowing from the N.W., with high seas and some lightning. Such a concourse of vessels ran "no small hazard, being obliged to keep together, and yet not come too near one another".[1] By Saturday nightfall the storm was much more violent; the long night was endured but, with light on Sunday the 21st, confused signalling to the considerably scattered ships to return to safe harbourage began. The Prince's frigate 'den Briel' reached harbour with many other craft the same day. William went ashore at once, making his enquiries of Lieutenant-Admiral General Herbert next day, Monday the 22nd, as to the state of the expedition as a whole. At first, he ordered that the infantry transports be kept with the warships but that the cavalry transports be sent into Helvoetsluys. It was feared the loss of horseflesh was very great. Such an order suggested anxiety to be quickly again at sea; but Herbert's report was such that by night the whole fleet was enjoined to come close to Goeree. Some repairs were needed and several ships were still missing. No time had been lost in ordering the people of Voorne to bring in remounts for sale; which was a wise enough move, for a very few hours had revealed the fact that over 1300 animals had been lost to the expedition. Some said that the horses had been wrongly loaded with their heads and not their tails to the sides of their transports and that the poor creatures had been drowned through carelessness; others, surely needlessly, spoke of colic caused by bad drinking water.

For many days after the unlucky Friday, the 19th of October, the wind continued westerly and the weather varied wildly. The "lotesmen"[2] scoured the coast for straggling vessels; vessels one after another still came in. Though there was much for the sailors to do, the seasick soldiers were miserable enough afloat; the long nights gave opportunity for much discussion, for rumours about the English fleet's unwillingness to fight and for the expression of doubts, on the part of the faint-hearted, as to the possibility of any ultimate success.

---

[1] Burnet, p. 782.
[2] An exaggerated picture of the storm is given by Whittle, who praises the skill of these pilots. de Bostaquet also describes his experiences.

The problem in warfare which the Prince's determination to intervene in English affairs had set before him is easily pictured.

No ordinary war by sea and land against the English King and people, no series of great battles to be followed by the long and piecemeal subjugation of a united, hostile populace was held in view. A single expedition, not calling for the indefinite maintenance of a line of marine communications for the purpose of reinforcement and warlike supply, but, rather, an expedition which, from the moment of successful landing, if possible at a pre-arranged place, or at one of a few select alternative places, should serve as a great rallying centre for the forces of English self-liberation, constituted the Prince's aim. Therefore, on the face of it, the Prince's task was reduced to the preparation, passage and disembarcation of an expedition and the preparation of a plan of leadership on English soil; also common prudence dictated the provision of the means whereby the remnants of the expedition might get safe, if not unscathed, away, in the event of failure. Soldiers, equipment and stores once provided, the initial part of the task became wholly a naval affair; the campaign in England might or might not demand the use of the maritime arm; the means of contingent escape ranked wholly as a naval consideration.

The notion of the command of the sea is, perhaps, one with which no English reader will find himself wholly unacquainted. A *command* of a given area of sea (for, always, one must speak of a definite and given extent of sea) may be defined as *the power to use and the ability to deny to the enemy the use of the waters of the area in question whether for military purposes or trade.* It is a condition which is only assured when no enemy fleet can operate in the area; hence it can only be set up after a battle decision between rival fleets has driven a defeated combatant out of the area; or so long as one fleet, blockading the other in harbour, keeps it from all intervention therein. Even so, a command is seldom or never absolute; and its duration may be long or short. Once secured, it may be enjoyed and exercised. Its exercise is, of course, seen in the few or many ways in which its possessor employs his power to use the waters in question for military purposes or trade and the deprivation of the similar facilities which he inflicts upon his enemy. The variety in exercise will depend on the strength of the belligerent and the particular purposes which he has in hand. But if, in theory, the exercise of command waits upon the establishing of the condition of command by battle decision or by blockade, practice often ignores logic; there is, in short, always a tendency on the part of a combatant to act as though possessed of a command which he has not yet made his own or which he may even know to have been definitely lost.

Two main courses are therefore open to a belligerent entering upon naval warfare. They may be called (1) the proper course of securing command by battle decision or by blockade, before attempting to exercise it; and (2) the assumption of an undecided or an adversely decided command in order to accomplish the purpose in hand—an assumption which may be either an *open* or a *concealed* procedure. These considerations, so well known to the modern naval officer, were not hidden from English and Dutch seamen of the later seventeenth century. It is quite true that the many extant Sailing and Fighting Instructions issued by that time[1] and such a work as *L'art des armées navales*[2] have familiarised the present-day reader with the *tactics*, the behaviour of ships actually entered upon battle, rather than with the *strategy* or broader considerations and plans underlying and governing the naval warfare of the period; but no one who has studied the operations of the three Dutch Wars can remain in doubt that the modern cardinal doctrine of command was, at least as an implicit notion, part of the stock-in-trade of the admiral and naval adviser of 1688. William would certainly be told that he ought to fight or blockade the English fleet before attempting to move his transports. The proper course would never a moment be doubted by the Prince's advisers.

But the whole question of contact between the two fleets raised political considerations of importance. Sedition existed in the English navy. The strength of that disloyalty it would

---

[1] See *Fighting Instructions* 1530–1816, Corbett.
[2] By le Père Paul Hoste, published 1697.

be easy to foster; no failure to defer to English susceptibilities in such a matter as the claim to the salute of the flag by foreign, and especially Dutch, shipping need be allowed to occur to alienate a single friend; everything that could be done to "strengthen...the weak hands and confirm the feeble knees" among the English sailors, who would be called upon to shot the ship's guns and stand awaiting the hoisting of the bloody flag of action, might indeed be done and done thrice over; but that the fleets could approach within speaking range without the interchange of gunfire was a hope which the rumours of English disloyalty did not bear up; and no man could say what might follow the awakening of the guns. Though English captains should desert their colours rather than go into action, it could scarcely be hoped that random shooting would not be followed by the loosing of whole broadsides, or that a few detached ship-actions would see the end of the day. It was far more to be feared that, in a smother of smoke and a familiar stink of gun-powder, away over the North Sea, would be rekindled all the old Anglo-Dutch bitterness and a conflagration lighted, the end of which no Dutchman and no English Protestant could, with any remaining hope, foresee. A triumphant voyage to English shores over the wreckage of the English navy would cause the inter-vention issue to be utterly misunderstood by waverers in England and alienate not a few outright supporters of the Prince. Writing to Bentinck on September 16/6, William asked Bentinck to represent this fundamental difficulty to Herbert and his words were quite unequivocal. "Ce n'est pas le tems de faire voir sa bravoure, ni de se battre si l'on le peut éviter. Je luy l'ai déjà dit: mais il sera nécessaire que vous le répétiez, et que vous le luy fassiez bien comprendre".[1] A battle decision yielding only a barren gain, a blockade that might lead to the undesired battle, was not to be thought of.

There was therefore nothing left but to turn to the second alternative opening—the assumption, either in open or con-cealed manner, of an undecided command for the purpose in hand. William's advisers no doubt allowed that he could assume the undecided command and sail in open manner, fleet and

[1] Quoted by Macaulay, II, p. 482.

transports together, to attempt to establish communications
with his ally; but they must at once have urged two objections,
arguing first that a fleet and transports, so sailing, would constitute an unwieldy, slow-moving mass, highly liable to detection, a detection which would lead to compulsion to fight; and
secondly, that, in meeting the attack he could not avoid, the
Dutch Admiral would find himself placed at a most serious
tactical disadvantage, inasmuch as his defending fleet would
be forced simultaneously to fight the attacking English and to
protect from sinking or capture a whole threatened drove of
worse than helpless transports. Under such conditions of
restricted manœuvring, William could not fail to realise how the
advantage in attack would rest overpoweringly with the English
enemy. The idea of a concealed rather than an open sailing
offered little more comfort. Practical sailors, such as those
around the Prince, would need no reminder that gales, fogs,
tides and sands—the chances of the sea—might provide a
calculating admiral with opportunity, or set up a fortuitous
concurrence of events to give even an unskilled admiral a
snatched success; the expedition might conceivably steal a
passage to the coast of England; but the risk involved in such an
attempt could only be likened to the desperate throw of a game-
ster's dice. Moreover, it could not fairly be argued that, disembarcation begun, the fleet would forthwith be free from further
restraint. The fleet, while continuing to protect unloading or
even emptied transports, would be more surely located than
when it moved with its convoy over the high seas; and its
admiral might find a particular anchorage uncomfortably
cramping when he came to make his dispositions to counter
an enemy attack. The Prince would need therefore to reckon
that the massed fleet and transports, even if a stolen crossing
could be made, would be discovered at some stage long before
the success of the land operations could make it reasonable to
send back the transports to Holland, and, therefore, long before
encounter between the fleets could be regarded as an unlikely
or unimportant thing. There can be no doubt at all that the
Prince's advisers urged strongly the professional unwisdom of
striving to conduct war by the means of peace. They must

have pictured their leader compelled to fight, sooner or later, at a needless disadvantage; they could only picture a latter end of the fleet and transports together which would be worse than either the loss of a fleet in battle decision or the relinquishment of the whole invasion design could ever be.

Facts such as these once set before William and pressed with all the cogency of conviction, it had been his duty to make his choice—a choice no man could envy. No doubt the more His Royal Highness had thought, the more he had been confounded by his own paradox and driven to hope that sedition would contaminate into sheer mutinous ineffectiveness the guns and canvas of the English fleet; that so, he might try the second and wrong opening, either in open or concealed way, essaying it with the practical certainty of not being called upon for real fighting nor need to consider carefully the risks he would run were he dealing with a loyal fleet. The choice which he had reached will at once be plain to the reader; for the orders which Herbert received at sailing upon October 27/17 were as follows:

Instructions for Lt. Ad. Gen. Herbert, and the further Head Officers of the Fleet.[1]

(1) That the Fleet is ordered to convey His Highness, with the ships transporting the land army, protect and defend them from all attack of the enemy, to the coast of England, and there to facilitate the disembarcation of land troops as far as possible.

(2) Having put to sea, and the fleet for transport of troops sailing in their order, the frigates of His Highness shall sail thus;— the Squadron of Lt. Ad. Gen. Herbert behind; that of Lt. Ad. Evertsen to the starboard and that of Vice Ad. Almonde to larboard.[2]

(3) When an enemy fleet shows itself, the war fleet shall place itself between the enemy and the transport ships....

(4) When the disembarcation is done, a detachment of several frigates will arrive in order to convoy all the transport ships again for the Maas and Texel.

---

[1] de Jonge, Appendix III.
[2] See p. 37. The engraving referred to puts Evertsen to larboard and Almonde to starboard; the contradiction is immaterial.

(5) When the weather permits, the Fleet shall sail to Scotland and there try to make a diversion; and, after that is done, they shall, with the first favourable wind, sail to the west of England and there try to make similar diversions.

(6) If Lt. Ad. Gen. Herbert in concert with the chief officers of the Fleet see occasion for the promotion of His Highness's designs that is not set out here in these instructions, they shall, as soon as they see it, do it themselves, employing all soldiers and sailors.

(7) If it happens that, in an action with the enemy, some of the captains do not do their duty, His Highness authorizes Lt. Ad. Gen. Herbert and the chief officers in his squadron to... supersede the officers and appoint others whom they can trust.

Helvoetsluys 27th Oct. 1688.

The Instructions indicate that the Prince looked at his task as a whole and issued a single set of orders to cover the naval operations involved. Sections 1, 2, 3 deal with the naval side of the passage of the expedition from shore to shore. Clearly, the proper opening plan of battle decision or blockade was rejected; but whether an open or concealed sailing was intended is not easy to decide. Section 4, picturing the return of the transports to Holland, suggests that the Prince meant, metaphorically speaking, "to burn his boats" and not to worry about failure; it also raises the thought that the cost of transport hire may not have been absent from the Prince's mind. Section 5 makes arrangement for demonstrative assistance to be given to the land campaign—assistance which could scarce be offered while the fleet remained hampered with transport-protection duties. Sections 6 and 7 are of general character; Section 7 is merely a necessary authorisation to give Lieutenant-Admiral-General Herbert a power which was not conferred by his Dutch naval rank alone. The proposed place of landing is not specifically named; but Section 5 points unmistakably to a disembarcation to be attempted somewhere upon the east coast of England. No thought of French intervention is reflected into the orders.

The terms of the Instructions represent a quite inevitable choice; but, inevitable or not, nothing could justify the issue of orders which, in main conception, set at defiance the gravest considerations of naval doctrine and common sense—at least nothing short of the possession, by William, of a miraculous foreknowledge that the prevailing winds and tides, throughout a whole campaign, would prevent the meeting of the rival fleets, or, alternatively, a reasonably placed and implicit confidence that the disloyalty of the English fleet would ensure that no appreciable conflict would follow, even if the antagonists encountered each other. It remains to add that it is known that the Lieutenant-Admiral-General and other seamen were opposed to a landing in the North of England (which area, because of Danby's influence therein, many advices from England represented as the most convenient rallying centre)[1] because of the disadvantages inseparable from an attempt to land in an easterly gale on an exposed coast and because of the danger of leaving open the Channel to any French design.[2]

When the men-of-war sailed out upon the 19th and 20th of October with their flock of shepherded transports, the choice which the Prince had made became plain to all. Blown back, thwarted, the massed sailing seemed more than ever unwise to those who, from the professional standpoint, had from the first considered it a gamble. "Rooseboom said that there was much deliberation whether H.H. should go with all the ships " (that is just before the next move came to be made) " or whether the warships should go first to see what the attitude of the British fleet would be" writes one reliable informant in his diary,[3] and another has recorded how, in these adverse days,

Wildman created a new disturbance....He possessed some of the English with an opinion that the design was now irrecoverably lost. This was entertained by many, who were willing to hearken to any proposition, that set danger at a distance from themselves. They were still magnifying the English fleet, and undervaluing the Dutch. They went so far in this, that they proposed to the Prince, that Herbert should be ordered to go over to the coast of England, and either fight the English fleet, or force them in: and in that case the transport fleet might venture over; which otherwise they thought could not be safely done. This some urged with such earnestness,

---

[1] Burnet, p. 777. Burlington (= Bridlington Bay) was commonly spoken of—" very good anchoring and clear ground ". *Great Britain's Coasting Pilot*, Captain Grenville Collins, II, p. 11.

[2] Burnet, p. 777.   [3] Huygens's *Journaal*, Nov. 9, N.S.

that nothing but the Prince's authority, and Schomberg's credit, could have withstood it.

Indeed the Prince "rather silenced than quieted them."[1]

It is worth while noticing that precautions were taken by William in these weeks to prevent passengers carrying news to England[2]—with what success will be observed later; and that a French privateer was once reported vainly spying in the vicinity of the Dutch fleet.[3]

It is time to take up anew and fully the English side of the story. It has been seen that the formal Instructions issued to Lord Dartmouth began with the recognition of the nature of the Dutch menace as one of invasion, referred to the ordered concentration for reinforcement at the Buoy of the Nore as to an enjoined task already begun and closed, by commending into the Admiral's hands, in wide discretion, the thwarting of the enemy's purpose. Any tendency to regard the Instructions as a model of their kind suffers, however, a rude shock when the consequences of the choice of the particular place of rendezvous, the Buoy of the Nore, are fully realised. At the Buoy of the Nore the fleet was useless; and, even calculating upon efficient scouting and speedy transmission to headquarters of all intelligence of Dutch activity, there could be no guarantee that the open sea could be regained at will from that anchorage. For, conversely, as it had been esteemed tactically dangerous that Strickland's squadron should be forced back from the Gunfleet, among the sands in the converging estuary, so it would be known that it might, in certain winds and states of tides, prove impossible for the new Admiral to work out from the Buoy, or, working out, prove tactically perilous for him to fight in emergence from a narrow channel between the long parallel sands. It does seem indeed surprising that James could, of his own will, risk the complete immobilisation of his fleet or load his Admiral with a heavy handicap, should the fleet be forced to fight while making the open sea from the Thames against the enemy.

Burchett attributes the recall of Strickland's squadron to

---

[1] Burnet, p. 787; Wildman, Sir John (1621(?)–1693), the well-known "politician".

[2] Huygens's *Journaal*, Oct. 27, N.S.   [3] *Ibid.*

James's belief that the fleet was "not of strength sufficient to intercept the Dutch".[1] If James really believed Strickland's forces so small as to be in jeopardy of total destruction, he was no doubt right in bringing his fleet to an anchorage where best he could preserve and strengthen it, and whence he could best send it out again to sea—notwithstanding that the withdrawal would imply the acceptance of a Fabian policy. The Buoy of the Nore fulfilled the first two conditions though not, of course, the third. But it is hard to credit that bald interpretation. It has been contended in these pages, on the evidence of figures which James possessed, that, at the date of the issue of the Instructions, no appreciable numerical inferiority of the English to the Dutch fleet existed. Consequently it is unlikely that James could have believed in a great disparity of numbers. The reason for the amazing choice must be sought in another direction. Reinforcements were in any case needed in order that pace might be kept with the probable increments to the Dutch fleet. The new ships should, normally, have been fitted and dispatched to a squadron kept at sea. At sea Dartmouth should have superseded Strickland and there carried on defensive duty from a proper base. But those very qualities in Lord Dartmouth that made it so desirable that that particular Protestant nobleman-admiral should succeed Strickland afloat were likely to prove as indispensable for the task of hastening the work of reinforcing James's fleet from the yards of the Nore. Dartmouth could not be in two places at once. James brought him to the Nore.[2]

From the almost "pluperfect" sense of the first part of

[1] Burchett, p. 11.

[2] There were no Port Admirals till the eighteenth century. The regular succession of them began about 1745. In the seventeenth century there was no officer stationed at any dockyard port to exercise military command, and the "hastening out of the ships" depended on the more or less fortuitous presence of a flag-officer belonging to the Grand Fleet. Various instances can be collected of a Commander-in-Chief dropping all other work in order to go "to hasten out the ships", as Buckingham at Portsmouth in 1628 and the Duke of York, also at Portsmouth, in 1664.

From 1695 William III appointed "Commanders-in-Chief" at the Home Ports with the necessary powers; but these appointments were only for very short periods when a special emergency arose. This system, with other interesting alternatives (which are not now to the point), held the field till 1745.

the Instructions to Dartmouth,[1] it is clear that James thought of no risk likely to be long continued. Yet, unless he had sure and certain information that the Dutch would not, for some appreciable time, be ready to sail (and it is barely likely he could have been so perfectly informed) James, by this decision, courted a very grave liability. In withdrawing Strickland's squadron, he ran the risk of undoing all the defensive work for which, during the summer, the squadron had been kept at sea; and he compromised the success of the greater defensive mobilisation he had put in hand.

Whether Lord Dartmouth approved the scheme for the Nore rendezvous for reinforcements is not plain. The orders emanated from the King; but, satisfied or not, Dartmouth would need to decide what, if left undisturbed, would be the minimum quota for which he would delay his sailing and whether, if the Dutch suddenly should show signs of movement, he would leave his moorings with less than a certain size of fleet. One would not, in any case, imagine that a gentleman of sense and spirit would stay in such a trap waiting for the completion of the crews of the last laggard ships or for the last few hundred-weights of stores. One would expect him, upon receiving unwelcome reports of Dutch activity, to risk any armament not hopelessly outnumbered, rather than let the issue go by an early and possibly irretrievable default.

The Vice-Admiral's squadron was indeed sufficiently well provided to be sent at once to anchor somewhat in advance of the rest of the fleet between the Red Sand and the Oaze-Edge,[2] Strickland's flag—the Union—flying from the foretop of the 'Mary';[3] and Dartmouth, while the winds blew strong and westerly,[4] addressed himself to the task of hastening the rest of his fleet.

Dartmouth would not expect great disappointment in respect of the hulls or the forwardness of the work of rigging. As Master of the Ordnance he could himself directly handle matters of ordnance and ammunition supply and eliminate the delay

---

[1] See p. 28.   [2] Dartmouth MSS, XI, 5, p. 141.
[3] *Memoirs...Torrington*, p. 23.
[4] Dartmouth MSS, XI, 5, p. 143 and several other places.

incident to the process of dealing with the Tower officials through the Secretary of Admiralty. For the rest of his needs, that is to say for the making up of complements of officers and crews, for stores and for victuals, he depended, of course, on the co-operation of the King-Lord High Admiral and Mr Secretary Pepys who appointed the officers, enlisted or pressed the sailors, and who, to provide supplies, operated through the Navy Board and the subsidiary officials at the Victualling Office and the Yards. It happened that two of the members of the Navy Board, Captain Sir Wm Booth and Rear-Admiral Sir John Berry, had been appointed to executive commands in the fleet (not that they thereby vacated their Commissionerships) and their presence in the fleet, no doubt, considerably aided the Admiral.[1]

As events proved, Dartmouth had little cause to complain of the state of the hulls and the work of the riggers.

The Ordnance Office was, however, struggling to meet the simultaneous demands of fortresses, regiments and ships, and its stock doubtless ran low. "I persuade myself I need not trouble the officers of the Ordnance from here", wrote Pepys on October 3rd;[2] but that he did not consider himself absolved from all care of oversight is shown in a letter to the Admiral-Master upon the 8th, "I cannot omit to give you Sir Richard Beach's words relating to the backwardness of the shipps at Portmouth", he said, in complaining of gun-carriage misfits and the want of tackles.[3] Dartmouth was not blind to the unsatisfactory despatch of Tower business. On the 17th, in a letter to the King, he wrote: "I humbly desire your Majestie to look a little into that office when they wait on you, for much of your service both by sea and land depends upon their well ordering and management of their business".[4] The unsatisfied vigilance of the Secretary led him to speak much more plainly upon the 20th.

My Lord, I must pray your Lordshipp, as Master of the Ordance to forgive me the discharging myself of what I cannot but hold my selfe accomptable for to the King in you as Admirall of his fleet, by

---

[1] Dartmouth MSS, XI, 5, p. 147. [2] Ibid. p. 140.
[3] Ibid. p. 151. [4] Ibid. p. 260.

observing to you, that however matters may be represented to you from the Office, there is not one shipp now behind you, from whose Comander I doe not daily hear of want of gunns, carriages, shot, or something else relateing thereto, notwithstanding (as the captains averr) their gunners' dayly attendance for them. And yet I am doubt-full whether, after what I have heretofore noted hereon, and your answers thereto, I should have troubled you with any more mention of it, but that upon my attendance this morning at the Cabinet, severall of the Lords there, did of their own accords (without any particular introduction to it) enquire of mee before the King, whether the shipps that should now be with you, had all their gunns and carriages abroad or noe, recomending to mee to inform myself thoroughly in it, for that their Comanders had declared to them their wants thereof at this day.[1]

There certainly were great difficulties in securing ordnance supplies; but presumably the demands of Dartmouth received priority in execution and were approximately satisfied. The Office went from bad to worse; but its delinquencies after mid October are here not relevant.

Ordinary stores are much more readily supplied. But when the captains of ships sent in requisitions in the hope of getting some, at least, of the things for which they asked, Dartmouth desired the assistance of a member of the Navy Board to deal with the lists submitted. He had also in mind the help that such an officer could give in other directions and, in par-ticular, he seems to have desired the presence of Sir Richard Haddock.[2] That, in view of the fact that Sir Richard was perhaps the most important official of the Board, and since Dartmouth had two members of the Board already with the fleet, was a little unreasonable. His wish was not granted; for scarcely a quorum of overworked Navy Board officials remained accessible in London.[3] Captain Wilshaw, the Master Attendant at Deptford, left London on the 7th to act in the place of one of the Commissioners.[4] Boatswains' stores, slops and signal flags, necessities and medicaments for the sick and wounded, were, in course, supplied—the latter through Mr Pearse the Surgeon General.[5] But the Navy Board very properly demurred to one

---

[1] Dartmouth MSS, XI, 5, p. 169.
[2] *Ibid.* p. 146.   [3] *Ibid.* p. 142.
[4] *Ibid.* p. 146.   [5] *Ibid.* pp. 152 and 161.

effeminate request—they could not find that beds for the soldiers were ever supplied by the Navy and therefore presumed they either made use of "hamaccoes" or had beds from the Tower.[1]

Victualling was a much bigger affair. In a letter of October 2nd, Dartmouth seems to have proposed that the ships being victualled should receive three months' supply instead of four. The suggestion was calculated, so Pepys's letter of the 3rd makes plain, to please the Victualling Commissioners, who had taken it not as a complaint that the extraneous duty of feeding the garrisons had been put upon them. The King approved the idea. Pepys wrote: "he with the Lords are most forward in their agreeing with it, as seeming to wish the fleet out, though it were but with 2 monthes provicõn, rather than have it stay but two hours for two months more".[2] Possibly also Dartmouth suggested that a Victualling agent should be sent to the fleet in order to facilitate business, for, after "a solemn meeting" at the Navy Board (October 4th) where the Commissioners for the Victualling were requested to submit an exact report of the state of supply to individual ships, they were asked to suggest a suitable agent.[3] They despatched an experienced purser as agent before the evening of the 7th, when the Commissioners were summoned to the King's presence and made to tell the exact state of their deliveries to the ships. They alleged that Strickland's squadron had been victualled in the Downs, that the Portsmouth ships were fully supplied, and that the rest were stocked so far as the list they produced would show. They were subjected to much exhortation. Pepys, writing these things that Sunday night to the Admiral, closed with the reflection that he could not "but wish that some other hands had had the providing for the land work elsewhere than at the Magazines of the Navy" for he had just discovered that three third rates might have been victualled for two months on what the garrison needs had devoured.[4] Possibly, the Commissioners were taken by surprise, when, on the evening of the next day,

---

[1] Dartmouth MSS, XI, 5, p. 152, "Bed" means "mattress".
[2] *Ibid.* p. 140.
[3] *Ibid.* p. 142.   [4] *Ibid.* p. 147.

once more they were summoned before his Majesty and found him much affected because of a complaint from his Admiral. Equal to the emergency, "they presented him with a fresh state differing from the other by soe much as they had performed... of what was then undone", and said that four more ships—two third and two fourth rates—would be victualled by Saturday and "the only two of the list then remaineing" would be dealt with as soon as possible.[1] On the 11th, Pepys could add no more to what he had told Dartmouth.[2] But the Victualling Commissioners had not done with sudden and solemn meetings. Again, on the 14th, they were brought to the King. They protested they had accomplished all they had declared. Unfortunately for them, on the table, lay a memorial from their agent which showed that foodstuffs had not got to the fleet. The practical Pepys suggested the despatch of an officer to "scoure the river of all their victualling vessels that shall bee found anyway truanting aloft" so that he might go to Dartmouth with "the only visible evidence of the truth of them, namely, the victuall itselfe spoaken of in those accounts". He was almost persuaded to spare Sir Richd. Haddock; but another supplied his place.[3] On October 20th, Pepys was able to say: "I am very glad to observe your Lordshipp's satisfaction in the business of the victualling and water-boats for the fleet".[4]

It has been pointed out that, in order to supply the deficiency of men, the press had been set in operation by an Order in Council of September 23rd,[5] which allowed pressing to be undertaken by the Admiral, certain other officers, and the heads of the Watermen's Hall and the Company of the Free Fishermen. Requisitions were made to the Companies by Pepys; and, writing on October 4th to Dartmouth, he said that the "Governors" of the Fishermen had reported to him that they had six vessels at work collecting men and that the "Rulers" of the Watermen peremptorily affirmed that their whole quota

---

[1] Dartmouth MSS, XI, 5, p. 150.   [2] Ibid. p. 155.
[3] Ibid. p. 159.   [4] Ibid. p. 168.
[5] See p. 25. Demand made by Pepys, Sept. 25th—each man sent by the Company to the fleet to be paid 12d. and 1d. per mile conduct money, the money repayable at the Navy Office to the Company. Records at Watermen's Hall (uncalendared).

of 200 had actually been sent to the fleet; they showed catalogues of names and lists of the ships to which the men had been assigned. Pepys doubted the list but could not say certainly where the pressed-men would be found. The same letter stated that a hundred soldiers were on their way to the ship and that over three hundred in all were under orders for service afloat. A few men were to be pressed in Sussex.[1] Pepys contended, in a letter of October 5th, that the watermen and fishermen were actually being put aboard the fleet;[2] but Dartmouth remained as sceptical about the delivering of the men as of the receipt of provisions;[3] and Pepys could do little to reassure him either on the 8th[4] or on the 10th.[5] The Rulers of the Watermen re-averred that they had delivered their quota of 200; and the Fishermen protested that 300 of the 500 required of them were actually forwarded. On the 11th, the Watermen were required to supply another 200 hands,[6] perhaps as a result of a letter from the Admiral to the King.[7] This time they were told to send them in a single body. It was anticipated that such a quota would require a search in the West Country—a week's task. By the 18th Pepys wrote that the Fishermen reported their work even more than complete, while the Watermen alleged themselves clear of their new quota.[8] But the actual deliveries continued to be matters of dispute.[9] Dartmouth was naturally anxious to secure these men. He could have no better sailors.[10] His lordship had decided by this time to secure a Mustermaster; and his brother, having made an attempt to prefer himself to Pepys for the post, discovered that Dartmouth would not forward his interests. The choice was left to Pepys who regarded the appointment as highly important.

The truth is, my Lord, as there is hardly any one Ministeriall officer appertaineing to a fleet, the well performance of whose work may be emproved to better use either to the Admirall or Prince then that of the Muster-Master, soe I must declare to you that in all my (near) thirty yeares service I never saw it, (or not above twice) soe executed,

---

[1] Dartmouth MSS, XI, 5, p. 141.
[2] *Ibid.* p. 145.   [3] *Ibid.* p. 257.
[4] *Ibid.* p. 149.   [5] *Ibid.* p. 154.
[6] *Ibid.* p. 157. Records at Watermen's Hall (uncalendared), Oct. 10th.
[7] *Ibid.* p. 257.   [8] *Ibid.* p. 167
[9] *Ibid.* p. 168.   [10] *Ibid.* p. 257.

as that either one or the other had the fruit required from it, but has alwayes been made, either a by-work, given for the profit sake to somebody that had other business to doe, and could not, or to some other that for want either of experience, diligence or interest, either could not, would not, or durst not adventure upon the executeing it with the strictness necessary to render it effectuall. In consideration of which it is that I have been soe slow, and am not yet fully prepared to propose anybody for this imployment.

At the writing of that, Pepys had only got as far as refusing the post to several persons, among them Mr Bowles the Admiral's Secretary, who received a reminder that Pepys knew from experience the work of an admiral's secretary and couldn't allow this duty to be done by deputy.[1] But eventually Mr Bowles did get the office.[2]

The first duty of an officer commissioned to a ship is to go aboard her at the earliest opportunity; if he be the commander taking over his ship from the dockyard authorities, his activity in preparing her for sea should be unremitting. From the first the conduct of certain officers left much to be desired. "Pray think of sending up Captain Coffin, for in truth nothing but such an officer...will be able I fear to prevent the delays that will be made, under one pretence or other in Commanders getting their shipps down". Thus Pepys to Dartmouth in his first letter.[3] Next day the 4th, Captain Cotton, going down to Dartmouth, was ordered by Pepys on his way to rouse the laggards.[4] On the 5th Pepys reflected that a certain ship (the 'St Albans') would "be more in the way of forwarding, had her Comander taken his leave of the Court".[5] On the 7th, he got the King's orders to write to the captains "still walking in Whitehall".[6] On the 11th he harked back to the same topic,[7] on the 17th regretted that "gentlemen are got above being jealous of any censure, or else they would not appear to the King every day at Court, complaineing that their shipps are not ready, while nothing is wanting towards making them ready but their own attendance on board".[8] Allowing both for

---

[1] Dartmouth MSS, XI, 5, p. 173.   [2] Ibid. p. 227.
[3] Ibid. p. 140.   [4] Ibid. p. 142.
[5] Ibid. p. 145.   [6] Ibid. p. 148.
[7] Ibid. p. 156.   [8] Ibid. p. 166.

the fact that Pepys can find no excuse for a half-hearted obedience to the commissions of Admiralty, and for the circumstance that some officers held their appointments *in commendam*,[1] the lack of zeal to which Pepys refers remains, if not exactly novel, at least inexcusable, and in such a crisis it might indeed be considered ominous. As a set-off, it is pleasing to learn of the excess of zeal which prompted the captain of the 'Tiger' to take away to sea a number of riggers who were at work on his vessel,[2] an action which brought on him a stingless reprimand.[3] And mention of other zealous service might be made.

In concluding these observations on personnel, it may be noted that Dartmouth took steps to secure more chaplains, their fewness being in his eyes "a scandal to our religion".[4] He was anxious to provide a sufficient number of surgeons and surgeons' mates;[5] he demanded pilots.[6] He dealt of course with the routine matters of recommendations and appointments within the limits the Service allowed. He had with him a Judge Advocate to assist at courts martial.[7] An attempt to make a correct table of officers' seniorities caused much trouble to Dartmouth and Pepys and some heart-burnings to captains who had been lax in registering their earlier commissions.[8] It is amusing enough to note that Dartmouth did not find the Secretary quiescent at an entry of 50 servants upon an official return, that total being the allowance of personal attendants which he, the Admiral, claimed for his rank. Pepys speedily, but tactfully, objected to an establishment equal to that allowed only to the Lord High Admiral of England and would not cede the point that more than 30 servants could be allowed to the flag.[9] While his ships were equipping, Dartmouth drew an instalment of contingent money from the Treasurer of the Navy.[10]

---

[1] Dartmouth MSS, XI, 5, p. 171. [2] *Ibid.* p. 173.
[3] *Ibid.* p. 182. [4] *Ibid.* XV, 1, p. 59.
[5] *Ibid.* XI, 5, pp. 148, 152. The Surgeon General was J. Pearse. See also pp. 217, 223.
[6] *Ibid.* p. 148. [7] *Ibid.* p. 166.
[8] *Ibid.* pp. 162, 174. [9] *Ibid.* pp. 149, 156.
[10] *Ibid.* p. 164. "Contingent money" was normally devoted to securing information as to the enemy's dispositions and strength.

Such, to the end of the third week in October, is our information as to the business of equipping the original fleet reinforcements for service. Much of the work had been done beside the wharves; part of it had been effected after this or that vessel had dropped down stream to join the rest of the fleet; doubtless many things which were desirable were, for each ship, never completed. The middle of the three weeks had seen the work well advanced; the end of the period witnessed its approximate completion. The fleet still lacked (be it allowed) its full paper strength of 61 vessels, the 12 thirds, 25 fourths, 18 fireships, 3 sixths and 3 yachts of the schedule. But nearly all the Channel ships were come round;[1] and, actually, the Admiral had with him 31 of the 37 ships of the line together with 14 of the fireships as well as other vessels. It was a fleet smaller, of course, than many sent out to represent England in this same era; but it constituted an adequately manned armament which, unless appearances mocked the truth, its Admiral could be rightly expected to consider it an honour to command, and which, unless official calculations were badly astray, seemed likely to prove adequate for the work in hand.

But, in these three weeks, had the slowly nucleating fleet indeed got out from the original place of rendezvous, the Nore Buoy, as surely James had expected it to do? And, if so, what new plans had been laid and what moves, if any, made against the Dutch?

Dartmouth, at once on taking command, had turned his attention to the conduct of the forthcoming campaign.

In the first place, he, or rather he and Pepys, had taken the precaution of concluding with a delegation of Trinity House Brethren, arrangements for dislocating the Estuary buoys and the Harwich light[2] in such a way as to pay due regard to legitimate shipping, it being agreed that no mark should be altered if the enemy should not appear.[3] Also Dartmouth had continued constant scouting services.

Probably too the work of the issuing of Sailing and Fighting Instructions had been early disposed of. Anyway, two papers,

---

[1] Dartmouth MSS, XI, 5, p. 259.   [2] Ibid. p. 140.
[3] "Journal of Captain Grenville Collins", Dartmouth MSS, XV, 1, p. 55.

one concerning the squadronal divisions of the fleet and the other touching the line of battle, were in the King's hands by October 14th.[1] There are still extant a squadronal divisional list for fifty ships, a system of signals for calling aboard the Admiral any captain of any ship, as well as full Sailing Instructions and complete Fighting Instructions.[2] From these it appears that the squadronal divisions were to be the usual three, the white, red and blue; the Vice-Admiral the white, the Admiral the red and the Rear-Admiral the blue; but that there was no attempt to subdivide the squadrons each under a Vice-Admiral and Rear-Admiral in the traditional way. Of course it was not to be a large fleet and, as has been remarked, would contain no first or second rate ships. The Sailing Instructions are seen to be of the usual character, the Fighting Instructions in harmony with the "Model" Instructions drawn up by James in 1673. In the Fighting Instructions, the only innovation referred to the handling of the line of battle, an innovation suggested probably enough by Dartmouth's previous experience.[3] The full squadronal list—anticipating some 50 sail to come under command—is herewith printed:

ADMIRALL DIVISION

A Redd Flag ensigne staffe.

3	Plymouth	... ...	Capt. Rd. Carter.
4	Dover	... ...	Capt. Cloud. Shovell.
4	Bonaventure	... ...	Capt. Tho. Hopson.
4	Nonsuch	... ...	Capt. Jam. Montgomry.
4	Centurion	... ...	Sir. Fran. Wheeler.
3	Montague	... ...	Jon. Ld. Berkeley.
3	Resolution	... ...	Capt. Wm. Davis.
3	Pendennis	... ...	Sr. Wm. Booth.
4	Advice	... ...	Capt. Hen. Williams.

---

[1] Dartmouth MSS, XI, 5, p. 160.

[2] B.M. MSS, Sloane 3560, defectively entitled "Lord Dartmouth's Instructions", contains all these and other matter. This is an undated MS, but internal evidence shows that it cannot have been compiled before 1689. It contains fine water-colour marginal illustrations of signals. According to Pepys's table (see Perrin, *British Flags*, p. 96) a small fleet of only three squadrons with all the flag officers flying the union, was to wear the red ensign throughout. This seems to be the only exception.

[3] Reprint and discussion in *Fighting Instructions* 1530–1816, Corbett.

	4 St. Albans	...	...	Capt. Constable.
	4 Crowne	...	...	Capt. Robt. Robinson.
	4 St. David	...	...	Capt. Wm. Dodham.
Fireships	⎧ Dartmouth	...	...	C. Wool. Cornwall.
	⎨ Guardland	...	...	C. Jon. Jenifer.
	⎩ Rose Sally Prize	...		Capt. Edmd. Elyott.
	6 Fire Drake	...	...	Capt. Jon. Leake.
	6 Quaker Ketch	...	...	Capt. Tho. Allin.
Fireship	Guensey	...	...	Capt. Robt. Arthur.

VICE ADMLL. DIVISION

A White flag on ye Ensigne Staffe.

	3 Rupert	...	...	Sr. Wm. Jennins.
	4 Jersey	...	...	Capt. Jon. Beverley.
	4 Bristoll	...	...	Capt. Tho. Leighton.
	4 Assurance	...	...	Capt. R. Mc.Donnell.
	4 Diamond	...	...	Capt. Ben Walters.
	3 Dreadnought	...	...	C. Steph. Akerman.
	3 Mary	...	...	Capt. Jon. Laton.
	3 Cambridge	...	...	Capt. Jon. Tyrewhitt.
	4 Newcastle	...	...	C. Geo. Churchill.
	4 Portsmouth	...	...	Capt. St. loe.
	4 Swallow	...	...	Capt. M. Aylmer.
	4 Deptford	...	...	Capt. Geo. Rooke.
	⎧ Richmond	...	...	C. Staffd. Fairborne.
	⎪ Speedwell	...	...	Capt. Bolton.
Fireships	⎨ Halfemoon	...	...	Capt. Jon. Munde.
	⎪ Signett	...	...	Capt. Jon. Shelly.
	⎩ Larke	...	...	Capt. Jor. Grymsditch.

	4 Mordant	...	...	Capt. John Tyrrell.
	4 Ruby	...	...	Capt. Fred Froude.
	4 Constant Warwick	...	...	Capt. Chas. Shellton.
	4 Greenwch	...	...	Capt. Ralph Wrenn.
	3 Yorke	...	...	Capt. Ral. Dalavall.
	3 Elizabeth	...	...	Capt. Nevell.
	3 Defyance	...	...	Capt. John Ashby.
	4 Foresight	...	...	Capt. Ed. Stanly.
	4 Woolwich	...	...	Capt. Arth. Hastings.
	4 Anthelope	...	...	Capt. hugh. Ridley.
	3 Henrietta	...	...	Capt. Rd. Trevanion.

Fireships	Pearle	...	...	Capt. Tho. Cole.
	Swan	...	...	Capt. Tho. Johnson.
	Sophia	...	...	Capt. Xpher Minngs.
	Eliz. & Sarah	...	...	Capt. Dove.

REAR ADMIRALL'S DIVISION

A Blew Flagg on the Ensigne Staffe.[1]

The reader already knows that Dartmouth wore the Union at the main of the 'Resolution', that Vice-Admiral Strickland flew the Union from the foretop to the 'Mary'. Rear-Admiral Berry's flagship, the 'Elizabeth', which got into the Nore on the 7th, hoisted the Union at the mizzen.[2]

Passing from these two matters, his precautions and that more or less mechanical side, the tactical aspect of his dispositions, one finds that there is also every evidence of early thought applied to find a proper plan for the campaign ahead. "I need not mind you to lose no tyme to gett out from amonge the sands", the King had written on the 5th[3], and Dartmouth had suitably replied.[4] James's next letter on the 8th, had brought out the

---

[1] The foregoing list gives many fewer ships than Burchett's table summarises (see p. 29). It omits:

2 fourth rates
'Tyger' (Capt. Matthew Tennant, Dartmouth MSS, XI, 5, p. 138).
'Faulcon' (Capt. Thos. Smith, *ibid.*).
1 sixth rate
'Saudadoes' (Capt. John Graydon, *ibid.*).
6 fireships
'Roebuck' (Capt. Francis Wivell, Dartmouth MSS, XI, 5, p. 216).
'Sampson' (Capt. Pooley)
'Charles and Henry' (Capt. Harris) — These names are supplied from Pepys's list of commanders on December 18th, 1688, in *Memoires.*
'Unity' (Capt. Stone)
'Charles' (Capt. Potter)
'St Paul' (Capt. Boteler)
3 yachts not named by Burchett.

But, as against Burchett, it includes:
Sixth rate...'Quaker Ketch'.
There were, operating with the fleet, a number of miscellaneous vessels, over and above those named in any list. Such are mentioned, where desirable, in the text, among them certain yachts.

[2] Dartmouth MSS, XV, 1, p. 55, and Sloane MS cited, p. 51. The flag was, for a short while, round about October 14th, borne on the 'Defiance' as the 'Elizabeth' was not fully ready for the emergency of that day.

[3] Dartmouth MSS, XI, 5, p. 144.   [4] *Ibid.* p. 256.

first suggestion for a really calculated campaign. The King had said,

tho' all (the ships) that are in the Hope should not be quit ready, consider well whether you should loze the opportunity of this westerly wind to gett out from amongst the sands or ventur to have the Dutch come and find you posted somewhere neare the boye of the Oze edg, amongst the sands, for you must expect they will come out and be looking for you, with the first easterly wind; and by letters which came this day on their 9th. I am informed they will send most of their (men) of war to look you out to engage you, whilst they send their forces to land some were els and 'tis believed, that it may be northward.[1]

Dartmouth had replied on the 12th,

Your Majesty cannot be more desirous to have me from among the sands then I am impatiently endeavouring to get out.... I will be on sea upon the first alteration.... I do not doubt but they will endeavour to attacke me with a considerable force...they will not venture out with their land forces while I can keep to sea and be hovering over them....I believe it for Your Majestie's honour and service if the weather be anything reasonable, to show myselfe upon their coast as nere as conveniently I can in the daytime, still standing off to get good sea room every night while I shall see it reasonable to stay thereabout. I have discoursed with the ablest men and pylots I have with me particularly, and they are all of opinion that there is no attempting anything in their ports at this time of yeare.[2]

It will therefore be seen that Dartmouth held, as the King also believed, that the Dutch would seek him out to win command by battle (hardly by blockade) in order that they might effect the movement of their transports. It seems he had not entertained the idea that the enemy would assume undecided command, and risk the moving of their transports either in an open or concealed way. The Admiral had even spoken of seeking the enemy coasts. Into the treacherous shallows of the Dutch Weilings it would have been hazardous at any time for Dartmouth to have penetrated. Slighter in build and less of draught, the Dutch ships could swing where there was no water for an Englishman to follow. And as, at that time of the year, entry into Dutch ports was out of the question, so a long preventive

---

[1] Dartmouth MSS, XI, 5, p. 152.   [2] *Ibid.* p. 258.

blockading stay on the Dutch coast was equally unthinkable. But demonstrative cruises of quite short duration might, none the less, he seems to have continued to believe, be undertaken. These projects of operating towards the enemy coast have, however, considerable historical interest.

In 1217, when Eustace the Monk, essaying to bring support to Louis of France in England, appeared off Dover, Hubert de Burgh went out and attacked him at sea. John, at Damme, had burnt the collected transports of an earlier intended invasion. By the attack he made upon the French ships at the port of Sluys, Edward III settled that the Hundred Years' War should not be fought on English soil. Drake singed the King of Spain's beard by attacking the convoying fleet in the harbour of Cadiz; and, but for a turn of the wind which swept Lord Howard of Effingham from the coast of Spain, likely enough the Armada would never have quitted the port of Corunna. This new danger had set an English admiral thinking on identical lines. It is perhaps too much to say that "forward play", to borrow a cricket expression, had become the traditional attitude to adopt towards the menace of invasion; but Dartmouth's wish to get upon the enemy coast was an instinctive English gesture.

While the deliberations of the Admiral stood thus, alarming news reached the flagship. By Sunday the 14th instant the wind had changed; and Dartmouth had learned that "the Dutch were at sea and resolved to come for the coast of England the first opportunity, being about 50 sail of men-of-war and fireships and 250 sail of flyboats and small vessels to transport their army".[1] A council of war was held[2] at which, doubtless, after a review of fighting strength, emergency decisions were taken. Dartmouth got under weigh,[3] behaving as the commander of a fleet not hopelessly out-numbered might confidently have been expected to do. The size of the fleet he had so far collected cannot be exactly estimated; though it was well under 31 ships of the line and 14 fireships.[4] Nor is the emergency plan he proposed to follow recorded; but it is safe to say it

[1] "Journal of Captain Grenville Collins", Dartmouth MSS, XV, 1, p. 55.
[2] *Ibid.*   [3] *Ibid.* p. 56.
[4] See p. 58.

cannot have amounted to more than an intention to work the fleet down the Swin (see Chart at the end of this work)[1], to make the best of whatever space of water the enemy's dispositions allowed for English manœuvres, and, in the fight at hand, to do all that the fleet might be found capable of accomplishing. Next day, the 15th, found Dartmouth little further on his way out of the river, no further indeed than the Black Tail and Oaze Edge Sands. There he had cause to believe that fate had dealt kindly with him, a fishing smack reporting that the returning westerly winds had driven many of the Dutch into Goeree.[2]

Every consideration of patriotism and professional interest laid it upon Lord Dartmouth to ensure that such a partial respite should not have come to him in vain. But no reader, who recalls the manner in which the proposal of Vice-Admiral Strickland to use the Gunfleet anchorage as a base of operations had, at the Windsor deliberations of August 26th last,[3] been vetoed in favour of a base between the Kentish Knock and the North Sand Head, can be prepared to learn that, on this 15th instant, Dartmouth, who, with Pepys and the Rear-Admiral, had been present at the Windsor meeting, in rounding off plans which were intended to serve not merely as emergency measures, decided to base himself on the Gunfleet roadstead![4] He informed Pepys.[5] There is no need to return to discuss the merits of the rival anchorages.[6] It can only be supposed that Dartmouth had, upon that August Sunday, held a minority view; or changed his opinion since, upon examination and representations made, he had come to prefer the facilities for quick information which the Gunfleet afforded and the advantages it offered for the undelayed launching of a blow, especially should the Dutch aim northwards, more than he feared the risk of being trapped or any inability to get quickly away to southward against the east wind and the flood.[7]

---

[1] The Black Deep and the Barrow Deep were not buoyed for navigation till this (20th) century.

[2] "Journal of Captain Grenville Collins", Dartmouth MSS, XV, 1, p. 56.

[3] See p. 19. [4] Dartmouth MSS, XI, 5, p. 165.

[5] Ibid. [6] See p. 20.

[7] The King had written on October 8th (p. 59) that the latest information said that the Dutch would attempt a landing to the northward. Against such a movement the Gunfleet was clearly the better position.

The 16th saw no progress. On the 17th Dartmouth held a council of flag officers and others "about going down the Swin". It was their opinion "not to adventure down without a fair wind". So the fleet rode in battle order in case the Dutch attacked unexpectedly.[1]

On the 17th, Dartmouth wrote to the King.[2] He had received a letter from his Majesty, dated the 14th, which complied with a request for an expression of the King's views upon his Admiral's plans. James had said,

As for your going over for to shew your self to their ships on the coast off Holland, I thinke you aught to consider well of it before you do it....By the last letters from Holland which were of the 6/16; 'tis sayd that Herbert who commands their fleett in cheef, is to look you out and observe your motions, whilst the Prince of Orange having Trump with him with eight men of war is to go with his army to land where he designs doing it; tho' this is not certain 'tis likely enough. I had ordred before I had yours, six thirds and all the remaining fourth to be fitted.[3]

It was a letter not to be construed as more than a warning to Dartmouth not to forget the assumed primary aim of the enemy —that defeat or smothering of Dartmouth's fleet which conditioned the safety of the Dutch work of transport; and it implied that the King did not desire Dartmouth (to quote words of Dartmouth's own using which were at the moment before the King's eyes) to "peeke" himself "or be provoked to do any rash thing",[4] it avoided all constraint and properly concluded "you will do what is best for my servis, which you that are on the place are the only judges of". Dartmouth observed the warning, replying,

upon the caution your Majestie hath given me I will not venture over on the coast of Holland without I see settled faire weather, which is not impossible after so much bad, but I thinke our appearance after this great hectoring would make a populous government change their vaunting. The light moones are comeing on, and it may be fit at least to see what use they will make of it.

---

[1] "Journal of Captain Grenville Collins", Dartmouth MSS, XV, 1, p. 56.
[2] Dartmouth MSS, XI, 5, p. 259.
[3] Ibid. p. 158.
[4] Ibid. p. 258. Dartmouth's last letter (of the 12th instant).

But the interest of the letter lies less in this acceptance of advice than in the reasoned statement contained in the following lines:

I shall take all the care imaginable now your fleet is likely to be in soe good a posture to keep it so till I see it absolutely necessary to undertake something for the preservation of all that seems to lie at stake, but upon the best advice I can take here we are all now of opinion that upon the first slatch of winde and faire weather we should fall downe to the Gunfleet where, tho' it be hard roadeing, yett the ground is good and we shall be well found. There we shall be ready to cover Harwich as well as the River Thames, be able to go to sea if occasion be, or we can but come up againe at worst. We shall be ready to looke towards the Channell, have very good anchoring between the Kentish Knocke and the North Sands Head, and the Downes allwayes to friend upon bad weather. This, Sir, with the humblest submission to your Majestie's better judgement is the present measures I thinke of till anything offers better for your service. I am even now grieved to be hooked here, though I thinke myselfe safe.

The sentence had a surprising continuation, in no way concerning his plan, which will receive notice later.

A letter from Secretary Pepys crossed with that reply to the King, for, on October 17th, Pepys despatched a letter intended for delivery to the Admiral by way of Harwich.[1] Pepys wrote just after leaving the King who had received from a person, present in Helvoetsluys on Sunday last (the 14th),[2] information which he, the King, quite accepted.

"The purport of which", said Pepys, "is this; that the Dutch fleet" (and here in a parenthesis he remarked that the evidence squared with the scout intelligences already reported to the 'Resolution' and confirmed at the Admiralty) "went into Goree the same Sunday, and arrived at Helversluce that evening, very much disordered with the late fowle weather, and particularly Mr. Herbert's Shipp (the 'Utrecht' if the King remembers her name right) soe belaboured with the sea, that she had 7 foot water in hold, and with some difficulty preserved from foundering. That he saw Mr. Herbert and Benting together upon the key at Helversluce on Sunday night; that Mr. Herbert was then busie in getting another shipp the 'Maiden of Dort' bought to the side of the 'Utrecht' for the transferring into her the guns, stores, provisions and everything else out of the 'Utrecht'. That the informant does beleive by all that he coold

---

[1] Dartmouth MSS, XI, 5, p. 164.   [2] O.S.

hear or judge, that the shipps thus come in could not be putt into a condition of comeing forth againe till to-morrow or Friday at soonest. That Herbert carried the flagg at the maine topp, namely the Holland's flagg. That they work night and day, Sunday and all, Munday last only excepted, as being a day of solemn fasting and prayer all over the provinces for good success to their undertaking. Lastly, that (to say nothing of their other known preparations) they doe certainly bring with them an incredible number of coates and other clothing for the men they expect to raise here, and small armes without stint, even to the makeing it a difficulty to buy a hand gun, pistoll or sword in all the country, and are forced to impress even English shipping for want of imbarcations enough to be had of other nations; and after all this, a vast quantity of lime, to what uses your Lordshipp is much a better judge than my self".

One matter of which his informant spoke, "the want of imbarcations", had for the King a special significance. To that question it will be necessary to return subsequently.

Dartmouth no doubt found the news of interest. It was not strictly coincident with fact,[1] but it does show that the surveillance of travellers leaving Holland had not prevented this particular traveller's report to the English King. The news, to be sure, did not long engross Dartmouth's attention. For the Secretary had continued

And this having said, as to the maine occasion of this express, I cannot omit to mention a particular or two in answer to your forementioned letter.[2] And first, that though I had noe comands at all from the King to mention any such thing to you, as declareing himself resolved to putt noe restraints upon you, by any advice of his in a matter where he judges himself soe safe, in his comitteing it entirely to your prudence, yet I cannot (as to my own particular) but think it fit for me to observe to you, that upon my reading to him that paragraph of your letter that speaks of your purpose of proceeding directly from the Oaze-edge to the Gunfleet, he imediately said to me, I wish that may be soe well as his remaineing where he is at the Oaze-edge, for fear he should be surprised while there by the sudden coming of the Dutch fleet, as being a place he cannot well gett out to sea from, while the wind remaines easterly. But I know my Lord Dartmouth will consider all that. My Lord I dare not undertake

---

[1] Herbert was not in full command till October 27/17. The 'Utrecht' was at this time Van Almonde's ship. He changed into the 'Maagd van Dordrecht'. Herbert hoisted his flag on the 'Leyden'. (Cf. p. 36.)

[2] Of the 15th instant Dartmouth MSS, XI, 5, p. 165.

that I have exactly repeated the King's words, but being as near as I can remember, and sufficient (I suppose) to lead you to judge of the King's thoughtfulness and thoughts herein, I did beleive it could be of noe injury, if it proved of noe use to you to know them.

So what the King would be likely to think of the Admiral's reference to the Gunfleet in the dispatch that night on its way to London is here, in anticipation, told. It may be added that when the King did write to Dartmouth on the 20th, he did not mention the matter.[1]

In spite of the commotion of the 14th instant and the terrible warning implied, the stay at the Black Tail and the Oaze Edge lasted through and beyond the third week in October. At first sight it seems an unnecessarily long delay, for, supposing that the Dutch were no longer expected to lie in the vicinity of the exit from the Swin, there remained no tactical danger to be feared, if a single tide and the prevailing winds not serving to bear out the whole fleet together to the sea, Dartmouth had fallen down the Swin in separate squadrons on successive ebb tides. But second thoughts tend to suspension of judgement. The winds, on the Dutch coast at least, blew from the eastward on the 18th and 19th of the month, blew therefore to hinder the English Admiral's emergence; and storms from the opposite quarter raved during the days next following. Dartmouth himself, in a letter to the King, on the 22nd instant,[2] referred to the bad weather.

It was not until October 24th that a four hours' run took the three squadrons to the Gunfleet,[3] to a base which, for good or evil, the Admiral still (it must be assumed) continued to regard as necessary to the carrying out of his command-disputing, command-asserting plan.

It was natural that, once he had reached the open sea, the Admiral should pass in review his collected strength; and that his thoughts should dwell upon the plan he cherished. On the 24th, one finds Dartmouth thus addressing the King as to the efficiency of his fleet.

I could wish I had more force if the enemy be so strong as I am told

---

[1] Dartmouth MSS, XI, 5, p. 169.   [2] *Ibid.* p. 260.
[3] "Journal of Captain Grenville Collins", Dartmouth MSS, XV, 1, p. 56.

tho' I belive we are as good a winter Squadron as ever England put to sea at this time of the year and as nothing shall be wanting on my part for your Majestie's service so upon the best enquiry I can make I apprehend nothing but a readiness in all the Commanders to do their duty by your Majestie. Sir we are now at sea before the Dutch after all their boasting.[1]

Of course, of the dramatic irony of his last sentence Dartmouth could not be aware! But he expresses satisfaction with ships and men. An armament of 31 of the 37 ships of the line and 14 fireships as well as smaller vessels,[2] though it did fall short of the full paper quota, was appreciable enough against an enemy believed to muster "50 sail of men-of-war and fireships". Dartmouth had no reason, when he wrote, to suppose that he suffered appreciable numerical inferiority. He knew, moreover, that he could expect without delay the backward ships; and six of the third and all the remaining fourth rates were to be taken in hand in the yards—a reinforcement and reserve in case of need. But what of the men? It is difficult to believe that he could "apprehend nothing but a readiness in all the Commanders".

The reference to caballing made by Dartmouth on the 17th instant in his letter to the King must now be quoted; and to that added the information conveyed in the further letter of the 22nd to his Majesty. In the letter of the 17th,[3] the continuation of the sentence which was said to have nothing whatever to do with the outlined plans, ran thus,

I would be glad to have more sea room and keep my commanders now they are in good order as much as may be aboard their own shipps and not liable to be caballing one with another, which, lieing idle together they may be apt as Englishmen naturally do to fall into, especially being in the way of dayley pamphlets and newes letters.

On the 22nd Dartmouth said,

I must acquaint your Majestie that on Friday last I had some hints of dissatisfaction in some young men in the fleet, and hearing Mr Russell is gone for Holland (if it be so) makes me more jealous then of any interest Herbert can have here....The Duke of Grafton was

---

[1] Dartmouth MSS, XI, 5, p. 261.
[2] "Journal of Captain Grenville Collins", Dartmouth MSS, XV, 1, p. 56.
[3] See p. 64.

down here a little after my comeing tho' he would not let me know it. My Lord Berkeley I am told is very pert but I have taken him in next shipp to me and shall know more of their tempers in a little time.

But he was able to say

I look upon most of the Commanders to be men of honour and will peek them that we are to be steady to your service tho' I feare they have other advices and still thinke all our mischiefes spring directly or indirectly from the old conduit of Whitehall. This I believe your Majestie finds more of and 'tis fitt I should endure my share.[1]

Of those captains who had been most active in caballing, Captain Matthew Aylmer of the 'Swallow' was perhaps the chief. On the way down from London, where a meeting had been held, he had taken into confidence Lieutenant Byng ("1st leftenant"—of the 'Defiance') whose sympathies General Kirk had been able to vouch for.[2] Byng, told of the meeting and informed that men such as Russel and Kirk intended declaring for the Prince, had become an adherent to sedition. But it is not surprising, perhaps, that, demurring from the attempt to convert Ashby, his own captain, he had put Aylmer, when on a visit to the 'Defiance', into Ashby's cabin and had left Aylmer to the work himself. Aylmer's persuasion had not had immediate success, Ashby at first replying that, in their profession, they were not taught to turn against the King. But having taken time to consider it and been in conversation with Byng (whose name no doubt Aylmer had in the discussion dragged in), Ashby had become at least a "well-wisher" to the cause. Seemingly, after that, Byng had waxed bolder and assisted in the more difficult task of winning over the violent-tempered Captain Woolfran Cornwall (of the 'Dartmouth'). Cornwall was moved from the standpoint that to desert the King was, to one who owed much to the King, a great villainy, by a parading of the names of the great adherents to the desertion scheme. The name of one captain in particular had carried great weight; and Byng had at length schemed that the two captains, Cornwall and the

---

[1] Dartmouth MSS, XI, 5, p. 260.
[2] For Byng's early career see *D.N.B.*, article "Byng, George; Viscount Torrington, "and Dalton's *Army Lists*, vol. II.

particular captain, should meet at a supper specially arranged to that end. From the night of that supper, Cornwall was an active supporter to the party of defection.[1] Of course Dartmouth would not know of these happenings. In particular he would not know why the "chiefest and most considerable" captains had supported the Gunfleet project, or be conscious that they could possibly count his decision to sail thither as the fruit of their persuasion and a "point artfully gained".[2] Again, a manifesto by Herbert supplementing a circular letter from the Prince of Orange[3] was almost certainly being read in the cabins and forecastles of the fleet. "I as a true Englishman and your friend exhort you to join your arms to the Prince for the defence of the common cause", it ran; it pointed to the adherence of the "best part of the Army as well as the Nation" to the undertaking and pleaded "prevent them in so good an action whilst it is in your power, and make it appear. That as the Kingdom has always depended on the Navy for its defence so you will yet so further by making it as much as in you lies the protection of her Religion and Liberties".[4] Dartmouth may or may not have seen that letter. Some things Dartmouth knew, of others he was evidently ignorant; but he cannot have been unconscious of the atmosphere which disaffection created. And if the leaven of disaffection were at work among those who were commissioned from the King, it must have fermented all the more violently through all the common ratings. Dartmouth's satisfaction with his command, real enough but too optimistic in the light of even his limited knowledge of sedition, naturally projected itself into contentedness with his plan. Such was his self confidence (to quote again from the letter of the 24th instant) that he could write—though he remained conspicuously silent still as to the Gunfleet choice—"if I may have leave to say so (between your Majestie and I only) your statesmen may take a nap and recover, the women sleep in their beds, and the catle I think need not be drove from the shoare".[5] From this point onwards, the Admiral's task was simplified.

[1] *Memoirs...Torrington*, p. 27. [2] *Ibid.* pp. 26, 27.
[3] Pamphlets in Bodley; 1688, 1, 2435.
[4] *Ibid.* 2433. See also Kennet, pp. 492–4.
[5] Dartmouth MSS, XI, 5, p. 261.

He had a considerable and still growing fleet with which he professed to be reasonably satisfied; his single legitimate aim was to make plain to himself and his captains his intentions and to put his plans to the test of the guns.

By the 24th, a ship of each division (i.e. squadron) was sent to cruise to the eastward—the 'Bonadventure', 'Swallow' and 'Foresight', under Captain Hopson of the 'Bonadventure'.[1]

It yet remains to carry the "English" side of the narrative from the 24th to the 29th of the month; and it may at once be said that those days saw a remarkable development in the Admiral's plans.

On the 26th, Captain Allin of the 'Quaker Ketch',[2] of whom Pepys had observed that he was glad this present service gave him "an opportunity of attoneing for his errors abroad (said to be great both in number and weight)",[3] reported "20 sail of men-of-war and fireships at anchor without Goree one of which let slip and gave him chase but could not get up with him". In the afternoon a council of war was held.[4]

By the 28th,[5] Dartmouth was in possession of news which had reached the King on the night of the 26—27th,[6] and which Pepys had passed on in duplicate (one letter despatched for Harwich between 4 and 5 a.m. on the 27th, the other sent by yacht later the same morning)[7]—authentic news of the first sailing of the Dutch expedition, of its buffeting and forced return to harbour. Dartmouth's receipt of this intelligence must have raised unpleasant memories of entrapping sands; but there is no hint of a disturbed equanimity in the reply which the Admiral sent off at once to the Secretary.[8]

"It is very manifest," Dartmouth began, "from the extract of [the] Marquis D'Abbevill's letters of the 30th of October and 2nd of November (new style) to the King, and the 31st of October to my Lord Sunderland that the Dutch put to sea on Friday, the 19th inst. our style, with a very considerable fleet, on which was embarked the Prince of Orange and his great land forces, and

---

[1] Dartmouth MSS, XV, 1, p. 60.
[2] "Journal of Captain Grenville Collins", Dartmouth MSS, XV, 1, p. 56.
[3] Dartmouth MSS, XI, 5, p. 156.
[4] "Journal of Captain Grenville Collins", Dartmouth MSS, XV, 1, p. 56.
[5] Dartmouth MSS, XV, 1, p. 60.   [6] Ibid. XI, 5, p. 175.
[7] Ibid. p. 176.   [8] Ibid. XV, 1, p. 60.

preparations, and that, the next day, they met with such contrary winds and ruffling weather as made them glad to retire to their own ports again...."

He passed by without comment d'Albeville's estimate of "the whole fleet" at 52 "men of war", and the transports at 400—500,[1] a circumstance which makes it fair to assume an absence of all surprise or alarm on his part at receiving this news of Dutch numbers and gives ground for the presumption that Dartmouth thought his fleet equal to the work in hand, even if it does not permit the inference of believed equality of strength. Nor over d'Albeville's remarks on the enemy objective did he think it worth while to delay.

"I cannot", he simply commented, "from any of [the] Marquis D'Abbevill's advices make any judgment as to what part of our Isle they will make their descent as believing—notwithstanding the suggested notions of the pilots mentioning, in their drink, Sole Bay[2] and some of Mr. Herbert's ships talking of Essex—the Prince would not trust the knowledge of a secret of that importance to his designs to above two or three of his private Council and therefore I believe myself very well posted here...".

With that, he left the matter to take note of something in Pepys's letter which dealt with the more vital present; "you tell me his Majesty seemed to think it might not be unuseful that I went with the fleet towards their coast", he continued; but only to show that the idea hardly pleased him. Rather, he said, he was

of opinion that the keeping of this fleet together and entire, is so essential to his Majesty's service, that, considering the season of the year, as the winds stand now, it is not advisable to venture over. The experience we have of the mischief to them, is reasonable advertisement to us, to avoid, as much as we can the same evil; for should we go over, and meet with such weather as should separate or damage us, they would, all the while, be safe in their own ports and ready to attack us, probably disabled, on the first fair invitation out.

It is a little perplexing to find the King half hinting through Pepys a course of action Dartmouth had earlier suggested to

[1] Dartmouth MSS, XI, 5, pp. 177, 178. D'Albeville also wrote to Dartmouth direct, p. 181.
[2] Sole Bay = Southwold Bay, Suffolk. See also p. 45 note (1).

the King and he, the King, had feared then to support; it is surprising to find the recommendation now being turned aside by its originator. But Dartmouth had, at this later date, the lesson of the storm before him, and, when he formerly made his proposal, he had not.

At first sight, succeeding parts of Dartmouth's letter scarcely remove the perplexity. Remarking that three frigates were out, he continued:

I hope for such intelligence as will enable me to do the best I can in attending[1] and attacking the enemy, with regard to the season, and utmost devotion to his Majesty's service, but because in a matter of that weight to the Crown as the preservation and conduct of this fleet is, wherein I find his Majesty wholly reposes and relies on me, I would not depend on my own single judgment....

and then,

I have this day had a consult with the Flags, and after that, a general Council of War of all the Commanders of the fleet before whom I laid every material circumstance and intelligence, whereon it was unanimously advised, Sir William Jennings excepted, and in terms I thing not very proper, at a more seasonable time of taking notice of it, that we should not, as the winds are, go over to that coast, but send scouts, as I have already observed to you, and if the wind comes up easterly or southerly with fine weather I will go to sea, and look out for them, [in] which case, considering the time must be spent in moving of such a body as their sea fleet, and the ships that carry their land forces must make, I cannot miss them on any probable conjecture.

It really does seem that contradiction could go no further! But, though Dartmouth had not receded from his original position, an outlook about which his correspondence had been more or less silent since the 17th, his position was not quite that of the earlier date; time and the latest news had made it firm, explicit, final. He does not now intend to go upon the Dutch coast in *any* wind that may blow (perhaps it is gratuitous to suppose he ever did mean to do that); he does not purpose to risk being driven upon their shores by, say, a westerly gale, while they, having waited safe in harbour, can come out on the change of

---

[1] "Attending" has a nautical meaning = "waiting upon for hostile purposes", "shadowing" (see *Oxford Dictionary*).

wind to attack his disabled ships. Such an operation would be especially perilous on the coast of Holland at this time of the year. Only when the winds set fair in east or south can they spread their sails. Then, and only then, does he undertake to "go to sea and look out for them". And apparently, it is not too much to hope, having read the letters of d'Albeville, that the Dutch, after all, even if led by Herbert, may be found about to ignore the securing of command, about to commit openly the folly of attempting to do two things at once—to beat the English fleet and convoy the transports—or, alternately, perhaps, to essay a concealed sailing. An expedition so sought could scarce be missed, so encountered could scarce escape destruction. Thus it might well befall that the decision of command (in the defeat of the enemy fleet) and the exercise of the same (in the destruction of the Dutch transports) would fuse into simultaneous operations, and double victory crown an ever-memorable day. But the circumstances which, in the thought of the Admiral, made possible this coalescence of the "command-disputing", "command-asserting" aspects of his plan is an important and somewhat startling conception. The doctrine of the proper use of adverse winds in the face of a near threatening invader is, through the story of the long watch kept by Hawke over the port of Brest until at last the enemy tempted him to the wintry battle of Quiberon Bay, familiar. Lord Dartmouth deserves the praise due to the pioneer officer. Yet, one disquieting spectre Dartmouth could not lay: "I hope", he concluded, "all the officers will do their duty honestly with regard to his Majestys Service, which by all the endeavours that I am capable of, I shall keep them to". The sentence is ominous.

For Dartmouth to have reached an explicit plan of campaign was an all important thing; to have begun to doubt seriously the merits of his Gunfleet base as a place whence to operate the plan was no less an important matter. With Captain Wm Jennens of the 'Rupert' Dartmouth may well have been, as he told Pepys, displeased. That ardent sailor, on the 26th, had written his Admiral advising him not to wait the Dutch coming to him but to take the opportunity of a fair wind and the light moon and go over to them; he had suggested that, if Dartmouth's hands were tied, a safer place than the Gunfleet should be found for the fleet.[1] Next day he had again taken up his quill,[2] not being able to "forbear giving his advice, although not sought for" and he might "be not believed capable of giving any". Under seven heads he had elaborated it; and politely hoped that it would be said of his lordship as Caesar said of himself of old "I came, I saw, I overcame". Incidentally the Admiral was no better pleased to hear that the Duke of Grafton was to be allowed on board Captain Hastings's ship, for the purpose of the expected fight, and then sent ashore.[3] But, though Dartmouth were indeed displeased with Jennens, possibly the fact did not prevent him from taking a useful hint[4] and asking himself again, whether the Gunfleet was the proper anchorage in which to lie. Whatever the cause of reconsideration may have been, in a communication to the King on the 29th, Dartmouth passed from the cheerful prognostication: "as your Majestie was almost too late before you would believe the designe... soe they by their owne delatariness lost their time for this yeare", to a recapitulation of his views about lying on the Dutch coast, and then to the question of his rendezvous, the Gunfleet, about which the King had never said a word. He declared,

Tho this be an open road yett there is many conveniences in it. I thinke we are well posted for security each way but as the moon grows older I believe they will grower sicker of their designe and the growing mad shall not provoke me to follow their example. Sir, when the light nights go off unless by some intelligence I see something better to be done I am advised to secure the fleet better in the Downes for it will not be safe here after the moon is over and there is noe other place unless we goe backe to the Buoy of the Nore which cannot be fitt till we are sure they are laid up first.

It would be a mistake to suppose that he is wondering whether, while he has still definite work in hand, the Gunfleet base is the right one. Of that he has no doubt. But he is not blind to the

---

[1] Dartmouth MSS, XI, 5, p. 170.　　　　[2] Ibid. 174.
[3] Ibid. p. 176; and XV, 1, p. 61.
[4] See D.N.B. article, "Jennens, Sir William", for early career. His advice became well known (see Burchett, 1720 edition, p. 414; Rapin-Thoyras, II, p. 776).

fact that the nights will shortly darken and soon the weather grow more wild. Presently he will have to consider whether the Downs, with their friendlier harbourage, must not be preferred to the more strategically satisfactory Gunfleet. That is all. He closed cheerfully, "I hear they wear English colours and talke of treateing with us, but pray, Sir, be assured I will suffer no language to be spoke to them but out of your guns".[1]

At 9 that night, Pepys wrote a long letter to Dartmouth,[2] elaborating a bitter complaint against the conduct of the Captain of the 'St. Albans' whom he found "within this half hour in his Majesty's bedchamber". He told Dartmouth how he protested to the King against the irregularity. "I added", he wrote,

that I tooke it, and still shall take it (to make it at all supportable), that he had his Majesty's leave for it; though I observed to his Majesty that if leaves of that kind be signified to Comanders by any other hand then mine while I have the honour of serving him in my post, it would be to noe purpose for me to pretend any longer to give him the account I ought, and he expected from me of his fleet.

Pepys affirmed that he had told the King that such absence without leave "was more then ever presumed to be done by my Lord Sandwich, Penn, Lawson, Harman, or my Lord Dartmouth himself, or even by his own self, without the leave of the King, his brother, dureing the whole time of his being High Admirall of England". To which the King returned, "that it was very true as to himself" and he gave the same credit in the case of the others. When Pepys had at length cooled his disgusted anger, he enclosed a further letter from D'Albeville November 2nd/October 23rd[3] which concluded with the words, "if the wind serves, the Prince will stay for nothing". But it mattered little whether Dartmouth got the complaint or the news. It mattered little—for the testing time had come, the time for the trial of a sound plan from a doubtful anchorage.

It remains to say in what way the Dutch "want of imbarcations"[4] had influenced King James's policy.

---

[1] Dartmouth MSS, XI, 5, p. 262.   [2] Ibid. p. 179.
[3] Ibid. p. 180.   [4] See p. 65.

By Order in Council of October 19th an embargo was placed upon the shipping of the port of Harwich; and on the 22nd, a further Order imposed restrictions on shipping in all the harbours from the Thames to Berwick.[1]

The nature of an embargo is worth passing attention. If all the ships, whether English or foreign, to be found in certain harbours were forbidden to sail, it followed that such vessels could not be used by the enemy; the sailors aboard them could neither serve the foe nor carry him tidings, and English seamen, in such ships, could not evade the operation or impressment for service in the King's Navy; moreover, were the time one of great stress, the detained ships might be made to submit to serve the urgent need of the state. But such advantages as accrued from the imposition of an embargo were countered by definitely recognised drawbacks; a loss to the Customs inevitably followed any drastic interference with sea-borne trade; the detention of foreign shipping might easily lead to this misunderstanding or to that cause of offence; and annoyance to English merchant interests was bound to arise.

The laying of an embargo was, quite properly, a matter at the discretion of an authority superior to the Admiralty—however that office might be constituted—and, of course, the purpose or purposes the Privy Council held in view dictated the incidence of the order it promulgated, the effectiveness and discrimination of the work of detention at the ports involved, and the duration for which restrictions should hold good. In practice, no sooner was the most limited interference authorised, than the owners and masters of individual ships sought passes to clear port, or protection certificates for retention of part or all of the Englishmen among their crews. Special cases multiplied and so worked against a long continuance of the imposition.

In this particular instance the purpose sought may readily be guessed; the lack of "imbarcations" of which the King had heard would alone account for it.

It is convenient here to anticipate the course run by this embargo and so dispose of the question. On the 22nd of the

---

[1] Admiralty papers in P.R.O.; Orders in Council, Ad. 1, 5139.

month an Order, which referred to its predecessors, defined the embargo and made it inapplicable to port-to-port British or Irish traffic. On the 25th, an Order in Council allowed exemption for a Hamburg voyage; a succeeding Order, dated the 28th, gave exemptions for French, Spanish, Portuguese, the Straits[1], Asian, African and American shipping. On the 3rd of November, an Order lifted the embargo from all foreign shipping, the Englishmen being first taken out of the crews; and a final Order of the 5th removed the lingering restrictions.[2]

*   *   *   *   *   *

Concerning the question 'what would have happened if the winds had not swept back to Helvoetsluys the Prince's expedition?' it will be sufficient to say that, had the winds remained fair from the 19th of October onwards to bear the Dutch ships outward, the English fleet would, in all human probability, have remained temporarily immobilised at the Oaze Edge and Blacktail, all the work of the summer cruising of Strickland would have been undone and the whole issue of the sea campaign very considerably prejudiced. One reputation is involved— that of the King; and, unless it is to be held that, although ordered to reinforce at the Nore, Admiral Dartmouth both could and should have got under weigh before the 14th of the month (the day on which he did leave the Buoy) and, further, that he both could and should have got to sea by the critical 19th instant, the reputation of the King must bear the adverse judgement. Certainly the contention against Lord Dartmouth cannot be sustained.

[1] Straits = Mediterranean.
[2] Admiralty papers in P.R.O.; Orders in Council, Ad. 1, 5139.

CHAPTER III

The Successful Sailing of the Prince
October 30th to November 7th

ON Tuesday October 30th, Dartmouth weighed from the Gunfleet with "32 sail of fighting ships and 13 fireships"[1] "to look for them";[2] for the wind, having first blown from the northward, settled in the south-east and gave the conditions he desired[3] for the execution of his plan, conditions which would bring out the Dutch and falsify his yesterday's half prophecy as to their growing sick of their design. Helped by the afternoon ebb, he hoped "to get clear of the Galleper before night";[4] but he did not succeed. His Master recorded the anchorage of the 'Resolution' with professional accuracy, as "between the Sledway and the Longsand Head, the Naze bearing W. and the Church of Bawdsey N.W. $\frac{1}{2}$ N."[5] Three yachts were put out, to north and east and southward.[6] The purpose for which Dartmouth had stood to sea must have been realised by all his fleet and, doubtless, when sail was shortened that October evening, those "chiefest and most considerable"[7] captains, whose voices at the last council of war had been loudest in satisfaction at the advantage of the Gunfleet as a base of operations, were speculating as to whether, after all, a point so "artfully gained" would be lost to their design. The wind and sea got up; and, when morning broke, no sail could be made.

On Wednesday the 31st instant Dartmouth was windbound.[8] On November 1st he could not sail; and his "frigates that were sent a cruiseing" came in before the wind, and anchored a league and a half to windward; they consisted of

1 "Journal of Captain Grenville Collins", Dartmouth MSS, XV, I, p. 56.
2 Dartmouth MSS, XV, I, p. 61.   3 *Ibid.*   4 *Ibid.* XI, 5, p. 262.
5 "Journal of Captain Grenville Collins", Dartmouth MSS, XV, I, p. 56.
6 *Ibid.*   7 See p. 69.
Dartmouth MSS, XV. I, p. 61.

the three ships originally sent out upon the 24th ultimo, the 'Swallow', 'Bonadventure' and 'Foresight,' under Captain Hopson of the 'Bonadventure'; and the 'Sandados', 'Katharine Yacht', 'Kitchen Yacht', 'Kingfisher Ketch' which had been added to them. One of the frigates had lost her fore-topmast, another her main-topmast and the whole fleet rode with yards and topmasts down, tugging at two and a half cables.[1] There was nothing else for it to do.

Tuesday, October 30th, had been in the Dutch ports of expedition a day of renewal of hope and purpose; at last the Protestant wind had returned; and, moreover, the weather in general had appeared more settled.[2] For some reason, perhaps not quite sufficiently explained by the statement that it was "so hard a thing...to set so vast a body in motion", "two days of this wind" had been lost by the Prince.[3] Then, at 10 on the morning of the Thursday November 1st, Lieutenant-Admiral-General Herbert had been signalled by the Prince. "Mon intention est de sortir encor en mer que le vent le permettra"[4] and the expedition had, on the evening tide, put to sea, exercising great care in picking up a proper formation.[5] The Prince was well informed of the position of the enemy war vessels.[6] The original Instructions issued to Herbert on the 17/27th ultimo still applied[7] and the size of the expedition had not appreciably altered. Thus the Dutch fleet and transports re-emerged to sea with the wind which proved more than sufficient to hold in the English warships.

Herbert steered a northward course. His Instructions, overriding, it must be remembered, his professional objections to a disembarcation in an easterly wind on the English east coast, implied an east-coast landing; though, whether at putting out

[1] Dartmouth MSS, XI, 5, p. 263. 'Cable' = about 100 fathoms.
'Katherine Yacht'—Captain Clements, Dartmouth MSS, XI, 5, p. 168.
'Kingfisher Ketch'—Captain Swaine, *Ibid.* p. 164.
'Kitchin Yacht'—Captain Cotton (?) *Ibid.* 153 and elsewhere.
[2] Burnet, p. 787; Huygens's *Journaal*.
[3] Burnet, p. 787. D'Albeville afterwards reported that the Prince waited the return of Zulestein (see Dartmouth MSS, XI, 5, p. 201); but that is doubtful.
[4] B.M. MSS, Egerton 2621.   [5] Huygens's *Journaal* (for Nov. 12/2).
[6] Huygens's *Journaal*, Nov. 11/1 "between Harwich and the London River".   [7] See p. 43.

an exact objective had been fixed, either a place within the sphere
of Danby's influence or some spot nearer London, is not
apparent. Then, after noon on Friday November 2nd, the whole
expedition turned south-west and sailed large. It may be that
the wind "so strong and full in the east" that they "could not
move that way" prompted the change. Such is the reason
stated from the Prince's own ship; and it is, no doubt, credible
enough if the word "east" is not read with too great exactitude.
If however, that reason were not advanced, one would be
tempted to suppose that, towards noon of the 2nd, Herbert had
learnt exactly the position of the English fleet, deduced from his
intelligence that Dartmouth's station would hinder an English
pursuit should he, Herbert, head for the Channel and, all the
more forcibly because of his dislike of the whole east coast
operation, had asked sanction for a different move.[1]

All that Friday the English fleet's position remained unchanged. Some of the tenders parted company; ships broke
their cables; one lost her longboat; the wind continued.[2]

Through the night, carrying shortened sail in the boisterous
wind, the Prince's expedition remained fairly compact and
made good way; but no attempt to bear up for an east coast
landing place was undertaken.[3] The soldiers did not relish
their experience; for still the vessels "would throw themselves
from side to side all the people in them after a sad sort".[4] On
the morning of Saturday November 3rd, when the sunbeams
"had dissipated the Mist, and dispersed the Fogg",[5] those
aboard could plainly see the land of the Thames Estuary. A
council of war was held, at which steps were taken to make
sure of the English fleet's position; then, in all probability, the
question of a possible landing place was settled.[6] Before noon,
"half seas over",[7] the new Armada was entering the Dover
Strait, gazed at by concourses of the people on the opposite

    Burnet, p. 787. See p. 45.
[2] "Journal of Captain Grenville Collins", Dartmouth MSS, XV, 1, p. 56.
[3] "Expedition of the Prince of Orange to England 1688". Somers Tracts,
IX, p. 276 and Harleian Miscellany, I, p. 449. Signed "N.N.". (Burnet.)
[4] Whittle's *Diary*, p. 23.
    Ibid. p. 30. There certainly was fog as well as wind. See Burchett, 1720
edition, p. 414).
[6] See note 3, *supra*.   [7] *London Gazette*; Nov. 1–5.

shores. The disposition of the ships was altered to make the spectacle as imposing as might be; the vessels to the convoy reached within a league of either shore, the fleet carefully protecting them. The Prince led the van. "His flag was English colours; the motto impaled thereon was, "The Protestant Religion and liberties of England"; and underneath, instead of "Dieu et Mon droit", was "Je maintiendrai".[1] The reflection of one of the many refugees aboard the Dutch fleet is worth quoting: "La France trembla à sa vue, et l'Angleterre, voyant son libérateur venir à pleines voiles à son aide, tressaillit de joie".[2] Guns saluted Calais and Dover and there was made a goodly display. For three hours or so "tunes" were played on the trumpets and drums. With oncoming night the ships entered the Channel.[3]

The story of that black Saturday in the English fleet is perhaps best told in the words of Captain Collins, the English Admiral's Master.

"At daylight we espied several ships to windward, close-hauled under their low sails, but immediately heaved out their top sails. Our windward ships" (these were the frigates) "let slip and stood after them to the southward. We discovered 13 sail of them. We had weighed with the whole fleet after them, but the ebb tide being almost spent, we could not weather the Longsand Head and the Kentish Knock. In the evening came into the fleet an English ship, which came last Wednesday from Hamburg, bound for London, but could not give us any account of the Dutch fleet".[4]

The Admiralty was not left long ignorant of the magnitude of the disaster; for, from the Downs and Dover, reports, the same evening, came to hand. Past midnight Pepys despatched copies of reports to the Admiral, in case he yet remained in ignorance (as in the state of the weather the King believed possible) of the fact that the Dutch had gone by. Pepys reminded Dartmouth of the importance of countering any danger to the fleet, and the customary shipping, which might be caused by the

---

[1] "Expedition of the Prince of Orange to England 1688." Somers Tracts, IX, p. 276 and Harleian Miscellany, I, p. 449. Signed "N. N." (Burnet). Also Rapin Thoyras, II, p. 776; and elsewhere.
[2] de Bostaquet, p. 214.   [3] See note 1, *supra*.
[4] "Journal of Captain Grenville Collins", Dartmouth MSS, XV, I, p. 56.

removal of the Gunfleet Buoy. The King hastened troops to Portsmouth, firmly believing that the landing would take place there.[1]

The dawn of Sunday, November 4th, the Prince's birthday and the anniversary of his marriage, saw the Dutch fleet and transports still standing on in good order, the Wight astern to starboard.[2] A signal note taken from the 'Brill' to the 'Leyden', in Russell's hand and terrible spelling, informed Herbert that, by the advice of his pilots, the Prince intended landing most of his forces at Dartmouth and the rest at Torbay, and requested protection from the English fleet. Apparently Herbert advised Exmouth; but Mr Gilbert (a pilot) considered the wind and sea unfavourable and his Highness held to his decision.[3] Russell and the pilot went aboard the leading ship of the fleet. The fleet proceeded under easy sail.[4]

Again the story on the English side is best told in the words of the famous hydrographer:

"At four in the morning", that is, of Sunday the 4th of November, "we made a signal for weighing anchor, and at break of day got under sail. At 8 o'clock the 'Foresight' Capt. Stanley which was one of the ships that let slip yesterday, came into the fleet, and told us that the Dutch fleet were gone to westward, and sailed by Dover yesterday, and that he had taken one of their fly-boats which had lost her rudder on the Gabbard Sand....We made all haste possible after them. At eight at night we got up with the South Sand Head, staved and pulled down all cabins, cleared our ship and made all ready for fight. At 12 at night, the light of Dungeness bore N."[5]

An estimate puts the number of the ships which went in pursuit, at 28 men-of-war and 12 fireships.[6]

Monday, November 5th, opened with a threat of something approaching disaster for the Prince of Orange's venture, daylight revealing to those aboard the leading vessel that the pilot,

---

[1] Dartmouth MSS, XI, 5, p. 183; see also a tract, "A declaration, 1688" Somers, IX, p. 269, which alleges the news "was brought to London by an officer of the 'Swallow' frigate so exhausted by fatigue and so affected by the tale he had to deliver that he fell speechless at James's feet". The 'Swallow' was in the Downs (see p. 84).
[2] Huygens's *Journaal*.   [3] B.M. MSS, Egerton 2621.
[4] Burnet, p. 788.
[5] "Journal of Captain Grenville Collins", Dartmouth MSS, XV, 1, p. 57.
[6] *Memoirs...Torrington*, p. 29.

in spite of careful calculations, had overshot the marks of Dartmouth and Torbay. Russell "was in no small disorder" at his pilot's mistake and told one who voyaged on that vessel, Burnet (shortly to become bishop of Salisbury) to go to prayers for all was lost. Russell's disorder was not surprising. Plymouth lies to the south-west, Torbay to the south-east of the wide desolation of Dartmoor; and Russell recognised that even if the landing could safely be made at Plymouth, commanded as it was by a governor whose sympathies were more or less with the Prince of Orange,[1] how certainly a "long and tedious campaign in winter through a very ill country" would prove a most serious obstacle to the cause. However, Russell was strangely saved from the effects of a too long continued fit of choler or the need to disturb the Prince's fatalistic phlegm; for, before Russell could order out his boat to go aboard the Prince, "on a sudden, to all our wonder, it calmed a little. And then the wind turned into the south; and a soft and happy gale of wind carried in the whole fleet in four hours' time into Torbay".[2] The fleet continued to protect the convoy from all molestation from the sea; a few war-ships went close in to the land. Then the 60 boats detailed for the duty of disembarcation began their work. Mackay's six English and Scottish regiments under the guard of the 18-gun 'Little Porpius' were the first detachments to receive orders to go ashore. The reception of the invader being in no way hostile, William landed immediately.[3]

Through the small hours of that Monday morning, the English fleet had still stood on in strong pursuit of the enemy. Yet though, with the full coming of day, Beachy and not Dungeness had lain abeam, the winds had shortly proved so fitful that the pursuit had perforce been stayed.[4] A council of war having been held, despatches were prepared for forwarding immediately to London. One of the two despatches was addressed to the King, the other to the Secretary of Admiralty.[5]

[1] John Grenville, Earl of Bath.
[2] Burnet, p. 788. See also Whittle, p. 33, de Bostaquet, p. 215.
[3] "Letter to a person of quality", previously cited. Accounts of the landing vary considerably.
[4] "Journal of Captain Grenville Collins", Dartmouth MSS, xv, 1, p. 57.
[5] Dartmouth MSS, xv, 1, p. 61 (to Pepys); xi, 5, p. 263 (to King).

Each paper, to a great extent, duplicated the matter of the other, though that to the King was the more complete and less formal of the two. The latter—the despatch to the King—opened with a concise and correct report of what had occurred in the last few days. The Admiral's lament that he took himself "for the most unfortunate man liveing", though confident that his majesty would be "too just to expect more than winde and weather will permitt", followed; and thereafter the despatch continued to read despondently to its close. For next his lordship wrote:

"if their fleet lie at St. Hellens whilst the rest land in Stokes Bay and Hampton Water their fleet being soe very much superiour as I finde they are both in number and quality", (notions which he had picked up from the captured fly boat)[1] "I am at a stand what to doe for on calling the Flagg Officers and Commanders they unanimously advise me[2] against attackeing the Dutch fleet if all possibility of hindering their landing be over, tho' everybody I assure you, Sir, I thinke are so exasperated at the Prince of Orange's proceedings that I am once more confident they will venture their lives very heartily in your Majestie's service. I consider the success of their landing and beating your only fleet together with the destruction as I may say of the flower of the English fleet or so many of them at least as are here at present. I confess Sir, the thoughts of this with the consequence it may have in London and all over England checks my inclination of setting upon them without your Majestie's farther orders, but I resolve to endeavour to fall in with the Isle of Wight at breake of day to-morow morning, and see what advantage it will please God to offer me, takeing the caution not to shute too far to the westward in the night nor to engage your fleet unreasonably, or at least after I see some hopes of doing so.

Then he went on to tell how, when he was about to seal thus much of his report and hand it to special courier, Strickland, Berry and Davis (Vice-Admiral, Rear-Admiral and Commissioner of the Navy, and "Flag-Captain" respectively) came to urge inaction in view of the weakness of the English fleet which, at the moment, appears (to continue quotation of the despatch) to have lacked "the 'Swallow'[3] and 'Tyger' in the Downes,

[1] See letter to Pepys. Stokes Bay is at the north-west extremity of Spithead.
[2] Opinions being taken separately; see letter referred to in note 1, *supra*.
[3] That she had sprung a leak (Dartmouth MSS, XI, 5, p. 263) is substantiated

the 'Dover', 'Foresight', 'Bonadventure', and 'Sandados' not yet come to us from cruising, since we came into the channell, the 'Speedwell' and 'Sally Rose' fire ships missing, as in all the small craft except one Ketch of the two yachts besides the 'Yorke', 'Woolwich', 'St Albans' and 'Newcastle', so that at present we want twelve". Finally, on the advice of these officers, Dartmouth pointed out, he had sent scouts to the westward;[1] had decided to "jogg easily" till they could bring him word of the enemy, till he could know his Majesty's pleasure; the case being "much different now and from what it would have been if we had been soe happy to have met them before they were discharged of their great convoy". His rendezvous he had fixed at the Naze (?)[2] or the Downs. As a sort of postscript he added, "I understand the Prince of Orange changed his measures upon his last coming aboard, when he heard your Majestie's fleet was at the Gunfleet, for before that he intended for the river".

So marked a change in the Admiral's outlook as the foregoing despatch reveals demands the closest scrutiny.

It is not to be gainsaid that the English Admiral's forces at hand at Beachy were much less than those that had lain round the 'Resolution' at the Gunfleet Buoy. At the Gunfleet some 32 or 33 capital ships and 13 or 14 fireships had been available for service. 32 ships of the line and 13 fireships had actually sailed thence on the 30th ultimo "to look for" the enemy. The number of vessels which, a day since (November 4th), had rounded the Long Sand Head to begin the pursuit now interrupted, had certainly been less; 28 capital ships, 12 fireships and other smaller craft made up the quota.[3] But it is fairly certain that two more capital ships were at the time cruising ahead in the Downs awaiting the fleet,[4] and that three others, away also

by a letter of Nov. 4, seemingly from Captain M. Aylmer to the Navy Board, the vessel then off the Foreland with 8 feet of water in hold, Dartmouth being to leeward. Admiralty Papers in P.R.O. Secretary's In-Letters (from Navy Board), Ad. 1, p. 3557.
 [1] 'Ruby', 'Centurion', 'Portsmouth' (see letter to Pepys).
 [2] Naze = Ness = Dungeness? Rye Bay is under it and he asked for the reply to be sent there.   [3] See p. 82.
 [4] 'Swallow' and 'Tiger'; see note 3, p. 84 for 'Swallow' and observe that the two vessels are associated in Dartmouth's despatch to the King.

on cruising service,[1] were expected to rejoin the Admiral without much delay. Thus at least 30, and, with good fortune, the full 33 ships of the line were expected to be available when contact with the enemy came to be made. As events turned out, all the five vessels were missing at Beachy; and a strength of 28 ships of the line, 10 fireships and, of the smaller craft, but "one ketch of the two yachts" represented all that the Admiral could muster if he chose to continue his pursuit of the Dutch. A depletion which, in the course of the six or seven days between October 30th and November 5th, could be represented, as far as capital and fireships were concerned, by the figures 33 : 28 and 14 : 10 respectively, naturally caused great misgiving.[2] Unfortunately, the Admiral, when he sought to relate his depletion to the probable strength of the Dutch fleet, found his misgiving intensified; for, already, before he had realised the full extent of his loss, reports picked up from the flyboat had led him to consider his previous estimate of the Dutch effectives much too low. Yet, it must be observed, this conviction of inferiority was nowhere, in the despatch, allowed to stand out as a separate consideration; first and last Dartmouth related it to the consequence of a further item of flyboat news—to the thought that Herbert's position had improved by the disembarcation which, as it seemed, quite close at hand, behind the Solent, the Dutch had been able to carry out. The nature of the improvement Dartmouth appears to have regarded as too obvious for elaboration. Clearly no new and sudden immunity from discovery by the English fleet had fallen to Herbert's lot. Herbert, at anchor with his transports in some near bay, could still be discovered with the utmost ease and precision; but Herbert's transport-defending task, so Dartmouth believed, and so, without laboured explanation, he expected the King to understand, had been considerably lightened. And it is not to be denied that if, as

---

[1] 'Dover,' Foresight', 'Bonadventure', (not 'Sandados' which was a sixth rate).

[2] The text of the despatch quoted on the preceding page, so far as it concerns smaller vessels than fireships, cannot be interpreted to complete satisfaction. All the yachts and ketches attached to the fleet have, however, been named in this narrative, except the 'Cleveland Yacht' (Captain Hoskins according to Pepys's December 18th list. See p. 59, note 1.)

Dartmouth supposed, he would find, should he follow up the Dutch Admiral, the convoyed vessels emptied of soldiers, horses, artillery and stores, lying partly sheltered by the land of Stokes Bay or by the protecting shores of Southampton Water, then their vulnerability to his attack would prove far less than would have been the case had he "been soe happy to have met with them" upon the open sea. A beating off of the English forces could no longer be regarded as an utterly impossible thing. A defeat at a time of grave political crisis might draw on the most alarming consequences. In the light of these facts, it is not, perhaps, surprising that the Admiral's continuity of purpose should have been checked, that he should have determined upon a brief delay, and a reference of the whole matter to the better judgement of the King. But, while he purposed thus, and declared that he would "jogg easily" till the ships astern rejoined the squadrons, till the scouts reported, till the advice came, he did not close his mind to the possibility that the receipt of some unexpected intelligence might make it reasonable for him to attempt something upon the enemy.[1] In other words, he allowed to pass into abeyance but he did not relinquish his "command-disputing", "command-asserting" plan. That his suggested base lay in his wake signified little, since the enemy, he thought, held the next available harbour to the westward.

Before leaving this despatch, it is necessary to draw attention to the disquieting sentence, "I am once more confident they will venture their lives very heartily in your Majestie's service" which the Admiral had used in speaking of his captain's loyalty. One, present in the flagship, to whom reticence was second nature,[2] has indeed declared "had the Admiral come fairly up with the Dutch, it would not have been in his Power to have done much against them; altho I have reason to believe, that, in such case, his Lordship, and some of the Captains, would have done their utmost". Another,[3] even better placed, has written:

It was well known that my Lord was to follow them; so there was a meeting of such captains as were inclined to the Prince, to consult

---

[1] Both despatches of the 5th make that clear.
[2] Burchett, p. 18.   [3] *Memoirs...Torrington*, p. 29.

what measures they should take upon coming up with the enemy. Some of them were of opinion that if my Lord attacked them, that in honour they shoud do their duty against them. But the (general) opinion, to which they agreed, was upon such an occasion to leave him, (and to range themselves on the other side). When the fleet was off Beachy Head my Lord brought to, and called a council of war, to have the opinions of the captains of the fleet, if in case they met with the Dutch they shoud fight them; which was so managed, that the result of it was not to fight them, if in honour it coud be avoided.

The foregoing statements are plain evidence of sedition. Yet it is not warrantable to argue that, at the council of war, the ulterior motive of sedition affected the terms of the advice tendered. The opinions of the officers were asked separately; and men would be chary of self betrayal at a gathering of that kind. Though coteries and cabals existed, at the most, disaffection could scarcely do more than add an emphasis to the terms of individual expression. In any case it is impossible to attribute to Vice-Admiral Strickland, Rear-Admiral Berry and Captain Davis, acting together, a desire to further an interested intervention.

The afternoon of that memorable day November 5th 1688 passed on into a bright sunset and sunset into a warm nightfall.[1] As long as the light lasted, the putting ashore of men and war supplies went on apace, some 2000 men being disembarked upon that day.[2] Indeed the bustle of camp activities continued even after the night had fallen and the moon, waning in her last quarter, had risen over camp and sea.[3] That night, from the port of Dartmouth, from Berry Pomeroy and Brixham, messages reporting the invaders' descent were speeded to London to the officers of the King. But neither sunset nor the late moonrise saw any forward movement of the English fleet. Over the waters lay a level haze; no wind stirred;[4] and at the dawn of a new day, November 6th, the position of the fleet remained unaltered.

The work of disembarking troops and equipment took up

[1] Burnet, p. 788.   [2] "Letter to a person of quality"—previously cited.
[3] de Bostaquet, p. 215, notes the moonlight. For fragments of orders about this date, from William to ——?, see State Papers Domestic (King William's Chest) uncalendared.
[4] Dartmouth MSS, XI, 5, p. 265.

at least two further days of the Prince's time, Tuesday and Wednesday, November 6th and 7th. It is said that some 12,000 soldiers in all had been brought hither, about a quarter of the forces consisting of cavalry.[1] The horse and artillery were the most difficult to put ashore; but local conditions were in favour of the invader; fishermen found a safe place for the horses to be put overboard and the artillery was run up into the Exe estuary.[2] The Prince had already on the 6th begun to consider the returning of the transports to Holland.[3]

The wind freshened a little in the afternoon of the 6th and Dartmouth determined to work up with his scouts. All night, in a small gale veering between S.E. and S.S.W., he sailed, steering first W., then S.E., "to get a better offing from the oares"[4] and finally N.W. till a storm came up from the S.W. and compelled him, shortly after dawn of the 7th, to relinquish his purpose. For the 'Assurance' had put out signals of distress, the 'Mary' had borne up, the "paunch" of the flagship's foremast was sprung and the "head of the mast wrung"; and to have strained the fleet further would plainly have been unwise. Before night, making a very fast time, the squadrons had run before the gale, in rainy weather, and moored in the Downs, their previously appointed rendezvous. The fleet came to in a defensive posture; attack however, was not believed imminent. Dartmouth then learned that the Dutch disembarkation had been made in Torbay. These things, omitting reference to the last mentioned fact, Dartmouth reported to the King and Pepys.[5] Certainly neither they nor any later critic could consider that

[1] *Somers Tracts*, IX, p. 269 cited p. 81; cp. de Jonge, Appendix IV, and engraving referred to, p. 37. P.J. Blok, *Prins Willem III naar Torbay*, citing Admiraliteitsarchief No. 251 (Rijksarchief), gives the paper figures.

[2] B.M. MSS, Egerton 2621. See Dr Firth's "Macaulay" for reduced facsimile of this particular letter, III, 1134.

[3] B.M. MSS, Egerton 2621.

[4] Doubtless the "Owers"—well known then, as now, "A dangerous big shoal surrounded by other shoals". "The Owers lie south south east from Chichester spire, and four leagues from the shoar....In little Wind or Calms you shall be drawn in here to admiration". Captain Grenville Collins, *Great Britain's Coasting Pilot*, I, p. 3.

[5] Dartmouth MSS, XI, 5, p. 265 and XV, 1, p. 62. See also "Journal of Captain Grenville Collins", Dartmouth MSS, XV, 1, p. 57, and *Memoirs...Torrington*, p. 29.

the Admiral had, between the 5th and 7th instant, exposed himself to the imputation of mere dilatoriness; but the Admiral,
who placed a continued regret for his misfortune at the fore-
front of his further reflections to the King, might have added
to his news by informing his Majesty that the 'Bonadventure'[1]
had come into harbour where also, presumably, the 'Swallow'
and 'Tyger' had rejoined his flag; he could also have reported
the 'Montague' and 'Dartmouth' in collision in the calms
and the former damaged.[2] He did remark upon his expectation
of the arrival of the three laggard vessels from the Nore and
declared that he had sent in "to take up six good vessells at
Dover etc. to make fire shipps, thinking it the quickest way...
to do them (there) with (his) owne carpenters and gunners
rather than expect the tedious delays from the rivers"—a line
of action which, he showed, had not, however, prevented him
from ordering Captain Wilford of Sheerness to send out all the
fireships in that depôt. He firmly professed his expectations
there in the Downs "quickly to gather the fleet"; but he did
not enter upon further discussions of his inferiority. Had he
written of inferiority, he would, no doubt, have been constrained
to set off against his re-accession of strength in the Downs the
several damages sustained in the pursuit westward.

As no change in the Admiral's belief in inferiority of strength
can have occurred, since the 5th instant, and more certain news
had supplemented the former false report of the Dutch landing
behind the Wight, one would scarce look to the remainder of
the despatches for any change in the Admiral's determination
to wait the advice of the King. Broadly the expectation is veri-
fied. The despatch worked up to this decision, "although I
cannot yett hope for more men of warre, this" (referring to the
three laggards expected from the Nore)[3] "will be a good reinforcement of this Squadron soe that I hope yett upon the first
easterly winde to be able to do some service, tho' at this time

---

[1] Dartmouth MSS, XI, 5, p. 194.
[2] "Journal of Captain Grenville Collins", Dartmouth MSS, XV, 1, p. 57.
Captains Lord Berkeley ('Montague') and Cornwall ('Dartmouth') were of
the "faction".
[3] 'Newcastle', 'St Albans', 'Woolwich', were still in the Thames, and
the 'York' at Portsmouth.

of the yeare I dare promise nothing more, but expect your Majestie's commands and that what strength can will be sent me by degrees ". The fact that he speaks thus of the east wind was no less significant than the reference to awaiting the King's orders; for it shows that the old aggressive design, though still in abeyance, was not relegated to the far background of the Admiral's thoughts. The Admiral noted a report to hand saying that the Dutch showed an intention of wintering upon English shores. Under such circumstances, he held that it behoved his Majesty to take counter measures that they should not ride "Lords" of his Majesty's seas.

*   *   *   *   *   *

It is convenient with the return of the royal fleet to the Downs to bring to a focus the causes of Dartmouth's failure to intercept the invader as he neared the coast of England—it being allowed that the high water which assisted Herbert's sailing in any case prevented his opponent from getting upon the Dutch coast to await the emergence of the expedition.

In the first place, Collins's "Journal", corroborated by all other documentary evidence, makes it quite clear that, the English fleet being in a certain position at a certain time, the tide and the wind prevented the fleet from steering the only possible course out to sea after the passing enemy. For the reader's convenience, the position of Dartmouth's flagship as logged by Captain Collins on the night of October 30th and therefore for November 1st and 2nd and the morning of the 3rd instant when the disaster occurred, has been marked by the letter A upon the Chart at the end of this work.[1] Near by, a long arrow points S.W. When it is high water at Dover the tide flows in that direction slowly or scarce at all. One hour later the ebb tide flows as the north-eastward pointing arrow indicates; at two hours and three hours after as the arrows (2) and (3) indicate; similarly for four, five and six hours. At the third and fourth hour the stream makes a mean rate of 1 knot at the neaps to $2\frac{1}{2}$

[1] The bearings were no doubt taken by Collins by compass, i.e. were magnetic. On the chart the position is calculated from true north. The variation at London in 1688 was 5° west; for Harwich it would be about the same.

knots at the springs. At the sixth it is almost spent. It was, presumably, at such a phase when, as Collins says, "the ebb tide being almost spent", the Dutch vessels were sighted at daybreak of November 3rd. If so, a period of slack water followed; then steadily towards S.S.W., at a rate of say, $2\frac{1}{4}$ knots, having regard to the day and time, accelerated by the easterly wind, the flood tide set. It is perfectly credible that to have attempted to round the Long Sand Head in such a wind, though it missed the force of a gale,[1] on such a tide, would have been to invite disaster.

It is interesting to note that, if the time of morning high water at Dover be calculated for November 3rd, 1688 (O.S.) the figure 2.11 a.m. Greenwich Mean Time is obtained or 2.33 a.m. Solar Time of the Long Sand Head. Such a calculation makes it abundantly clear that the ebb tide would be far spent at November daylight and the contention of Collins receives corroboration.[2]

Yet, because it is undeniable that wind and tide made it impossible for the English fleet to get from that place in which they were upon the morning of November 3rd, it is by no means to be admitted without question that Dartmouth should then have been exactly where he was. Really there are two enquiries. He had worked by the end of October towards a final plan of campaign which deserves not merely approbation but praise and one that should have brought him certain victory and honour; but (1) had he, in view of all the issues involved, blamably chosen the Gunfleet anchorage as the base from which to operate his plan? and (2) should he, in the space between October 30th and November 2nd have got beyond the Galloper or, at least, further out than he had?

As to (1) the problem is difficult. There is no need to recount

---

[1] The fact that the Dutch set their topsails on November 3rd shows that the wind was not *then* more than a strong breeze (see p. 81).

[2] I am indebted to Dr J. K. Fotheringham of the University of Oxford Observatory for this calculation. Astronomical data apart, it was reached by the use of *harmonic constants*, derived from analysis of observed heights of the tide at Dover. The method now used by the Admiralty for tide prediction, called the *equation method*, might give a more precise result; but any slight variation would not affect the argument.

the pros and cons that affected his choice between the only alternatives he had to consider[1]; but the reader will do well to revert to them[2] before, he, wise after the event, sums up. The more expert he is, the better he knows the North Sea, the more likely he will be to consider Dartmouth justified. (2) is even more troublesome. That an admiral, keenly intent on getting outside the Galloper in that time, the east wind blowing very high but not a gale, could not do so, or at least finish further out to sea, is not incredible; but it is hard to believe. Dartmouth was a zealous officer; and he must, in respect of (2), receive the benefit of the doubt.

James (as the next chapter will make plain), whether as interpreted by Pepys or read in his own writing, entirely avoided, at the time of the disaster, recrimination. Moreover, the later view of his "Memoirs" is not unkindly.

My Lord Dartmouth writ he was under sail designing to anchor somewhere to the east of the Galoper to be clear of the Sand, and so to be able to stretch it one way or the other as he pleased when the wind should come fair for the enemy and according to the course he steered but he stood not out so far but anchored a brest of the Long Sands head when the Easterly wind took him and blew very fresh.[3]

Pepys, although (as the next chapter will also show) actuated at the time by a fine sympathy towards Dartmouth, moved round later with time to hostile judgement and exclaimed,

What a pother was heretofore made about ye pretended Discovery of our Sands, etc., to Strangers. While it now appears how little Use wee were able to make of our supposed only knowledge of them ourselves, at soe Criticall a Juncture as that was when my Lord Darto could not tell how to gett his Fleet out of them, tho there by his own choice; and after all ye Cautions given him by ye King against ye very Evil hee betrayed himselfe and his Unhappy Master to by going thither.[4]

---

[1] Solebay was, of course, utilised during the Dutch wars but it was far too wild for winter use.

[2] See p. 20.

[3] *Memoirs of James II*, III, p. 286.

[4] *Naval Miscellanies*, p. 292 (quoted in note in article referred to. Note 6, p. 11).

In the second place, it is plain that the winds, which so strangely changed after Gilbert the pilot had overshot the promontory of Berry Head, which served to waft the whole expedition so opportunely and gently into a commodious bay, which, at the same time, fell away and produced hazy calms off the cliffs of Beachy, then, once more, and as suddenly, rose and grew too boisterous for the continuance of safe pursuit, had much to do with the further freedom from molestation which the expedition enjoyed.

Thus, in summing up, it may be said that, Dartmouth's not, *per se*, unjustifiable choice of the Gunfleet base, a preference which was either his before he set foot aboard the 'Resolution' or was reasonably arrived at on examination made and representation received (arrived at, indeed, so reasonably, upon the premises, that he might well have adhered to it, even could he have learned that the seditious officers smiled as he reached it) conditioned the Admiral's inability to clear the estuary of the Thames in an easterly wind on the morning of November 3rd; which circumstance, together with the vagaries of the Channel winds and breezes in the next three days, made impossible a meeting between the antagonists, and, so, completely assured the Dutch success as far as the Torbay disembarkation.

Among the older historians, Ralph,[1] and, among the later writers, Lingard,[2] seem best to have appreciated the truth about Dartmouth's situation in these days.

There is, of course, another aspect of this finding. In the preceding chapter, when criticism of the Instructions intended to cover the whole naval operations of the intervention design were discussed, it was pointed out that nothing short of the possession of miraculous foreknowledge of the winds and tides of a campaign or alternatively the placing of an implicit confidence in the advices received concerning the sedition of the English fleet could justify the issue of the Instructions. Under these Instructions a sailing had at length been made; and, as it has just been shown, sedition, working very subtly, had con-

---

[1] Ralph II, p. 1032.

[2] Lingard, x, p. 342. Devon's pamphlet (see list of Authorities) is a vindication going beyond the events dealt with in this work.

tributed, considerably though not wholly, to the success of the passage. It is natural to ask what was, up to the date of the actual sailing, the extent of William's knowledge of English sedition, in order to decide how reasonably he could put faith in such information as he held. It may at once be said that it is impossible to give evidence that the Prince possessed, at sailing, the promise of this or that individual English officer to do this or that particular thing; but it is a fair presumption, from the facts already advanced, that many captains were far committed to serve him in a general way. Whether William had received assurances of a "Gunfleet design" cannot be determined; but it is safe to say that no group of officers in the English fleet, however high placed or however numerous, could give reliable assurances that the English fleet would be immobilised at the Gunfleet on a certain day, to wit, November 3rd, in order that the expedition might go unmolested by. In any case the English fleet cleared the Estuary in time, but for baffling winds, to have made contact with the Dutch, busy at the work of disembarkation, a likely contingency. Thus the real crux of the enquiry, the question whether William had, at sailing, proper justification to believe that an encounter of the fleets would, whenever it should occur, occasion desertions so numerous as to make the meeting nothing but a great regrouping parade, a scene of friendly negotiations unaccompanied by any appreciable exchanges of angry artillery, is not, even thus early in the history of the campaign, to be avoided. And there is nothing to warrant the view that William had any right to place such overwhelming reliance upon any of the assurances he had been given.

How, the question may well arise, had a prince, of thirty-eight years of age, so phlegmatic, so wary, brought himself to take his amazing decision? How could the head of a modern state behave no less rashly than Alexander or Hannibal of old? The answer does not lie on the surface.

Macaulay has warned us that it is easy to allow admiration for the Prince as a statesman to prevent recognition of his shortcomings as a general. "Among his officers there had been none competent to instruct him. His own blunders and their consequences had been his only lessons. 'I would give', he once exclaimed, 'a good part of my estates to have served a few campaigns under the Prince of Condé before I had to command against him'. It is not improbable that the circumstance which prevented William from attaining any eminent dexterity in strategy...."[1] Or again: "I cannot deny myself the pleasure of quoting Massillon's unfriendly, yet discriminating and noble character of William. 'Un prince profond dans ses vues; habile à former des ligues et à réunir les esprits; plus heureux à exciter les guerres qu'à combattre; plus à craindre encore dans le secret du cabinet, qu'à la tête des armées'".[2] The distinction between the art of war by land and the theory of hostile operations by sea is not small; and though, in that age, it did, on occasion, happen that great military men turned with success from land to sea warfare, they had much to learn in the transition. William, albeit he had studied in the school of adversity the task of military leadership, had never, unlike such soldier-admirals as Blake and Monk, served an apprenticeship of failure afloat. To say that he had filled not only the office of Captain-general but that of Admiral-general also, since the difficult year 1672, is not to prove his critical appreciation of the plans of De Ruyter and Tromp. In any case one would not ascribe to William the flexible intellect which enabled his great contemporary, Marlborough, to understand the nature of amphibious operations. There is therefore a temptation to draw the conclusion that had William known more of maritime affairs he would have dared far less. But that conclusion would be wide of the mark.

Burnet says that, on landing, the Prince took him heartily by the hand and asked him if he would not henceforth believe in predestination.[3] There is more in the question than historians have hitherto perceived. William sailed because he was a Calvinist. The winds and tides, the chances of the sea he could not foreknow; nor could he, beyond a peradventure, be assured that sedition would facilitate his landing. But the

[1] Macaulay, II, p. 165.   [2] Ibid. II, p. 185.
[3] Burnet (edition with notes by the Earls of Dartmouth and Hardwick, etc.), III, p. 328.

conclusion is plain—he could and did believe that either the elements or English treachery, or both, would yield him his destiny. Fate established him in Torbay when he should have shared the lot of Medina Sidonia.

> They fought from heaven; the stars in their courses
> fought against Sisera.

No doubt the ancient paean, remembered by many a militant Puritan, won new meaning from the current hour. The gloss of Bishop Burnet and others,

> O nimium dilecte Deo, cui militat aether
> Et conjurati veniunt ad classica venti,[1]

certainly stands a fully pardonable hyperbole.

---

[1]   "O nimium dilecte deo, cui fundit ab antris
          Aeolus armatas hiemes, cui militat aether
          Et coniurati veniunt ad classica venti".

At the battle of the Frigidus (A.D. 394), fought on the River Wipbach, the Emperor Theodosius, aided by a local Alpine wind called the 'Bora,' overcame his rival Eugenius. Claudian addresses the Emperor Honorius, son of Theodosius and one of the two joint successors to the purple, on the strength of the fact that Honorius, though a boy at the time of the battle, and though not actually present at the conflict, happened to be the Consul under whose auspices the issue was joined. (Panegyric on the Third Consulship of Honorius, vv. 96–8.)

CHAPTER IV

Dartmouth's Attempt on Torbay
November 7th to 22nd

THE magnitude of the disaster which had befallen the
English fleet was well understood from the moment
that the news reached Whitehall; and the recognition
seems to have counselled in the mind of the King a policy
of extreme caution rather than of hurried revenge. For, on
November 6th, when Pepys wrote to the Admiral, in order to
voice the opinion of the King and court, that none, who knew
his lordship, would believe that any part of his "disappointment
in relation to the Dutch fleet" could "be charged upon anything with in" his "power to have prevented", and forwarded
the latest news, establishing the fact that the landing begun at
Torbay would continue in the Exe Estuary, he declared that he
had no orders from the King, except to observe that, as the
situation had changed in the direction of giving the Dutch
"entire liberty to receive or attack", the King trusted that the
Admiral would not lose sight of the need to avoid undue ex-
posure of the royal fleet.[1] That careful attitude was even more
fully demonstrated when the two despatches of the 5th (those
sent from Beachy) reached town on the morning of the 7th.
Having consulted the King, Pepys replied to the appeal for
guidance with a new assurance of the King's "full satisfaction
in beleiving that [Dartmouth] had done all that a prudent
and careful Admirall could doe"; he added a statement to the
effect that the despatches were welcome evidence of a coincidence between Dartmouth's outlook and the cautious official
point of view; and went on to submit a twofold advice;—first,
that Dartmouth should send in two or three fourth rates to
Portsmouth to answer there some vaguely hinted emergency;[2]

---

[1] Dartmouth MSS, XI, 5, p. 184.
[2] It is quite possible that the design which was put to Dartmouth upon
December 2nd (see p. 134) was already projected.

and, secondly, that he should consider whether the safety of the fleet and the need to guard well the Thames and Medway approaches did not suggest a withdrawal of the whole remaining fleet to the original rendezvous of the Nore.[1] When the two more or less duplicate reports of the 7th (those which, in the preceding chapter, were referred to as having been despatched by Dartmouth as soon as he had regained the Downs) came in upon the 8th, they were suitably acknowledged, producing from Pepys a further assurance of the King's satisfaction, a statement that the Navy Board would provide from the River the six vessels for fireships which Dartmouth appeared to be vainly seeking in the port of Dover, and a reference to the tardy sailing of the 'St Albans', 'Newcastle' and 'Woolwich'. But the letter gave no further advice to the Admiral.[2] Nor when, the same night, Pepys, moved by the fear that his assurances and reassurances might still have failed of their purpose, penned a personal note specially and solely devoted to the task of soothing the much exercised mind of the Admiral, and, moreover, was able to promise that the King would, on the morrow, if he could find time, write, in his own hand, to his lordship, was the advice of the 7th in any way improved upon.[3] It was the King's letter of the 9th that first gave indication of some change in the policy of excessive care. It stressed the need for conserving the fleet; but its terms at least indicated that the King had not wholly closed his mind to a recognition of the combative purpose for which his fleet existed. The King wrote:

I...am fully satisfyd you did all that you could and that nobody could worke otherwise than you did. I am sure all knowing seamen must be of the same mind, and therefore be at ease as to yourself, and consider of the best means of securing the squadron you have with you, and of being in a condition of taking such advantages upon the enemy, which may offer themselves to you. Whilst the winds continue betweene the S. and W. you must be very carefull of your self if you remain in the Downs, but where you can be els to be secured from the blowing weather, and to be able to take an advantage of E. wind I do not well know, nor will I at this distance advise,

[1] Dartmouth MSS, XI, 5, p. 186.   [2] *Ibid.* p. 187.
[3] *Ibid.* p. 188.

you on the place being best judg how to secure yourself from bad weather and an enemy.

The rest of the letter merely showed the King's preoccupation with land rather than sea affairs and his realisation that the advance of the Prince upon Exeter demanded countering. For that purpose the King indicated that he himself intended, at the end of the coming week, to leave "London well garded" and go to the westward.[1] This letter, a model of professional propriety yet a plain refusal of explicit advice, was ill calculated to aid the Admiral; and the effect it had upon his policy will presently be considered. It was duly committed to the post, together with a communication from the Secretary[2] acknowledging the receipt of papers, especially of a fleet list, captured from a Brandenburg vessel;[3] but it took two days to reach the 'Resolution'. In the interval, other correspondence proceeded from Pepys; and it is convenient to dispose of it before considering Dartmouth's reception of the King's guidance. In all, three further letters from the Secretary were on their way before or about the time the King's communication was delivered.

The first of these letters, written on the 10th,[4] followed the receipt of a despatch from Dartmouth, dated the 9th,[5] which chiefly discussed the condition of the fleet, and from which it may be gathered that the 'Dover' and 'Foresight' were come in from cruising. The chief value of this particular letter lay in the considered comparison of the two fleets which a scrutiny of the Brandenburger's papers had made possible, Pepys enclosing a tabulation in which he professed to demonstrate the odds only inconsiderably in favour of the Dutch, so far as mere numbers were concerned, and not at all on their side in the matter of quality; this letter also directed the Admiral, in answer to a request made by him in his despatch just referred to, to await the King's decision as to what should be done with the Brandenburg vessel and the captured flyboat[6] and not, in the meantime, make prizes of enemy traders. The second of

[1] Dartmouth MSS, XI, 5, p. 190.   [2] Ibid. p. 189.
[3] Ibid. p. 266; by Capt. Cole of the 'Pearl'.   [4] Ibid. p. 191.
[5] Ibid. XV, 1, p. 62.
[6] See p. 82. They were both set at liberty in due course (Dartmouth MSS, XV, 1, p. 65, and XI, 5, p. 202).

Pepy's letters, dated the 11th,[1] conveyed a report that 5000 more Dutch troops were waiting for transport, in 25 vessels under the convey of two men of war, to this island. The third, also of the 11th,[2] among routine matters of some importance, made reference to the receipt of further papers out of the captured Brandenburger (documents extracted and sent up by Dartmouth the day previously);[3] it demanded a court martial on an accident to the 'Centurion' (which, commanded by Sir Francis Wheeler, had gone ashore on the 9th under the North Foreland to be got off next day in a condition making it imperative for her to be ordered into the River to be docked);[4] and lastly, it gave details of a number of intended reinforcements to the fleet. These were to be the 'Phoenix' (Captain Gifford), the 'Portland' (Captain Geo. Aylmer), the 'Hampton Court' (Captain Priestman), the 'Tiger Prize' (Captain Smith), as well as the 'Kent' and 'Warspite'—one of the latter specially to replace the Vice-Admiral's 'Mary'.[5] It is curious but perhaps natural, in view of the fact that Pepys would assume that the King's communication was actually before the Admiral on the 11th instant, that the Secretary did not in this third letter, take up a remark which the Admiral made in sending up the second batch of Brandenburg papers on the 10th instant to the effect that he desired of the King fuller guidance than the commands of the Secretary had so far provided him with. In plain truth, as Pepys was shortly to infer from another despatch of the 10th,[6] then travelling towards him, Dartmouth had ignored the suggestion to retreat to the London River and had indicated a very different preference, namely that of sailing westward to the Spithead anchorage.

It was on Sunday, November 11th, that the important letter reached the fleet. By midnight Dartmouth had answered it.[7] He thanked his Majesty for "the greatest happiness of [his] life", for the opening sentences of exoneration but, as might

---

[1] Dartmouth MSS, XI, 5, p. 192.   [2] Ibid. p. 193.
[3] Ibid. p. 267.
[4] "Journal of Captain Grenville Collins", Dartmouth MSS, XV, 1, p. 57.
[5] Her "crankness" ("disposition to overset", Oxford Dictionary) was complained of.
[6] Dartmouth MSS, XI, 5, p. 64.   [7] Ibid. p. 267.

have been expected, he did not seize advice which would have served amply to justify pretentious inaction in the Downs or even complete withdrawal to his earlier Nore anchorage. He chose not to make the retirement of which Pepys had spoken and of the advantages of which certain officers had loudly argued. He desired, he said, to avoid a move which would "at best...argue some feare" and "hooke" him "within the sands againe". He held it preferable "to look towards" the enemy from the anchorage of Spithead. But, because he still felt the inadequacy of the guidance he had just been accorded, he asked, in closing his reply, for a reasoned pronouncement from the King—to reach the 'Resolution' if possible, before the fleet quitted the place in which it lay. The messenger who brought this communication to London presented a parallel despatch to Pepys.[1] It thanked the Secretary for the kindness of the special commiserating and reassuring letter of the 8th; it expressed some doubt as to the Admiralty interpretation of the intercepted fleet list; it put the English fighting strength at 29 ships of the line; and, like the letter to the King, asked for full and precise orders as to the future. In one respect it went further; for it suggested that the October 1st Instructions referred only to the prevention of an enemy descent and might, therefore, technically be regarded as lapsed in their application.

The terms of the answer to the King and the important observation to the Secretary left the initiative still in the hands of his Majesty. So, when Dartmouth's midnight reply of the 11th instant reached London (together with the letter to the Secretary) on the 12th, James found it necessary to decide a course of action. Roused to the seriousness of the situation, he answered the Admiral on the same day.[2] He began with references to matters which, he said, Pepys, in a concurrent communication, would be found to handle; but all the rest of the letter was directed definitely to meet the Admiral's appeal for advice. He said:

I think that the boy of the Nore ought not to be so much as thought on, without you were very much overpowerd by the enemy; you

[1] Dartmouth MSS, XI, 5, p. 268. There was another report of that date.
[2] Ibid. p. 194.

best know your owne strength and whether you are in a condition to make use of this esterly wind to attempt any thing upon them, at least I thinke there can be no danger of going to the Spit head, and I should thinke you in more safety there when the winds shall come westerly then in the Downs.[1] T'would be of some reputation even your going but thether, but of much more if you thought yourself strong enough to look out for them. Another convenience you would have, by going to the Spit head, if you are not in a condition to seek them out, which is the conveniancy of soner changing any of your ships that may be defective then in any other place, and as to their coming in upon you there by the Needles, I thinke there can be no danger in that, for the same wind which must bring them in there would carry you out by St. Hellens, and you could work to windward of them as De Ruyter did at Bullen bay[2] and the same fate, or worse, might happen to them as did to our fleet in that tyme,[3] and should the wind chop about to the S. or S.E. they would be in a very ill condition;[4] and now that I have sayd this to you I must leave all to your judgment who are on the place, who can judg best what is to be done...and I have not tyme to say mor, t'will be the end of this weeke before I thinke to leave this towne.

The additional information which the King had stated the Secretary would supply went with the royal letter.[5] Pepys drove home the Admiralty finding about the rates of the fleet's strength, the validity of which estimate Dartmouth's last letter had somewhat questioned. Pepys alleged that he could produce "two evidences...greatly to the coroborateing of the King's beleive of the present validity of the paper". He could say that the Deal postmaster had sent up figures which agreed with

[1] The Spithead, the "King's Bedchamber", is only open to south-east winds.
[2] "Bullen" = Boulogne.
[3] James refers to the first day of the Four Days' Fight, June 1666, when Albemarle made use of a S.W. wind to attack, from windward, De Ruyter's superior force lying in the Dover Strait, but was forced to tack back from the French sands on which De Ruyter had led him. Thereupon many of De Ruyter's vessels, left by the vigorous Albemarle in his rear, secured a windward position and did him severe damage.
[4] If the Dutch came in through the Needles and Solent with a S.W. or W. wind (as contemplated) and the wind then shifted to S. or S.E., their choice would lie between anchoring at Spithead and there awaiting attack, or beating out from Spithead by way of St Helens. To go back by way of the Needles would be impossible. That passage is so narrow and dangerous, that it was never attempted without a fair wind.
[5] Dartmouth MSS, XI, 5, p. 195.

those which a Scotch seaman "a mate in the Dutch fleet for 8 months past, and... now... deserted... to serve his Majesty both in his person and by his intelligence" had provided the King with. The deserter[1] put the Dutch fleet at 44 war vessels great and small, declaring it meanly manned and victualled for six months only. Other matters of routine interest the letter spoke of, the most important being a request (made as a result of Treasury representations) to provide for warning "divers rich shipps... within a little time expected home". But the chief significance of the letter was not in the marshalling of evidence as to the Dutch strength or in the subsidiary matters which it handled. It supplemented the King's own written word by enclosing an order direct from the office of Lord Middleton, one of the Secretaries of State, which amplified the October 1st Instructions and gave full authority to the Admiral to fight the enemy wherever he came upon him. Through hastiness of despatch the paper lacked "being directed in forme"; but Pepys undertook to secure and send on a perfect copy. The King's letter was delivered together with the Secretary's information and enclosure within the space of a day.[2]

Tuesday, November 13th, is therefore a significant date in the English story. The period of delay, caused by Dartmouth's reference to headquarters and welcomed in London because of the cautious policy which the King had entertained in the first few days following the disaster, came then to an end. Thenceforth the Admiral, amply reassured of the royal approval of all his past conduct, his choice of the Spithead specifically approved, the future referred to his sole judgement, resumed undivided responsibility for the operations of the fleet he commanded, operations which, for a week and a day, he had felt it too great a burden in unaided judgement to direct. But, in bringing into prominence the significance of the day, a single qualification must be added. Just as, immediately after the despatch of the urgent appeal to the King, on November 5th, from Beachy, his lordship had followed up his scouting vessels to see whether

---

[1] It is not improbable that he was an imposter (Dartmouth MSS, XI, 5, pp. 270, 218).
[2] Dartmouth MSS, XI, 5, p. 268.

any advantage upon the enemy would offer itself to his depleted forces, so, a veering of the wind to the east, during the week-end preceding this particular Tuesday, had so strongly tempted him to spread his sails to catch a fickle favour that there is little doubt, had the gale been less tempestuous, the Downs would have been quitted before the royal communication could have been delivered aboard the Admiral's flagship. That is to say, a second time in this period of reference and pardonable dislike of sole responsibility, Dartmouth, rather than allow an opportunity to slip by, to the prejudice of what he believed would prove the ultimate interests of the royal service, had refused to profit by the fact of reference to the King and had taken an interim decision to seek the Spithead with an expressed intention of early attack on Torbay. It was a decision which, in the circumstances, one would confidently have expected him, as an English Admiral, to make.[1]

Communications to the King and Pepys,[2] which the receipt by Dartmouth of the two new letters upon the 13th at once and gladly provoked, show that their perusal forthwith produced a marked effect. The Admiral was prepared to drop all discussion of fleet strengths; he was so confirmed in his anxiety to resume his campaign that he began to hope it might even prove unnecessary to put into the Spithead until he had "rendered (the) better service" he sought to perform.

It is natural to ask whether Dartmouth had reinforced his fleet sufficiently to achieve the "better service" he intended. The delay had at least given him the necessary respite for regathering his fleet. The 'Swallow' and 'Tiger', as has already been recorded, had been found by the Admiral on his return on the 7th to the Downs; thither also, it has been noted, the 'Bonadventure', 'Foresight' and 'Dover' had come in; and the three celebrated laggards, the 'Newcastle', 'Woolwich' and 'St Albans' having made their belated appearance just before the 13th instant (though the 'Newcastle' had leaked to

---

[1] See letter to King, Nov. 13, Dartmouth MSS, XI, 5, p. 269; see letter to Pepys, Nov. 13, Dartmouth MSS, XV, 5, p. 65.
[2] See n. 1, *supra*.

the extent of "23 inches of water a glass"[1] all the way round from the River and the 'St Albans' had contrived to bump on the North Sands Head in her passage),[2] Dartmouth, on this 13th instant, was only one capital ship (the 'York' at Portsmouth) short of his full paper strength. The 'Montague', 'Assurance', and 'Centurion' were not likely to keep the sea;[3] but, even in that case, while the 'Mary' stayed with him, he was, counting only third and fourth rates, of strength equal to that which was his upon October 30th, and five stronger than upon the dismal November 5th—or 33 third and fourth rates in all. His strength in fireships must also have been augmented to at least 14 since November 5th.[4] His fears for the loyalty of officers and men remained still suppressed; that is, if one is to judge from an isolated reference to the spirit of his command, made on November 10th when the second batch of Brandenburg papers was forwarded. He had then observed "great distinction to be made of men"..."some being willing rather to hide their defects then thinke of being from (His Majesty's) service ...but more...willing to be refitting".[5] Thus, then in point of numbers the Admiral was at least of tolerable strength; and, as for his distrust of certain officers, that, regrettably enough, was no new thing though perhaps a constantly worsening factor.

In turning to examine what the Admiral actually implied by his optimistic phrase "better service" little difficulty is to be

[1] "A glass". As a measurement of time at sea the glass was traditionally said to have been equivalent to an interval of "half an hour" and, in support of the view, the sound authority of Captain John Smith's *Seaman's Grammar*, 1627 edition, is quoted by the *Oxford Dictionary*. But while it is certain that larger and smaller instruments were employed—the four hour (watch), the hour and the minute glasses—it is not so evident that the half hour instrument existed. It is not to be credited that the vessel leaked 23 inches in half an hour and kept afloat.
[2] Dartmouth MSS, XV, 1, p. 66, and "Journal of Captain Grenville Collins", Dartmouth MSS, XV, 1, p. 57.   [3] Dartmouth MSS, XI, 5, p. 268.
[4] The 'Speedwell' and 'Sally Rose' missing on the 5th (p. 85) were in, for they were among the ships mentioned—Dartmouth MSS, XI, 5, p. 212(for both) and p. 217 (for 'Speedwell')—as scattered in the westward sailing about to be dealt with. Also the 'Half Moon' and 'Charles' had reached the fleet—Dartmouth MSS, XV, 1, p. 66 (for 'Half Moon' and 'Charles') and "Journal of Captain Grenville Collins", Dartmouth MSS, XV, 1, p. 57 (for Capt. Mundin who (v. p. 58 of this work) commanded the 'Half Moon'). Thus 10 (see p. 86) + 2 + 2 = 14.
[5] Dartmouth MSS, XI, 5, p. 267.

encountered. Dartmouth made it clear to the King[1] that the "better service" which he held in mind would not concern itself with the weakly protected convoy reported on Sunday last, by Pepys, as possibly coming from Holland. He could not spare detached ships for subsidiary purposes. Should the Dutch ships venture out, scouts should report them; likely enough they would run into his fleet in the Channel. By "better service" he meant "to finde them out and give...the best account God (would) please to bless (him) with". His latest intelligence had informed him that the Dutch fleet still hovered round Torbay but that the transports lay among the shoaling bars of the narrow five mile estuary of the Exe, some as far north as Topsham, a matter of over 15 land miles from the Bay. He therefore knew that it would be quite impossible to fall simultaneously on the Dutch fleet and transports which were not anchored in the same place; and he knew also that it would be quite unlikely that, if he neglected first to handle the Dutch fleet, Herbert would so fail to interpose his vessels as to allow the English to carry out the destruction of the transports. He may very well have reflected that, run close inland as they were, the transports would, in any case, be likely to prove inaccessible. The single possibility of the situation was to compel the enemy fleet to a decision in the deep water harbour of Torbay; if there he won, he could expect that the surrender of the embayed transports would automatically follow. Such, it may confidently be advanced, was Lord Dartmouth's scheme. It promised him his only chance of success. It is interesting enough to observe that, to all intents and purposes, the new plan was nothing more nor less than his lordship's original "command-disputing", "command-asserting" design—a design rendered, indeed, more difficult of application because of Herbert's freedom from the worst difficulties of transport protection upon the open sea, but, none the less, the true original scheme which, on November 5th, off Beachy, had fallen into abeyance, which on the 7th, on the return to the Downs, had begun to struggle for re-emergence in his lordship's policy and which had persisted because it was the only right scheme for a sailor to hold in

[1] Letter referred to at foot of preceding page.

view, the only possible alternative to inaction, remorse and ignominy.

The rough weather of the week-end subsided into a "starke calme";[1] and so Dartmouth was compelled to wait for three days beyond the 13th instant before he could sail to carry out his intentions. The enforced delay provided opportunity to hold the two courts martial. On the 14th, "John Oliver Master of the 'Centurion' for running the said ship ashore...was turned off and fined a month's imprisonment. The Pilot of the 'St Albans' was tried for running the said ship ashore, for which he was rendered incapable of piloting any of the King's ships".[2] Possibly at this time the Admiral did what he could to meet a request mentioned in Pepys's last letter that certain homecoming merchantmen should be warned of the state of affairs in the Channel. Dartmouth rounded off his plans. He, on the 14th, decided that his rendezvous in case of the separation of his fleet should, with an easterly wind, be St Hellens, but at Spithead or Plymouth Sound, according to circumstance, should a westerly wind prevail.[3] On the 15th, to Captain Lord Berkeley of the 'Montague' and to Captain Frowd of the 'Ruby', special copies of the general (?) instructions for the intended attack were, for special reasons, sent.[4] On the 15th, also he wrote the King and Pepys; but the letters are not important except to show his purpose, if attacked before he could sail west, to work out by the North Sand Head to get room before closing in battle.[5]

A long letter from Pepys, dated the 13th,[6] almost certainly reached the Admiral before he sailed westward. Pepys had laid upon his office table all his previous correspondence with the Admiral, so that the paper attempted a general clearing up of all outstanding matters between them. Anticipatory of the Admiral's needs for reinforcements, a complete survey of the mobilised and non-mobilised strength of the Royal Navy was presented—a survey calculated, indeed, to leave in the Ad-

[1] Dartmouth MSS, XI, 5, p. 270.
[2] "Journal of Captain Grenville Collins", Dartmouth MSS, XV, 1, p. 57.
[3] Dartmouth MSS, XI, 5, p. 202.   [4] Ibid. p. 203.
[5] Ibid. p. 270 (to King) and XV, 1, p. 66 (to Pepys).
[6] Ibid. p. 198.

miral's mind a sense of satisfaction. For besides the fourth rates about to go out—'Portland', 'Tiger-Prize', 'Phoenix'— the fourth rates, 'Sweepstakes', 'Mary Galley', 'James Galley', might be used; also, apart from the third rates due out—'Hampton Court', 'Kent' and 'Warspite'—the 'Dunkirk', 'Edgar' and 'Suffolk' were available. Indeed, on Dartmouth's demand, any of the other third rates (save two) could be put under his flag. The big third rates or still larger vessels, it was thought, Dartmouth would not desire to ask for. No doubt Dartmouth observed and appreciated the survey though, at the moment, it availed him nothing. Much else of incidental interest the letter contained, and the facts mentioned below are worth noting. Trinity House had been instructed to re-lay the River buoys. As to "demands touching stores, particularly anchors, cables, sayles, and longboates," Pepys assured the Admiral that he would keep the Navy Office at its work and, after the manner of a responsible official, he tacked on a reminder that the King expected "all wayes of good husbandry in the expense of his stores"; "formal warr" could not, he thought, be "long prevented"; the King's purse could not but be slender and "navall stores... by the scarceness of the market (would) be very soon brought beyond the power of money presently to procure". That reminded the Secretary to ask "whether the anchors and cables that were lately left behind by the 'Bonadventure', 'Swallow' and 'Foresight' had not buoys left with them, in order to their recovery". Dartmouth should see to that in the King's interest. And—not a matter disconnected with the inculcation of the need for economy—Pepys declared that, as for the general arrangements for supplies of stores at Deal—there or at Sheerness and Harwich where Dartmouth had thought perhaps yards might be "re-erected"—it had hitherto been the custom of the authorities to leave "one person only...at some small sallary under the name of storekeeper for the answering any little accidentall occasion which the officers of the Navy may happen to have of employing one in the intervall of warr".[1] Reference was made to the King's previously mentioned desires that the Dutch prisoners from the flyboat should be secured in the

---

[1] Dartmouth MSS, XV, 1, p. 63.

Tower.[1] There occurred also an expression of a desire to know
his lordship's views about the "performances of the fishermen's
and watermen's companies", Pepys having reason to think they
had "served the King very slightly; but especially the former"
(after all their brags and the King's large favours) by abusing
the press warrants in "rakeing up from all ends of the town,
and the most scandalously, persons of all sortes, but that only
which they should be of; namely, fishermen, or, at least seamen". There was a mention of Sir Francis Wheeler's bad luck
in nearly losing his ship and in having so much desertion among
his men. There was, at long last, a conclusion! Of course, if
there are many things to say they must be said; but Mr Pepys's
letters were seldom brief. Among the enclosures was a letter
from d'Albeville to James, dated November 16th (N.S.), in which
that ambassador sought to show that William, just before
sailing, had given up the idea of landing on the East Coast
after a secret consultation afloat with 'Eullenstyn' returned
"from some creek or place upon the coasts of England"; but,
though the ambassador's report was both interesting and
circumstantial, it probably carried no great conviction of
accuracy.[2]

The story of what befell the English fleet when, at the end
of the three days of provokingly calm, delaying weather, Dartmouth at length cleared the Downs, intent to redeem his fortune
and to serve the King, makes at best a melancholy tale. But
the episode is important; and it is well to follow its detail in
the actual despatches which the Admiral sent from Spithead,
one to the King and one to the Secretary, on November 22nd.[3]

November 22nd. Aboard the 'Resolution' at Spithead.

Admiral to Secretary.

After sailing from the Downs to the westward on the 16th instant
and encountering at sea, as I shall now proceed to give you a particular account of such variety of winds and storms, as frustrated all
my hopes and intentions for his Majesty's service, the fleet being
very much shaken and shattered, I returned with 20 or 21 sail of
ships and anchored in St. Helens road the 20th instant where with

[1] Dartmouth MSS, XI, 5, p. 194.   [2] See p. 79, note 3.
[3] Dartmouth MSS, XI, 5, p. 271 (to King); XV, 1, p. 66 (to Secretary).

very much wind at west, I rode till this morning and then had a...
to turn into the Spithead.

On Friday the 16th, at 3 in the afternoon, with the wind at N.E.
I got under sail with the whole fleet[1] and at 8 that night we were
abreast of the light on Dungeness, the wind being E.S.E. a fine gale,
we steered away all night W.S.W. Saturday the 17th in the morning,
the Isle of Wight bore N.N.W. distance about 7 leagues. At 10 in
the morning, we lay by and sent the 'Cleveland' yacht, into Portsmouth with a letter to Sir Richard Beach, to prepare and get in readiness, what ships he could to strengthen the fleet and particularly to
hasten out the 'York' and those ships I had ordered in there, as my
last advised you the 'Montague' being disabled, she went also at
the same time for Portsmouth with order to Sir Richard Beach to
man the 'York' completely from her company, if the said ship's
repairs should require any long time. At noon of the same day, the
body of the Isle of Wight bore W. by N., about 5 leagues off with a
fresh gale at S.E. and we stood away for Tor Bay, making such sail
as might bring us there early in the morning; but at 4, afternoon,
the wind came out at S.S.E. and S. by E. very much wind, when we
tacked and stood to the eastward to undlay (sic)[2] the tide of ebb; but
finding the winds to shrink,[3] that we could lie no better than east, at

---

[1] "Whole fleet" = "45 men of warre and fireships" according to the
parallel despatch. On p. 106, with 'Montague', 'Assurance', 'Centurion'
excluded, the available third and fourth rates were estimated at 33 and the
fireships at not less than 14. The 'Montague', as this despatch shows, went
into Portsmouth, the 'Centurion' and 'Assurance' had gone back to the
River for repairs (Dartmouth MSS, XI, 5, pp. 206, 207). But these three are
allowed for. It seems that 'Constant Warwick' also put into Portsmouth
("Journal of Captain Grenville Collins", Dartmouth MSS, XV, 1, p. 57) so
that not more than 32 capital vessels sailed west and there may possibly have
been just less than that number. In any case the difference between Dartmouth's and Herbert's forces was not appreciable.

[2] "Undlay". In a very general manner the Channel tides may be thought
of thus: In the North Sea the flood tide sets southward, in the Channel,
eastward. When the southward-setting North Sea flood has fully met, in
the Strait of Dover, the eastward-setting Channel flood, the former deflected,
at the meeting, over towards the English side sometimes as far south as
Dungeness, and the latter forced over to, and up, the French shore, then the
temporary equilibrium set up is high water at Dover. For the next six hours
the Channel tide ebbs west; for six hours thereafter there is the regathering
of flood water towards Dover. There are important local peculiarities, e.g.
at the Spithead and Solent. And meteorological conditions affect the bodily
movement of the water. "Undlay" is evidently a contraction of "underlay".
The term is possibly nowhere else extant in a sea sense. The *Oxford Dictionary*
shows the meaning of the word, when used as a mining expression, to be "to
slope or incline from the perpendicular". Here the sense is cognate—as a
diagram will show. In nautical language, it means "lee bow the tide".

[3] "Shrink" = to draw ahead, to become foul.

7 at night, we tacked, again and stood off S.W. with the tide of flood under our lee, to check us off the shore. At 12 at night, being much wind, we took in our foretop sail, and lay under a pair of courses[1] till daylight.

On Sunday the 18th, in the morning, we found that the flood tide under our lee had caused us to make a S.W. course good, by the Island of Aldnerney, bearing E.S.E., distance, about 7 leagues, then we bore up, and the wind increasing to a very great storm, we lay our head to the eastward, trying under a mainsail[2] till noon, to bring the fleet together there not being then in sight above 24 sail, the Rear Admiral with several men-of-war and fireships, being wanting.

At noon, we set our foresail, standing N.E. by N. and E.N.E. till 4 in the evening, at which time the land of St. Alban's bore N.N.W. about 6 leagues off, when we tacked,[3] and stood to the westward, the storm continuing violent, and at one at night, with a violent gust of wind and rain, our mainsail and mizen, blew away and some ships fired guns as signals of distress.

Monday the 19th, at 4 this morning we brought to another main sail and mizen, by seven in the morning, being less wind, at west we got up our main yard, set the main sail, heaved our top sail, and stood away to the eastward and at 9 in the morning, it clearing up, we saw the Start Land bearing N.N.E. distance about six leagues at which time we were 22 sail. At noon the Start bore N.W. We stood away towards Torbay, and at 2 o'clock we were close to the Berry, describing[4] the Dutch fleet in Torbay, but could not discover their number whereupon I ordered the 'Jersey' Captain Beverley, to stand near in, for giving me the better account of them, and, with the fleet, I steered away to the eastward towards the Isle of Wight. At 10 at night the wind came out at S.W. blowing very hard, so that we handed[5] our top sails and lay under a pair of courses till 12 at night, when we had a violent storm at W.S.W. so that we were forced to lie a try under the main course till break of day.

Tuesday the 20th in the morning, the storm continuing very hard,

[1] "Courses" = the lower sails; "The Main-sail and the Fore-sail is called the Fore-course and the Main-course, or a pair of Courses" (*Seaman's Grammar*, Capt. John Smith; 1691 edition, p. 31). Course = corps (body).

[2] A storm, let us lie at Trie with our main Course, that is, to hale the Tack aboard, the Sheet close aft, the Boling set up, and the helm tied close aboard". *Ibid.* p. 40.

[3] "Tacked" here means "hauled to the wind", a meaning which became obsolete soon after this date. Apparently they stood in to make the land in order to verify their position, and may be supposed to have altered course to E.N.E. to avoid any risk of getting into Portland Race. All this time the wind was southerly.

[4] In the sense of "descry"—not unusual; see *Oxford Dictionary*.

[5] Furled.

we bore away for the Isle of Wight and at noon anchored at St. Helens Road where the 'Jersey' came in to me giving an account, that standing close in with Torbay, he saw the Dutch fleet, being as near as he could tell, 57 sail of great ships,[1] their small ships being so far in, that he could not count them. I found here at anchor the 'Pendennis', Sir William Booth, who was forced in on Sunday with the loss of his foremast and having received other damages by his guns breaking loose in the storm, wherein also I understand that the 'Heldrenbergh'[2] hospital ship was unfortunately lost, and but 13 of her men saved in her long boat by Capt. Ashby, by some ships running on board her, which is supposed was the 'Bonadventure' she being seen at anchor, on the backside of the Isle of Wight without a head, bowsprit, or foremast, and was getting up a jurymast, so that not having yet had any further account of her, I hope she is got into the Downs. I found also Sir John Berry with other men-of-war and fireships at St. Helens and Spithead, and I fear most of the fireships have received damage, as well in their hulls, masts, and yards, as fireworks.[3]

We had much wind all night at west, which continuing also all Wednesday, kept us at St. Helens and this day we got into the Spithead, where was sent on board me, by Sir Richard Beach, yours of the 20th instant, whereto all the answer I can make, at present is that I shall endeavour all things for his Majesty's service to my utmost.

The despatch to the King traversed the same ground in somewhat less detail.[4] It sounded however a more intimate note. Thus: "if I had gone into the Spithead I knew many wants would be pretended and considerable time delayed, besides for other reasons I thought it best for your Majestie's service to bring the fleet to fight as soon as conveniently I could...". Further on:

By this they should have had some recruites but your Majestie may see how reasonable my coming upon them had been if it had pleased

---

[1] A very high estimate for "great ships" only; not to be reconciled with other facts. Counting from a distance perhaps partly explains it.

[2] This vessel was, presumably, captured from Monmouth's little expeditionary force, Macaulay, I, p. 572. The 'Heldrenburg' (Capt. Howell (?) —Dartmouth MSS, XI, 5, pp. 212, 146) and 'Antelope' were in collision. ("Journal of Captain Grenville Collins", Dartmouth MSS, XV, I, p. 58) but 'Antelope', a fourth rate, is incorrectly called by Collins (if he has been correctly copied) an hospital ship also.

[3] 'Pearl' (fireship) lost a foremast, 'Pendennis', Sir Wm Booth (third) bowsprit and foremast. "Journal of Captain Grenville Collins", Dartmouth MSS, XV, I, p. 58.

[4] See note 3, p. 110.

God to bless me so that the winde had stood and the weather continued faire, but there is noe resisting a storm in the Channell at this time of the yeare, and if I should not have ventured when the winde was faire and the weather promised well I might have been justly blaimed, for if nobody should go to sea when the winde is faire for fear of the winde shifting and a storm comeing down things would hardly ever succeed.

It also does amplify a little the laconic ending of the other despatch which concluded, "all the answer I can make, at present is that I shall endeavour all things for his Majesty's service to my utmost". For he told the King,

I believe several shipps that are missing are blowne to the Downes, whither I have writ to Mr. Pepys to send orders for those that are in condition with the first opportunity to rejoine me here, the rest to refitt in the river as soon as possible, for to my great disappointment Sir Richard Beach tells me there are very few stores for fourth rates which is the greatest part of this fleet. I will be sure to take all the care and pains I can to refitt and change such shipps as are necessary (if your Majestie will give me leave) for I am very apprehensive of their passing by me in the night (which is not to be avoided especially when it blows hard) and their going up the river while your Majestie is absent, but of this I will take the best care I can. Their fortune hath been extravagant for their hath been but three faire days since I came to sea and they had two of them to land in while I was becalmed off Beachy, but sure I shall have some luck at last for I will struggle all I can and endure with patience till I can compass that service you expect from me.

My business now shall be to gett readdie as soon as possible tho' the season of the year is intollerable, sixteen hours night to eight hours day with lea shoares in the Channell is harder workeing then any battle.

I am sorry to heare any have proved false to your Majestie in the army;[1] I not only wish, but will be watchful that it may have noe influence here. The Prince of Wales I am told is at Portsmouth, and tomorrow I will venture your Majestie's leave to pay my duty to him tho' it is the first time I have set my foot ashoare since I tooke this charge. It is some comfort to be near a part of you since I cannot be so happy to be at your owne side at this time. God protect you both, and enable me to serve as effectually as I earnestly desire it.

[1] He knew of the defection of the Duke of Berwick's, Lord Cornbury's and Lord St Albans' Regiments. (Dartmouth MSS, XI, 5, p. 204.)

The despatch to the King was forwarded direct to Salisbury.

At this point note must be taken of the fact that James had begun again to coquette with the idea of securing French assistance. Judging from the despatch sent by Seignelay to Barillon, on November 24th, James made, just before that date, overtures for a considerable number of ships from "l'armement à Brest". Barillon was told to inform him that they could not be supplied before the Spring. Barillon himself was reminded that much might happen before that time came. Louis, so Seignelay remarked, had wasted enough money on James and had no wish to bolster up a hopeless cause.[1]

It is necessary to turn once again to the Dutch side of the story.

The Prince of Orange had landed where he had been least expected; and it is, of course, a matter of common knowledge that the land design, at first, moved much less rapidly than his Highness had anticipated. Though his forces reached Exeter on November 19th, for several days the numbers of men of rank who came in to him were not so great as to dispel a certain disappointment at his slow progress. It was not that he considered he had cause to complain of the information he had received as to the state of the English parties. He assured Prince Georg Friedrich von Waldeck, who commanded his troops in the Netherlands, that he was satisfied on that score;[2] but one sentence of the letter written upon November 26/16 to Waldeck, "Il est facheux que nous avons este obligé par le vendt de mestre pied a terre de ce coste icy du West", shows that the Prince continued for many days to be fretted by what he regarded as the misfortune of a westward landing, the undeniable cause of the tardy incoming of his friends.

On the whole, little is known of the naval affairs of the Prince for the period which, on the English side, has just been handled —i.e. for the interval between November 7th and 22nd. From the first, William was concerned for the covering of the dis-

---

[1] *L'Italie en 1671...*, Pierre Clément, p. 338.
[2] *Wilhelm III von Oranien u. Georg Friedrich von Waldeck*, P. L. Müller, II, p. 118.

embarcation, though he was no less interested in the disposal of the transports and fleet. By the 20/10th, he evidently desired to send back the transports and wished Herbert, unless the royal fleet should be known to have passed the Strait, to bring ashore with him "Adml. Everse" so that a consultation might be held. Incidentally he spoke of the danger to be apprehended from French privateers.[1] The same day Herbert proposed that he should seek the English fleet and drive it into some port. William, on the 22/12th, from Exeter, approved the plan.[2] But the letter of approbation contained significant terms:

Ainsi je crois qu'en vous aprochent de la flote Anglais vous luy pouries donner le salut ordinaire que la flote d'Hollande est accustome de donner en temps de Paix a celle d'Angleterre et tacher ainsi a venir a un pourparler. Mais si elle n'y veut point entendre vous saves ce que vous aves affaire, et qu'il faudra user de force. Au reste je laisse toute l'affaire a vostre·conduite, estant impossible de donner des ordres precis en une telle affaire.

The English fleet disposed of, Lieutenant-Admiral W. Bastiaensze was to convoy the transports and Lieutenant-Admiral Evertsen take back the fleet.

The orders, which modified considerably the terms of Section 4 of the Instructions given on October 27/17 to Herbert before sailing, would, at first sight, suggest that, late in the day, the Prince had been converted to the professional outlook and desired to plan the rest of the naval undertaking on orthodox lines; that he wished to win command by battle decision or blockade before moving his transports, and to risk fight where previously he had avoided it. Circumstances alter cases. The Prince had, in the first place and before sailing, calculated that his transports could be evasively convoyed back to Holland by the special ships which Herbert's Instructions spoke of as appointed to sail from England in due course for that duty; but, contrary to his then expectations, which had pictured an east coast landing, he saw himself disembarked far

---

[1] B.M. MSS, Egerton 2621. Prince to Herbert, 20/10. *London Gazette* (Dec. 3–6) reports from the Hague (Dec. 10) a vessel arrived on the 5th at Rotterdam bearing word that a Dutch squadron had met five St Malo privateers, of 30 to 40 guns, and taken two and sunk three.

[2] B.M. MSS, Egerton 2621. Prince to Herbert, 22/12.

to the westward and probably realised, as clearly as his Admiral, that it was most unlikely that transports returning could be so convoyed as to evade the English all along the Channel, or, in any case, in the narrow waters of the Strait. Therefore the risk of fight had to be taken. But, when it is added that Russell professed to be able to tell Herbert on November 13th[1] "8 capts was resolved to salute Dartmouth and come over to us" and that "Berry, Deane, Hastings[2], Churchill, Aylemer, Shovell and Barkly" were named on the paper, the simple construction of a clean conversion to the professional opinion cannot, and need not, so easily be put upon the matter. It is likely that upon the inferior *moral* of the royal fleet the Prince had begun, about that time, to calculate with such an enhanced confidence as to believe that the English fleet could, on the merest show of force, be driven into harbour where desertion could be relied upon to accomplish all he desired to obtain. However, no move was made by Herbert against the English enemy; and, for the time being, the transports remained where they were. The Dutch merely manifested a certain liveliness. In evidence of their alertness, it may be added that, late on the 6th, the 'Dove' of London,[3] bound from Lisbon to Amsterdam, had been stopped five leagues from the Start and the master taken before Herbert. Then the vessel was searched and three royal letters were found. The master saw twenty of the Dutch ships that wore ensigns bearing the words "For the Protestant Religion and liberty of England". He was released, on the 9th, on condition that he sailed straight for Amsterdam. An extract from a report written by Thomas Phillips at Portsmouth to Lord Dartmouth on the day he weighed from the Downs shows similarly.[4] Having estimated the Dutch fleet in Torbay at "70 men of war and fire ships"[5] and mentioned two Dutch flyboats that had recently gone on, under convoy of a man of

---

[1] B.M. MSS, Egerton 2621.

[2] Another name occurs here following that of Hastings, but it is indecipherable.

[3] Dartmouth MSS, XI, 5, p. 213.

[4] *Ibid.* p. 204.

[5] Another very high estimate—against which might be set that of "never above 42 sayle of men of warre and not so many now" given by Sir Robert Holmes of Yarmouth (Isle of Wight) Nov. 28.

war, though the 'Fanfan'[1] had drawn them into shoal water on the Horse,[2] Phillips said:

On Sunday last came in a Vice-Admiral chasing the 'Mary' yacht,[3] about 12 of the clock, and stood for Stokes Bay to discover where their fleet was at Cowes. We shot from the upper stone platform out of one of the two angle guns which reached him and fell very near his stern; he struck his flag and topsails, saluted and came to an anchor to view the ships and the harbour. He weighed in the evening and went to sea....Preparations at Portsmouth....Dick Wharton gone to Plymouth, having orders to put himself in there, but now it is too late. The writer told him to burn his papers and instructions and go towards Bristol, but it is now said that they are in parties as far as Bridgewater, so there is no passage for him that way, and by sea they spread over to the Casquetts that no vessel can pass without examination.

In Torbay, this letter said, Herbert lived "very splendidly". On the 14th, according to the *London Gazette*, 25 sail of Dutch great ships were off the Lizard.[4] On the 27/17th, the Prince acknowledged, from Exeter, a letter from Herbert and concluded, "je suis bien marry que le vent contraire vous oblige d'y rester".[5] The *Gazette*, from Weymouth, on the 21st instant reported: "We have no news of the Dutch fleet only that they had left Torbay".[6]

*   *   *   *   *   *   *

It is perhaps a matter of some interest to ask whether Dartmouth's delay in the Downs, however desirable or necessary for the purpose of reconditioning his fleet, involved a sacrifice, for the time being, of any opportunity to proceed against the Dutch fleet and transports. The evidence as to prevailing winds from November 7th to the 13th, that is, from the date of the Admiral's return to the Downs upon the adverse gale which

---

[1] 'Fan-Fan' sloop (Capt. Henry Turvill) was captured by the Dutch before Dec. 2nd (Dartmouth MSS, XI, 5, p. 222, and "Journal of Captain Grenville Collins", Dartmouth MSS, XV, I, p. 58).

[2] "Horse"—off Portsmouth. "The Horse is hard ground and in some places not above seven foot water at low water". *Great Britain's Coasting Pilot*, Captain Grenville Collins, I, p. 3.

[3] 'Mary Yacht' (Capt. Fazeby), *Memoires*, Pepys, stationed at Portsmouth.

[4] *London Gazette*, Nov. 19–22.

[5] B.M. MSS, Egerton 2621. But the idea of taking the fleet to Plymouth, which the Prince hopes shortly to possess, is in mind.

[6] *London Gazette*, Nov. 22–24.

stopped his pursuit beyond Beachy, to the date of his attempt, just before the receipt of the conclusive advice from the King, to weigh and make for Spithead, is strong in the direction of suggesting that, after the 7th and before the 13th instant, he could not, in any case, have put westward. From the 13th onwards, there is, of course, no question of lingering in the Downs even for reconditioning the fleet. Thus it seems that the interval of by no means unreasonable delay in the Downs involved, as winds blew and weather continued, no loss of opportunity to attack the enemy.

It is of course impossible to check a very natural sympathy with the Admiral in the upshot of the venture from which he had hoped so much and from which nothing but a new disappointment had followed. This further and critical set-back involved in no way any moral turpitude or lack of professional skill. The Admiral had failed because wind and tide and weather had fought remorselessly against his fleet.

CHAPTER V

Inaction in the Royal Fleet
November 22nd to December 1st

THE two despatches which Dartmouth sent to the King
and Pepys upon Thursday, November 22nd, show that
the English Admiral looked forward to the future with
faint and chastened hope. Henceforth fast succeeding events
darkened his outlook.

To begin with, on coming in, he learned, through a letter of
the 20th instant, that his acceptance of the Secretary's offer of
the 13th instant to fit out the remaining third rates had been
a waste of time; and that the promised fireships were not yet
found for him. Much else of colourless routine interest, over
which there is no call to delay, the letter handled. The only
satisfaction it can possibly have provided for Dartmouth lay in
a comment upon an enclosed draft of a warrant, which the
King had prepared, but which, so great had been his trust in
his Admiral's discretion, he had never signed, a warrant intended
"in explanation of" the important Supplementary Order of
the 12th instant issued from Lord Middleton's office, and on
the strength of which the recent futile sailing to Torbay had
been made. Perhaps, in the light of a new, if undeserved,
failure, even the flattering comment read ironically.[1] The
above-mentioned letter, Sir Richard Beach, Commissioner of
the Portsmouth yard, had handed on.[2] He, at the same time,
reported his cheerless prospect for lack of funds to pay the
hands needed to repair the vessels in dock and his shortage of
essential stores.[3] Next, a "short and melancholy account" of
the bankrupt affairs of the Ordnance Office made dismal reading
for its Master.[4] Then, on the 24th,[5] Lord Berkeley, who had

---

[1] Dartmouth MSS, XI, 5, p. 205. The letter grants a request that a storeship
shall follow the fleet.
[2] Ibid. XV, 1, p. 68.   [3] Ibid. XI, 5, p. 211.
[4] Ibid. XI, 5, p. 211.   [5] Ibid. XI, 5, p. 210.

communicated on the 17th,[1] in by no means convincing language, the reason why he, allowed by orders of the 16th[2] to go into Portsmouth to change or refit his damaged ship, the 'Montague', had not, on receipt of modifying instructions of the 17th[3], followed the fleet to Torbay, reported a probable long delay in dock and related all the news and rumours of the shore. His budget declared that the Prince of Wales had been brought, the night before, into Portsmouth, under guard of Irish dragoons; that Lord Cornbury had taken his regiment over to the Prince; that the Duke of Berwick's horse and the Lords St Albans and Colchester had deserted, that Lord Lovelace had attempted to change sides, had been captured, yet had defended himself very well; that the first captain of Sir Edward Hales's regiment and Frank Russell were missing from the King's side; that the Duke of Berwick's foot regiment, Sir Edward Hales's (regiment)?, the Irish and the Irish dragoons were in Portsmouth and that the King was with the army.... Of part or of all this news Dartmouth was already cognisant; but, on top of the letter of the 17th, this of the 24th must, on account of its general tenour, have read unpleasantly. On the 24th[4]—it matters not at all whether before or after Berkeley's letter reached him—the Admiral set foot ashore, for the first time since taking up his commission to command the fleet;[5] and, attended by his vice and rear admirals and most of the captains, waited upon the baby Prince. The 'Resolution' fired a 21-gun salute; the rest of the fleet followed suit. For his lordship, the payment of such respect can only have called up distressing emotions and increased his wonder at the curious presence of the royal infant in Portsmouth town. The next communication from the Admiralty, dated the 24th[6] and delivered before or on the 25th,[7] brought, it is true, the satisfying news that the 'Henrietta', 'Antelope', 'Bonadventure', 'Crown', 'Lark', 'Guernsey' and 'Sally Rose' had reached

---

[1] Dartmouth MSS, XI, 5, p. 205.　　　　[2] *Ibid.*　　　　[3] *Ibid.*
[4] "Journal of Captain Grenville Collins", Dartmouth MSS, XV, I, p. 58.
[5] See p. 114.
[6] Dartmouth MSS, XI, 5, p. 211.
[7] *Ibid.* XV, I, p. 68.

the Downs, that the 'Speedwell'[1] and 'Cignet' were in Portland Road, the 'Portsmouth' and 'Ruby' safe in the Isle of Wight; it expressed also a warm approval that the reconditioning of the fleet had been put into a "true method", by requiring the two members of the Navy Board with Dartmouth then afloat, namely Sir John Berry and Sir William Booth, to co-operate with the resident Portsmouth Commissioner, Sir Richard Beach, to constitute a Navy Board fully empowered there, on the spot, to take all necessary steps to refit the fleet; but, to mar any satisfaction it could bring, the same letter reported the suspicious rumour, current upon Exchange, that Captain Churchill[2] had taken the 'Newcastle' into Plymouth. There was also a second communication of the 24th[3] from the Secretary, delivered on the following day. It dealt with preparing reinforcements; it confirmed the rumour about the 'Newcastle'; and it stated that the "Lords of the committee for foreigne affaires", who were deputising for the King during his absence with the army, having read a full report from the Admiral, dated the 23rd[4], preferred not to offer "any advice". For, until the ships could be "putt againe into a condition of service", which would "require some time", "noe advice" could be of any use "in reference to their future disposal"; and, more particularly, they remarked that his Majesty was expected back in town in a few days and would then be able to take resolutions "in relation to the whole of his affaires". The attitude of the "Lords of the committee" surprised the Admiral.[5] It raised, in view of the issue of the Supplementary Order of the 12th instant, the terms of the King's letter of that date and the King's decision not to sign an explanatory further

[1] The crew of the 'Speedwell' had deserted in the storm, leaving the captain, chirurgeon, gunner and five boys without a boat at the mercy of the gale. Captain Poulson had cut his main mast and that had carried away the mizzen; with help from passing vessels he had made Studland Bay and Poole. There, unfortunately, he "was inveigled into the Antelope Tavern" and made a prisoner. His ship was seized for the Prince. He made his escape to the 'Resolution'. (Dartmouth MSS, XI, 5, pp. 217, 233.)
[2] Capt. Geo. Churchill, brother to John.
[3] Dartmouth MSS, XI, 5, p. 212.
[4] Not preserved; several of the papers to and from the Admiralty are not extant.
[5] Dartmouth MSS, XV, 1, p. 68.

warrant—such being the trust he reposed in his Admiral—the critical question whether this reservation of advisory authority, by a committee acting on the King's behalf, did not amount to a cancellation, or at least to a curtailment, of the full directive control his Majesty had been so insistent to invest his Admiral with. Thus, at once, on the 25th, Dartmouth stated his difficulty frankly to the Secretary and demanded to be "positively and plainly instructed" as to the "fleet's disposal" and "all... other affairs of the fleet", that he might be "without any manner of doubt" in the fast changing situation. About the outlook he spoke with no ready ease, declaring that "unless great supplies of all things, at least of provisions" could be sent to him, he could not "so much as abide [there] much less proceed again to the westward". On the evening of the same day, Sunday, November 25th, Dartmouth probably learned how the King, relinquishing his purpose to make a stand against the Prince, had passed Andover on his way back to town; and at much the same time, no doubt, he heard of the defection of Kirke, Churchill and Grafton. Such news left little latitude for hope. Lord Dartmouth could only await with strained apprehension the meeting of the councillors and the King. The King re-entered his capital upon the afternoon of Monday the 26th; Monday the 26th passed by. Tuesday night brought the Admiral a long communication from the Admiralty.[1]

Dated the 26th[2] "by express direction of the King given... this night at the Cabinet-Councill" it was concerned to narrate the "withdrawing of the Princess of Denmark in the night (last night)... his Majesty's end in... telling... this being to prevent any wrong impressions that may be made in the fleet". How the Princess had been missed from her bed in the morning Pepys recited. Another branch of the story led up to the coincidence that Lady Churchill and Mrs Berkeley were also gone. A coach and six and a lady had waited for two other ladies in the street in the dead of night. Rumour was rife. But Pepys did not believe that the Papists were involved; rather it was natural that the ladies should follow their husbands'

---

[1] Dartmouth MSS, XI, 5, p. 273.
[2] *Ibid.* p. 214.

example,[1] though his Majesty did not think it becoming of him "to part with a daughter without some yet more solemn enquiry made into the ground of it". Dartmouth might expect more in Pepys's next. Enclosed Dartmouth was to find a warrant,[2] tallying with an oral commission which, given the day before by James at Andover, to Lord Dover, travelling to Portsmouth, to command in the absence of the Duke of Berwick, the new 'acting-Governor' would, no doubt, deliver on arrival. It was a warrant for the arrest of Captain George Churchill. James had seen and opened at Salisbury a letter addressed by Captain Churchill to Pepys and had so acted.[3] Nothing this time from Pepys except news of defection! Next day, Wednesday the 28th,[4] the Admiral acknowledged this letter. He could only express his surprise at the news concerning the Princess and voice the sentiment, "God grant so happy an issue as may put His Majestie in saftie, his great minde at ease and the whole nation and people out of that ferment and chrysis of dissatisfaction to his Government which (from the too many nobles and great men ungratefully deserting him) appears to be so universall". Thoughtful deliberation led him to decide not to send a frigate to arrest Captain Churchill. He knew, he said, that the Dutch were alert off the Start, and then pointed out that, if Captain Churchill had really gone over to the enemy, it might be expected he had prepared his men to make resistance. A sentence in the letter, "It will be a hard task for a single friggate to master him when probably now some of the men may not be so well disposed to it as I could wish" seems to suggest he had not a single frigate in the fleet to which he could have entrusted the duty! He decided to send the 'Quaker Ketch' with orders to Captain Churchill, if honest, a condition Dartmouth doubted (although, by that time, he had probably received a plausible account from the suspect himself),[5] to rejoin the fleet; or, alternatively, the captain of the ketch should

---

[1] Churchill and Prince George of Denmark; the Prince, together with Ormond and Drumlanrig, were missing from the King's retinue by Monday morning.

[2] Dartmouth MSS. XI, 5, p. 214, for text of warrant.

[3] Then he had sent the letter to Pepys; and that is how Pepys on the 24th had been able to confirm the rumour (Dartmouth MSS, XI, 5, p. 213).

[4] Dartmouth MSS, XI, 5, p. 273.   [5] Ibid. p. 210.

request Lord Bath, commanding Plymouth, to arrest the deserter. Separately Dartmouth wrote "a generall letter concerning the Fleet".[1] The same day he broke his week-long silence to the King;[2] for an absence of new orders in a political state so desperate demanded something beyond a merely passive loyalty.

Your Majestie will easily believe [he said] with what grief of heart I write this to finde what usage your Majestie hath received, and indeed I finde a great alteration in most people's faces since my comeing in hither not for want of loyaltie in most of your Commanders, but the dayly impressions they receive make them stand amased. For God's sake, Sir, call your great councell and see which way a Parliament may be best called for I feare nothing will give a stopp but that, and if others are the cause it cannot be done it will no longer lie at your door, and if it may be acceptable to you or a reall service you will soon have the thankes and approbation of your whole fleet with assurances of standing by your Majestie in it, but this your Majestie can best judge of, and I hope you will excuse the thoughts of a faithfull servant for such I have ever been, and by the blessing of God will persist in it till my live's end.

I have been endeavouring ever since my arrivall here to refitt your fleet, and tho' not to be effected according to my desires, yet I hope it will prove serviceable to you and I earnestly beg what orders you have farther for me may be sent when you thinke convenient. Your Majestie, knowes my victualling will not last long, but I hope for a month's recruite from hence which we are dayly getting aboard with all the dilligence imagineable.

Sir, I am dayly sensible you have reason to mistrust mankinde but if you should have hard thoughts of me it will breake my heart for I am and will be just to my live's end. I am in so great perplexity for you that I am able to say no more.

The second part of this letter, by giving information of the fleet in the matter of victualling, enables an inference as to one item of news that the "general letter concerning the fleet" sent to Pepys probably contained and shows that, at Portsmouth, somewhat more hopeful progress had been made, especially in the supply of victuals, than the Admiral could, a day or two since, have anticipated.

This most important letter amounted to a recognition of the

---

[1] Dartmouth MSS, XI, 5, p. 273.   [2] *Ibid.* p. 272.

widespread falling away of loyalty and of Dartmouth's inability
to hold the obedience of the fleet unless a summoning of Parliament came about immediately. As an admiral, straitened to a
realisation of the predicament in which he stood, Dartmouth
had every justification to state the bare dilemma of his situation; he could, however, address the King not merely as the
commander of an incipiently revolting fleet, but as a peer of
the realm, a privileged councillor and a friend. He gave, in one
respect, a piece of necessary information; in another, bold and
unequivocal counsel. Whether, considered as advice, his recommendation followed consistently upon previously held conviction is a biographical question away from the track of this
general enquiry. He told the King by what method he could
hope to avoid the mutiny of his naval captains; he plainly said
that, by that way alone, could the King hope to retain any
allegiance and rule within the state.

As it chanced, this important despatch of Wednesday,
November 28th, and the two to Pepys of the same date were
not immediately handed to a messenger. They did not leave
the 'Resolution' that day or the next. They were forwarded
at noon on Friday the 30th of the month.[1] The reason is told
both in a supplement to one of the despatches to Pepys[2] and in
a postscript to the letter to the King.[3] From the former it is
plain that Lord Dover, newly arrived to command Portsmouth
in the Duke of Berwick's absence, to the stupefaction of the
Admiral, "not only detained the money newly come for paying
the yard but countermanded the sending of any provisions to
the fleet". The motive is not elucidated; the consequence only
is told. The whole work of the yard was brought to a standstill;
and the responsible Navy Commissioners and port Victualling
Officers of course protested to the Admiral. Dartmouth had
some hope that satisfaction would follow the "intercessions and
reasoning" with which he intended to ply Lord Dover; and,
when that personage came aboard the 'Resolution' on Thursday
morning, Dartmouth was successful in securing the promise of
the surrender of the money so that the work could be resumed.
It was because he desired to avoid reporting the unsatisfactory

---

[1] Dartmouth MSS, XI, 5, p. 273.   [2] *Ibid.* p. 274.   [3] *Ibid.* p. 273.

news that Dartmouth held back the letters through Wednesday night, all through Thursday and during part of Friday. By Friday noon the trouble had subsided. But the supplement and the postscript tell of more than this unwarrantable intervention by Lord Dover. They make it plain that, during the night of Thursday, there came aboard a new letter from the Secretary.[1] It set out the great news that the King had declared for a free Parliament, to meet at the earliest possible date, viz. on January 15th; but, unfortunately, it included one item of bad report—Lord Bath had handed over Plymouth to the Prince. Dartmouth naturally assured Pepys he would make good use of the news concerning Parliament; he prayed that God might grant from that "great meeting" an "event" which should "establish his Majestie with honour and safetie in the sway of his dominions and people with lasting glory and peace". He closed the postscript to the King with a like prayer that "Almighty God" might "send a good end" to the intended deliberations. Dartmouth also told Pepys he would relinquish his design to send the 'Quaker Ketch' to Plymouth.

Now it will be quite obvious that his lordship, having heard of the promise to call Parliament, as soon as the writs could be issued and the necessary 40 days could run, needed not to have sent his letter of the 30th to the King, containing advice to call a great Council, preparatory to summoning Parliament. None the less he did send it. The news of the steps taken for convening a Parliament was announced officially to the commanding officers at a council of war on Saturday, December 1st;[2] and the meeting lingered to draft and sign a resolution of thanks to the King. The wording of the paper is not of special significance but it may be noted that the names of the signatories stand thus:[3]

> Dartmouth
> Berkeley
> Ro. Strickland
> J. Berry,

[1] Dartmouth MSS, XI, 5, p. 216 (dated 28th).
[2] *Ibid.* p. 275. "Journal of Captain Grenville Collins", Dartmouth MSS, XV, 1, p. 58. *Memoirs...Torrington*, p. 33.
[3] Pamphlets in Bodley 179/1688.

followed by thirty-seven others. Captains Lord Berkeley, Arthur
Hastings and Thomas Leighton, one captain from each of the
squadrons (though two[1] of them were, it seems, of the faction),
were deputed, next day, to ride to London to convey the
document to the King. The Admiral, in a covering note of
December 1st,[2] remarking that it might cause his Majesty
surprise that "men of warre concern themselves so much for
peace", expressed the hope that an address "that there was no
delaying" would prove neither "offence nor disservice...for
now if the Prince of Orange doth not desist it will show the
world he hath other meanings then are pretended". The note
continued in perfect candour:

I am still endeavouring to put the fleet in the best posture I can, and
it is no small endeavour I am putt to to make them in good humour,
for matters are mightily changed and must be again before it will be
fitt to sett upon the Dutch and it is plane they thinke it not time yett
to set upon us, but the best treaties are made with sword in hand so
that we must still be upon our guard. My greatest trouble is for your
person; for the rest, time will mend....

It was a curious trick of fortune which enabled Lord Dartmouth so unexpectedly to test the truth of his forecast as to
what effect the summoning of Parliament would have upon the
fleet. Be it noted, from the covering note to the congratulatory
address, that the consequence does not appear to have been all
he could have wished; for, after the publication of the news,
he still anticipated being put to "no small endeavour...to make
(his commanders) in a good humour"; and things, he declared,
would have to be "mightily changed" before he would be able
again "to sett upon the Dutch". Be it also observed that,
ignoring all idea of hostility, the admiral, peer, councillor and
friend looked steadily towards negotiated peace. By Saturday,
December 1st, the royal fleet, somewhat scattered, but (save
for the lost hospital vessel) intact as to numbers, in fair process
of refitting and revictualled to a considerable extent, had ceased,
under a loyal and brave admiral, to be of the slightest value to
the Crown of England. Had the English Admiral ordered his
captains to engage the Dutch at Torbay on November 20th,

[1] Berkeley and Hastings.   [2] Dartmouth MSS, XI, 5, p. 275.

there would, though he must have lost the battle, have been a greater measure of obedience than disobedience to his commands. It is certain that, on December 1st, Dartmouth would not have dared to have given the simplest aggressive orders to his fleet.

Before leaving entirely this eventful week, it is necessary to introduce a strange story, an interlude best presented in the language of a narrative twice already in these pages laid under heavy contribution, first in respect of fleet movements and, secondly, for certain details about the caballing faction.[1]

When the fleet was here and at the time the Prince of Orange was on his march from Exeter, those of the fleet who were well inclined to him thought it time to shew themselves, and even some that were timorous and silent hitherto; at a meeting they had, they determined to send him a message, and to assure his highness of their assistance and readiness to obey his orders. This was to be done in secrecy, and by word of mouth; and Mr. Byng was to undertake to execute this message, and to this purpose first address himself to Mr. Russell, who came with the Prince from Holland. Accordingly Mr. Byng obtained leave of Lord Dartmouth to be absent, on pretence of going (to a relation) into Huntingdonshire, upon affairs that very much concerned him. He then landed at Gosport, and, disguising himself like a farmer, set out to meet the Prince of Orange. Upon the road he was in some danger from a party of the Earl of Oxford's regiment of horse, who made up to him, for from the general acquaintance he had with the officers of that regiment, had he been carried before them he had been discovered, but from the meanness of his habit, they did not mistrust him. (When he got to Salisbury, his horse was so tyred that he went to the post house, where he lay, the weather being to bad to proceed then further; and, being furnished with another horse, left that place, tho' he was surprised when, as he was going, the postmaster told him he mistrusted him, and showed him a warrant to stop all such persons as he suspected carrying to the Prince; but they prouved to be in the same interest). When he was come within 10 miles of the Prince's quarters he stop'd at a place to bait (near Dorchester); where sitting in his disguise (in the chymney corner of the common room) Colonell Rooke's servant, knowing him, conducted him (up a back pair of stairs) into a room where he was surprised to find his uncle Colonell Johnson, Colonell Rooke, and several of his acquaintance; they having left King James army,

[1] *Memoirs...Torrington*, p. 20.

and had just come from the Prince of Orange; (and the like woud
have done Generall Kirk, had not his) intentions been discovered;
who was to have gone off with severall others the night he comanded
an out brigade; yet by a stratagem he deceived Generall Scarsfield,
who was sent by King James with a guard to seize him that night.
After expressing their joy to meet there, Mr. Byng desired of them to
produce him a guide, and so left them and went on (in a very dark
night; and coming into a hollow way), he was stoped by a party of
men who examined him very closely; and one of the officers, sus-
pecting he knew his voice, desired to know his true name, and if it
was not Byng; who desiring to discover his, and it proving to be
Colonell Wingfield, who was with Villars, two perticular acquaint-
ances of his that were with a party of the Prince of Orange's horse,
he was glad to find who they were and discovered himself to them.

The Prince of Orange had passed Exeter on his way to Salisbury,
and was at the Earl of Bristol's house at Sherbourn when Mr. Byng
came to him. The first person he met with that knew him was my
Lord Churchill, who was that day come with the Prince of Denmark;
and from the stair head asked him what he did there. Mr. Byng
desired he woud ask no questions, but carry him to a private room
where he might see Mr. Russell; who coming to him, he acquainted
him with his message, and was then by him conducted to the Prince
of Orange, all the company there retiring, except Mr. Russell; and
he delivered to his Highness the message from the officers of the
fleet, naming those who had engaged themselves to assist him:
(which was very wellcome to him, and) the Prince expressed great
satisfaction at such wellcome assurances, received Mr. Byng with
(great) civility and promised him, if he succeeded, he would take
care particularly to remember him. He sent him back with an answer
to the officers of the fleet, and with a letter to Lord Dartmouth, to
acquaint him of the necessity of his coming over, and of his intentions
to continue him at the head of the fleet; with promises that Admirall
Herbert (between whom there was some variance) should not be
advanced over him. This letter the Prince advised Mr. Byng to put
into the stuffing of his saddle, least in case he was seized it shoud not
be found upon him; but he thought it best to quilt it in the rowlers of
his breeches. So Mr. Byng, taking his leave, returned safely to the
fleet again. There was some difficulty how to give this letter to Lord
Dartmouth, whose zeal to the King was well-known; and therefore
Mr. Aylmer undertook it, and one morning took an oppertunity to
lay it upon his toilett.

Which morning? Unfortunately, while the authority so opportunely gives these details concerning the mission of Byng,

it omits wholly to date the day on which this invitation reached Dartmouth's hands. And, without a break, it continues, in the next sentence:

This letter had some effect on him, for from that time he seemed inclinable to the Prince's party, though his real thoughts coud no ways agree with the measures then taken; yet he was terryfied at the disposition of the nation and the fleet, that he thought it to no purpose to oppose them, and knew not what might be the consequences to himself, since the Prince of Orange advanced with such success, and all the people were daily rising against the King.

It declares:

He was the more cautious in his behaviour, from a deseign that was discovered to seize him on board the[1]...commanded by Capt. Hastings who had invited him to dinner for that purpose, in which case they intended to give the command of the fleet to the Duke of Grafton. But Capt. Davy Lloid (a strick plain man)[2] who had found himself neglected by his old friends, and from the favour he was in with the King's party having knowledge of it discovered their design to Lord Dartmouth; by which means he avoided their puiting it in execution, by excusing himself from going.

Then the narrative runs ahead: "He continued in great doubts how to behave with regard to the Prince's party in the fleet; and to act according to his principles and consistent with his duty to the King". But, at that place, in confused and interpolated manuscript, it adds: "(Yet an address being at this time (I think at a council of warr) draw'd up for the meeting of a free parlement, he coud not avoid signing it) seeing himself in the power of those of the other party, and not able to refuse his assistance in an attempt of the most dangerous consequence". What attempt? That, for the moment, must remain untold. What was the earliest date at which this invitation, penned at Sherborne upon Thursday, November 29th, carried by the rider, Byng, to the Spithead, and taken aboard, could be passed to Captain Aylmer and so on to the Admiral of the Fleet? Not before Dartmouth's advice had been penned—upon the 28th; postscripted—upon the 30th; and despatched the same day;

[1] The 'Woolwich', as the editor of the MS observes.
[2] It does not appear what ship he was on. The editor of the MS has a full note on him (p. 3).

scarcely before the council of war of December 1st, which received the glad news of the royal intention to summon Parliament and sent the loyal address to the King; if before December 2nd or 3rd (by which date the "attempt of the most dangerous consequence", not yet told to the reader, had begun to materialise) then with almost the least possible delay, indeed with a celerity which the expression "one morning" does not suggest. There exists definite evidence which shows that the letter was not delivered until December 12th; but the witness is in Dartmouth's own hand. That evidence as to delivery, evidence much more precise than the "one morning" of the narrative (which is much corrected and scored at this place) must carry weight, and the imputation as to the letter's influence, an imputation due to the backward glance of a *rédacteur*, must fall through. When December 12th is reached, the text of the invitation will be told.

There is no lengthy tale to tell concerning the naval aspect of the Prince's expedition from Thursday, November 22nd, to the end of the month. No further attempt was made to give effect to Lieutenant-Admiral-General Herbert's belated proposal to win command by blockading the English fleet, in order that the transports could be convoyed in safety along the Channel and so home—the plan to which the Prince's assent had been given, partly because of the necessity to modify the original Instructions once a west coast landing had been made, and more because of newly received advices as to the shaken moral of the English commanders. At most the Dutch fleet continued to manifest a liveliness which showed no tendency to pass into more definite action. It is natural to look for the explanation of the seemingly relinquished design in the course of the Prince's land affairs.

The Prince left Exeter upon Wednesday, November 21st. By Monday the 26th, the grand desertion from the King had taken place; and James had returned from Salisbury, a beaten man. On Wednesday the 28th, as the Prince came to Sherborne, hastening to Salisbury, Byng delivered to him his assurances from the officers of the fleet. Thence Byng was sent back with that message to Dartmouth of the terms of which the reader is shortly to be fully informed. It does not seem reasonable to suppose that, while events were moving as precipitately as they did in the days immediately following William's departure from Exeter, he (William) would be expressly anxious for any active prosecution of Herbert's design upon the English fleet. Byng having come to Sherborne, and the letter to Dartmouth having been sent away, obviously it was to William's interest to avoid provocation to Dartmouth's forces by Herbert's fleet, at least until sufficient time had elapsed for the English Admiral to have returned a considered reply. That Herbert was, for such a reason, stayed by the Prince from action is a conclusion hard to resist. What is clear is that the Dutch fleet lost no time in solving its provisioning difficulties by working into Plymouth; for the news of the surrender of that town reached the Prince about the time that Byng met him. Lord Bath, commanding Plymouth, writing on November 27th, said, "the Harbours of Plymouth and Falmouth shall be for the security of Yr. Highness ffleete whenever you shall have occasion to command them", and the same letter referred to the lucky accident of the driving in of the 'Newcastle'. Happily that reference reveals the truth about Captain Churchill. Like his brother, he was "entirely for the Prince".[1]

*   *   *   *   *   *   *

It is unnecessary to stress the importance of an interval in which the Royal Navy ceased to be of the slightest value to the Crown of England, and during which the Prince of Orange, in all probability, came to think of the naval side of his adventure as of an affair that might best be brought by a policy of calculated inactivity to a successful close. It rests to consider the manner in which the inevitable surrender came—inevitable because, as our forefathers well understood, a fleet must always obey the will of the dominant party within the protected shores.

[1] State Papers, Domestic (King William's Chest), uncalendared.

CHAPTER VI

The Surrender of the Royal Fleet
December 2nd to 14th

UPON the afternoon of Sunday, December 2nd,[1] the acting-Governor of Portsmouth, Lord Dover, paid his second visit to the 'Resolution', waiting on the Admiral to demand, in the King's name, adherence to a very desperate scheme. Dover unfolded the project through the presentation of two letters. The first, which he had received a week previously, upon parting with the King at Andover, he had, in full consonance with the sense of his instructions, delayed in delivery. It ran:

1688, Nov. 25th, Andover. I send this you by the Lord Dover, whom I send to Portsmouth to command in chief there,...I haue charged Lord Dover...to speake with you of my intentions concerning my sonne, and you must follow Lord Dover's directions as to what concerns our sayd sonne, by being assisting to him in what directions I haue giuen him by word of mouth. I haue not tyme to say more. James R.[2]

The second letter, which had not been long in Dover's possession, carried the request a stage further.

1688 Nov. 29th, Whitehall. This is the second letter I write to you upon the subject of my sonne....'Tis my sonne they aime at and 'tis my sonne I must endeauor to preserue, what so euer becoms of me, therefore I conjure you to assist Lord Dover in getting him sent away in the yachts, as sone as wind and weather will permitt for the first port they can gett to in France, and that with as much secresy as may be, and soe that trusty men may but (*sic*) put in the yachts that he may be exposed to no other danger but that of the sea, and know I shall look on this as one of the greatest piece of seruice you can do me.[3]

But an attached postscript, dated November 30th, stated that there would be a short delay before the Prince would be removed out of the country.

---

[1] Dartmouth MSS, XI, 5, p. 275.   [2] *Ibid.* p. 215.   [3] *Ibid.* p. 220.

For the Admiral the interview proved extremely painful. Striving with some success to control his emotions, he pointed out to the acting-Governor the seriousness of the contemplated course; and, it appears, tried to persuade him not to act precipitately. The rest of the day Dartmouth spent in drafting a strongly worded protest to the King. On the morrow, however, Monday, December 3rd, before the remonstrance had been despatched to town, Dover once more got into touch with the Admiral. He handed on two newly arrived notes from the King to Dartmouth, both of them dated December 1st. One acknowledged the Admiral's communications of the 28th and 30th ultimo, professed a most implicit trust in his loyalty and asked for a promise that Dartmouth would do all in his power to further the intended scheme.[1] The other demanded that the plan should be put into immediate execution.[2] Called upon thus finally to make his decision, the Admiral did not waver. He effected a few changes in the already drafted objection and advice,[3] then passed the packet into the acting-Governor's hands for transmission by a trusty messenger. He again and specially impressed on his brother officer the need for inaction.[4] After that, he waited for the next move from the King.

Dartmouth's protest is too long for full quotation.[5] He stated that "With the greatest dread and grief of heart imaginable" he understood his Majesty persisted in his "former intentions" of "sending away the Prince". He asked the King to reflect on the strict character of the laws; he demurred to being made "guilty of treason to (his) Majesty and the known lawes of the Kingdome", especially where the offence ranked of "so high a nature" as in this instance; on "bended knees" he begged James to turn to "other counsells". He had, he said, ever professed himself "of the Church of England", never pretending to be "of any other"; and he was bound "as such, and a faithfull servant, subject and councellor" to advise "that sending away the Prince of Wales without the consent of the

[1] Dartmouth MSS, XI, 5, p. 220.   [2] Ibid.
[3] See the King's reply of 5th: "yours of the 2nd which you say was not sent till the 3rd"; ibid. p. 224.
[4] Ibid. p. 277; letter to Dover.   [5] Ibid. p. 275.

nation" would be "at no time advisable". Least of all, he said, at that time could the contemplated sending into France be justified; it could only yield" a "fatal consequence" inducing subjects to "throw off their bounden allegiance" and, in addition, entail "a perpetuall warre...giving France alwayes a temptation to molest, invade, nay, hazard the conquest of England". The Admiral implored not to be made the "unhappy instrument of so apparent ruine" to James and to the country; he hoped his Majesty would not "suffer it to be done by any other". As the King knew, he had, in the past, "prophetically ...foretold...misfortunes" and indicated courses which the King "might have taken to have avoided them". He had no wish to reproach his Majesty with the past; but he did trust that the determination to call Parliament and negotiate a peace would not be tampered with. In conclusion, he disclaimed "disobedience" but insisted firmly that he would "not be instrumental in nor suffer" the Prince "to be carried into France if by any means" he could "prevent it". He said it would be essential for James to take the child again into his own custody. He thought it would be well for the King to order him to see the baby removed from Portsmouth immediately.

It is evident enough, from the outspoken terms of the protest, how well the Admiral had turned over in his mind the consequences which would follow obedience given to the King. And there is more than a biographical interest attaching to the fact that, Churchman and Tory as he was, he summed up those consequences as involving treason against the King *according* to the Law and that he did not choose to justify or excuse himself to his Majesty *apart* from the Laws of England.[1,2]

[1] The state of the law of Treason in 1688 may be inferred from *The Constitutional History of England*, Hallam, III, p. 154. Dartmouth would have been liable in good law on the several heads of a lengthy indictment.

[2] Before the page is closed upon the happenings of the 3rd instant, this letter deserves rescue from oblivion:—"Ship, Cambridge—Capt. John Tyrwhitt to Lord Dartmouth. His Lordship's generous charity, shewn in the interest he made on the writer's behalf with the late King, has kept him from wanting bread, and encourages him to make a further trial of his honour's kindness. Having lost by this late sickness most of his good head of hair, would beg of his Lordship to bestow on him one of his worst short periwigs to keep his head from the cold, and to enable him to come on board and kiss his Lordship's hands and give him humble thanks; for if

The Admiral soon had cause to distrust the court party in the port. Next day, Tuesday, December 4th,[1] he was, in spite of his so recent special appeals to the acting-Governor, forced to protest that the fleet had been "alarumed" in the preceding night "with the endeavours to carry away the Prince of Wales", a scheme engineered, so he conjectured, if not by "the folly or means of Captain Fazly"[2] then "by a gentleman of my Lord Powys, or one of the pages of the back staires"; and it is, at least, established that events had shaped so seriously, during the course of the night of which he wrote, that he had been forced to take sharp and appropriate action to burke the court party's scarce concealed design.

The evidence is twofold. It is known that Captain Geo. Rooke of the 'Deptford', coming in off the Culver Cliff at noon on Tuesday, after being led away "in chase of some Dutchmen", acknowledged orders, of the night before, requiring that he, with two other vessels, should watch any suspicious ship-movements and detain any vessel that might be suspected of having the baby Prince aboard.[3] Also, it is stated by the narrative which told the adventurous riding of Mr Byng, that the faction, round about this date, reported to the Admiral the rumour of the dock and town to the effect that the Catholic Vice-Admiral would undertake the spiriting away of the baby Prince in a yacht into France; and that, thereupon, Dartmouth ordered Captains Aylmer, Hastings and Shovel to prevent unauthorised egress from the harbour, and Captain Cornwall and the returned Lieutenant Byng to watch in armed boats the waterside.[4] These two pieces of information, that

periwigs were to be bought here for thirteen pence a piece he were not able to purchase one, having but two sixpences in the whole world".
[1] Dartmouth MSS, XI, 5, p. 277.   [2] See note 3, p. 118.
[3] Dartmouth MSS, XI, 5, p. 223.
[4] Memoirs... Torrington, p. 33. There is extant a letter dated 3rd instant from Captain Cornwall to the Admiral. "Going ashore to get provisions he saw goods going on board the 'Mary Yacht'. On enquiring was told they were Lord Dover's and that the Prince of Wales was going; and he saw several women go on board who were said to belong to him.... Sent his coxswain aboard to enquire, and they told him they were bound for St. Malo as soon as the moon was up; but the milk and pap were sent for ashore and he believed they would not go that night. It was kept a secret". There is also another letter, from same to same, in slightly different words.

concerning Rooke and the details of the activity of the faction, are more coincident than contradictory; for it is very probable that the 'Deptford' worked in so late that Rooke found three other vessels already upon station. Cornwall and Byng decided upon a plan which was certainly thorough. One undertook to wait near the house in which the Prince was known to be, while the other agreed to remain by the boats. Conferences, to take place at set intervals over the town walls, were arranged; and, on the first attempted moving of the Prince into a yacht, these officers, being empowered to secure the baby, intended to seize his person. They meant to do so even if they had to board the yacht and show credentials from their Admiral. They knew that their efforts would be seconded, in case of need, by the three ships of the fleet. Finding themselves selected for this service, all these of the faction not unnaturally considered themselves in high favour. They imagined that the Admiral had had no other option than to court their support. Thus, at length, is explained the reference of the Byng narrative, quoted on p. 131, to that assistance in an "attempt of most dangerous consequence" which, so the narrative boasted, the Admiral was compelled to give.

At this point it is necessary to digress a little to observe that, sometime during Tuesday, December 4th, Dartmouth found time to acknowledge in a single short reply to the Secretary[1] two letters, both dated the 29th ultimo, one from the King,[2] one from the Secretary,[3] which had been delivered in the fleet on the preceding Sunday.[4] They had been drafted as complementary advices; for whilst, among other things, the Secretary's communication indicated to Dartmouth that he could expect no further reinforcements to his fleet, a circumstance he had no doubt already taken for granted, the King's letter so far confessed to immobilisation as to say that the "preservation" of the fleet ranked as an affair of the "last consequence"; and that he desired only to know "speedily" where best the vessels could be caused to lie. Dartmouth, in his answer, told the Secretary that he had ordered Lord Berkeley and his crew

---

[1] Dartmouth MSS, XV, I, p. 68.   [2] *Ibid*. XI, 5, p. 219.
[3] *Ibid*. p. 217.   [4] *Ibid* p. 219.

out of the 'Montague' into the 'Edgar' and Sir William Jennens and his company out of the 'Rupert' into the 'Warspite'; he stated that his general reconditioning progressed both steadily and economically; but he did not proceed to satisfy the King's request. He could only tell the Secretary that he "had not yet come to a resolution what advice to offer his Majesty" about the disposal of the fleet. The inconclusiveness of the reply is not surprising. Lord Dartmouth was far too concerned over the affair of the baby Prince to devote care to a less important consideration. To him it was a matter of greater importance to prevent the perpetration of a terrible blunder than to bother about the disposal of an admittedly useless fleet. It is also worth while noting that, by Tuesday night, Captain Lord Berkeley's report of his mission to the King probably reached the flagship. Berkeley affirmed[1] that the King, upon the reading of the loyal and congratulatory address, at noon on the 3rd instant, had appeared "pleased withal". His lordship also said that, though "abundance of people" railed at the Admiral, the King "continually justified" him. Berkeley spoke of the Dutch fleet as gone to Plymouth and saluted at its entry "with above 40-guns". He handed on all the general news saying that Bristol had fallen, that the Lords Halifax, Nottingham and Godolphin had set out to negotiate; but that "the trumpeter that was sent before for leave they found drunk asleep at Reading". The items of general news had their value as filling out the recently scanty official sources; the depression they must have produced is not to be over-estimated.

The Admiral's protest against being made a party to the removal of the Prince reached Whitehall late on Tuesday night; but the King did not answer it before the following morning, Wednesday, December 5th.[2] The King then said that he could not "come to any positive resolution" with himself until his Commissioners to the Prince of Orange returned to report their reception. Twelve hours later however,[3] James had moved towards decision, directing, in a new letter, that if, by reason of any forward move of the Prince of Orange's troops, Dover

---

[1] Dartmouth MSS, XI, 5, p. 222.   [2] *Ibid.* p. 224.
[3] *Ibid.*

could not arrange for the safe conduct of the baby Prince to London, then the Admiral should provide for a yacht to carry the royal infant as far as Margate. So two letters left Whitehall on December 5th for the Admiral of the Fleet.

Wednesday, December 5th, passed quietly at Spithead. The two letters arrived in proper sequence on Thursday, December 6th.[1] As might have been expected, Dartmouth at once acknowledged them,[2] "rejoiced", he said, to see his Majesty "pleased to receive (his) poor endeavours" and doubting not that he would "judge charitably of the sincere sentiments of so faithful a heart", of the aims of one who held no "hope to see the face of God" if he studied "any other thoughts then (his) Majesties' true interest". For the King's decision to remove the Prince to London, he was profoundly thankful. He supposed that it would prove practicable to take the Prince to London by road, and thought that such would prove a far better course than to carry him round by sea. Yet, if the latter alternative were decided upon, he would, he said, himself escort the yacht to Margate.

From that point in his letter, he dismissed the affair of the Prince from his mind. He turned to discuss the preservation and disposal of the fleet and so harked back to the unanswered portion of the King's letter of the 29th ultimo. At the "latter end of next week", he said, he could be fit to move. The spirit of his command, he confessed, remained bad, the men's minds changeable. A few ships not in good condition for sea and smaller fireships, he supposed, should, in any case, be left with a serviceable advice boat at Portsmouth. He interpolated the remark that "too many sailors" did not agree with the Portsmouth garrison, for feeling had run high over the "late barbarous murther of the boatswaine of the Ossory" and other killing and mayhem. He said that he feared Herbert would appear off the town if the royal fleet departed; but he advanced that opinion rather as an argument for increasing the numbers of the Portsmouth garrison than for prolonging his own stay at Spithead. He mentioned the Downs, he spoke of the Nore. The thought that his Majesty might wish the fleet near by him

---

[1] Dartmouth MSS, XI, 5, p. 277.   [2] *Ibid.*

in the Thames while Parliament met, crossed his mind; but, in effect, he left it for James to decide on the place to which the vessels should be taken. He spoke as though he took his departure from Spithead for granted.

Dartmouth put this letter aside for despatch till the morrow, Friday, December 7th. When morning came, he was able to add a postscript[1] saying he had just heard from Captain Neagle (who had been ashore with the acting-Governor and his deputy Sir Edward Scott, and who would now act as bearer of this letter to his Majesty) that the Prince had been taken away from Portsmouth by Powis and Dover (the acting-Governor) by land. Dartmouth mentioned in the postscript (though quite briefly) the fleet disposal question. "Pray now consider where your Majesty will have the fleet be and what further commands you please to send me".

Before quite closing the episode concerning the baby Prince of Wales, it may be added that Captain Cornwall and Lieutenant Byng did their work thoroughly. On the Wednesday night, while Cornwall was in the town, he "observed a great hurry in Mr. Ridge's house, where the Prince was lodged". Eventually, he saw "the Duke of Powis's (Governor of the town)[2] his coach and six horses at the door; and approaching them in the dark, felt their leggs, which he found dry; which made him conclude it was not a coach come in but going out of town". The significance of the fact immediately dawned upon him. He realised that that, for himself and his companion, was "an end of the enterprise".[3]

Saturday, December 8th, was a day of no special significance either at the Admiralty or in the fleet. Glad that the affair of the baby Prince, which had so cut across his main business of preserving intact his immobilised fleet and of ordering its difficult routine, had at length been cleared out of the way, Dartmouth attended to the performance of commonplace duties. In particular, the likelihood of considerable disturbance in the town of Portsmouth worried him. Sunday, the 9th,[4] saw the

[1] Dartmouth MSS, XI, 5, p. 278.
[2] Powis was not Governor; Berwick, for whom Dover deputised, held the post.   [3] *Memoirs... Torrington*, p. 33.
[4] "Journal of Captain Grenville Collins", Dartmouth MSS, XV, 1, p. 58

return of Captain Lord Berkeley, his lordship able, and no
doubt very willing, to fill out for his Admiral and fellow peer
detail on detail of the news he had collected from privileged
and unprivileged sources during his stay of nearly a week in the
capital. Berkeley at once got new leave and went back to town.[1]

On Monday, the 10th of the month, however, events at court
moved suddenly towards a crisis. The Secretary was instructed
to forward a royal letter which was intended partly to tell the
Admiral that the Queen and baby Prince had been put beyond
the reach of harm and, partly, to command him to await certain
orders which the Duke of Berwick, setting out for Portsmouth,
would have charge to deliver.[2] Pepys enclosed a covering communication,[3] concerned not much more with routine than with
detailing the latest "occurrences of publick moment", such as
the seizure of Dover Castle by a rabble, a skirmish at Reading,
the alarm of the Catholics, the flight of Lords Salisbury and
Rochester and the secession of the Bishop of Chester and the
Attorney-General.

The packet was outstripped in delivery by a far worse alarm.
By the night of Tuesday the 11th common report and private
correspondence had bruited abroad not merely the startling
intelligence that the King had sent the Queen and her royal
infant out of the country; but that his Majesty himself had, in
the early hours of the morning, disappeared from his court and
capital, intent, as it seemed, to follow after his Queen and child.
Thus it befell that, on Wednesday the 12th, when the letters
from the Admiralty were handed to the Admiral of the Fleet,[4] a
belief in the truth of the whole threefold story obtained aboard
the royal vessels.[5] Long before the day ended, belief had
hardened into complete certainty.[6] And, through the hands of
Berwick, Dartmouth received no further orders concerning the
future of the fleet.[7]

[1] See note (3), p. 147.
[2] Dartmouth MSS, XI, 5, p. 225.   [3] Ibid. p. 226.
[4] Ibid.
[5] "Journal of Captain Grenville Collins", Dartmouth MSS, XV, 1, p. 58.
[6] It is not quite certain how Dartmouth got his news. See Dartmouth
MSS, XI, 5, pp. 229, 230 for letters, especially one from his companion in arms,
Lord Feversham.
[7] Dartmouth MSS, XI, 5, p. 226.

It was at this critical juncture in the affairs of the nation that the letter which Byng had brought away from Sherborne and handed to Captain Matthew Aylmer for delivery to the Admiral was deftly placed by the Captain upon his lordship's toilet table. The Prince's appeal to Dartmouth was as follows:

My lord, the Protestant religion and the liberties of England being now at stake, I cannot beleiue you will contribute towards the destruction of either. I therefore send you this letter to invite you earnestly to joyne the fleete under your command with mine and to declare as I haue donne in my Declaration for the Religion and Liberties. It will be an act so commendable that it will not only oblidge me for ever to be your friend but even to study which way I may shew my kindnesse to you in the most particular manner. I expect and desire you to consider well of this my proposition and advice and that I may speedely receaue the news of your compliance, which will make me your affectionate friend.[1]

Admiral Lord Dartmouth drafted his reply, making his choice and surrendering the fleet of England.[2]

Spitthead, the 12th of December, 1688. May it please your Highness.

Out of duty to my country and the Reformed religion of the Church of England, (of which as I am, I have allways professed myself a true son,) I imbrace readily the faire invitation given me by your Highnesses particular letter, of the 29th of November, (come just now to my hands) to dispose the fleet under my command to joyne

[1] Dartmouth MSS, XI, 5, p. 219.
[2] Quoted from Devon's pamphlet. The original cannot be traced. The editor of the Dartmouth MSS, XI, 5, states: "Pages 45 and 46 are cut out, and the following is a note at the end of page 44 in the handwriting of William the second Baron and first Earl of Dartmouth. 'The following leaves were cut out by my mother Barbara Baroness of Dartmouth before the book came into my hands.

(Signed) Dartmouth'".
Dartmouth MSS, XI, 5, p. 279.
There is an entry on XI, 5, p. 232, speaking of "copies" of letters of 12th and 20th which are not given. See also the entry of the editor of the MSS, XI, 5, on p. 284. "The next pages are torn out, and at the foot of page 56 is the following note in the handwriting of William the first Earl of Dartmouth.
'The following leaves were torn out long before this book came into my hands by my mother. When I asked her why she had done it she said she thought that they were better out. I told her I was very sorry she had because I had often heard my father say his journal would allwayes be his justification.

(Signed) Dartmouth'".

with your Highnesses, and concurre in the good ends you have hetherto pursued, with so much vigour and success, towards supporting our religion, laws, liberties and properties, not doubting, according to your Highnesses declarations, but you will prosecute the same with utmost regard and tenderness to the person and safety of the King my master, whose just commands all his Majesties subjects (but men of honour especially under his commission and pay) are bound to execute; and among that number, I held myself very particularly obliged, but to my great amazement (which I cannot but tell your Highness, with great confusion and griefe of heart) I understand just this moment, that his Majestie hath sent away the Queen and Prince of Wales (contrary not only to my advices, but ernest indeavours to prevent), and is resolved to withdraw himself, which (on a firme beleife of your Highnesses just duty and care of him) I cannot apprehend his Majestie can have any reason to doe, otherwise then that he is not willing to be a witness of, or consente to, what the lawes, and a free Parliament (which myself and the fleet addressed for 11 or 12 days agoe) shall inflict on his evill advisers, who have put the Kingdome into that ferment, which had invited your Highness to come and expose your person, for the re-establishing it, and routing out of the government all Papist officers, as well civil as military.

I have well deliberated on your Highnesses most mercifull proceedings hitherto, in preventing the effusion of Christian blood, and doe believe it not only a just, but commendable act, to joyne with your Highness in acquireing your declared purposes, which I promise to doe heartily, and to that end will purge the fleet of all Papist officers immediately.

I doe farther promise solemnly to your Highness, to doe my utmost to prevent any French forces landing, or making any descent, on these Kingdomes, and doing everything (like a true Protestant of the Church of England, and lover of my country) that may conduce to the safety of the King and his Kingdomes, and the religion, laws and liberties thereof, by all such means and councells as to your Highness and the Kingdome shall seem meet, and in full relyance thereon I put myself, and the fleet of England, under your Highnesses gracious protection; soe that both fleets being at your Highnesses disposal, in the joining whereof, and the time you think best and necessary, I doubt not but you will have a just reguard, that no distaits may be given, that either may be liable to.

I hope to receive your directions by the bearer, Capt. Aylmer, who is my very good friend, and is intirely devoted to your Highness, being a firme Protestant and an honest man; to him I pray your Highness will be referred for many particulars, as well in relation to the fleet as the garrison of Portsmouth, too long to trouble your Highness with here; humbly submitting all concerns to your Highnesses better judgement, as becomes....[1]

The Prince's appeal calls for no special comment; but considerable interest attaches to the little known terms of the Admiral's reply just quoted. There had come into being, on a sudden, a "state of nature". All bonds of rule had been cancelled. Dartmouth, unable any longer, in any practical sense, to give meaning to his allegiance to a wilfully absent King, had realised that he, in turn, could expect no continuance of obedience to orders given in virtue of the deserting monarch's commission. In such a predicament, a bigot, acting after his kind, would, no doubt, have commanded the impossible and brought upon himself, the fleet and the nation, disaster; a coward would have sought safety in flight; a flatterer made servile answer to the Prince. In his response, Dartmouth employed the language of deference but not of adulation. He, in no way, cloaked his disappointment at the going away of the King. He made it plain that he well realised that the only remaining service he could render to the King, to the nation and to his religion lay in immediate co-operation with the Prince for the purpose of the maintenance of order. So he placed "the fleet of England" under his Highness's "gracious protection"; and he promised to abide by the agreement to which the Prince "and the Kingdome" might, in a short space, be trusted to come. In telling the Prince that he would dismiss the Papist officers, protect the shores from a French descent and raise no difficulty to union with Herbert's fleet, Dartmouth gave the best guarantees of good faith that, under the circumstances in which he was placed, he could possibly have yielded.

On Thursday, December 13th, a council of war was held.[2] The fleet unanimously concurred with the project of communication with the Prince.[3] But Dartmouth, if he had not already sent his letter to the Prince, added no postscript. Sir Roger Strickland laid down his commission, and the other Catholics,

---

[1] The concluding formula is not in Devon.
[2] "Journal of Captain Grenville Collins", Dartmouth MSS, XV, 1, p. 58.
[3] Dartmouth MSS, XI, 5, p. 279. Letter to the Lords.

certainly not numerous, did the same. Sir John Berry became
Vice-Admiral in Strickland's stead and Lord Berkeley joined
the flags as Rear-Admiral.[1] Strickland's departure from his
flag-ship was so tempered to his misfortunes that he could only
tell the Admiral that "his heart and eyes were so full of grief
and tears" that he could not "make the least return" for all his
lordship's "extraordinary kindness in parting".[2]

From the prominent reference which, in his submission to
the Prince, the Admiral gave to the name of Captain Matthew
Aylmer, it is clear that the assiduous commander of the 'Swallow'
had been led to reveal himself to his lordship. Full details of
the manner in which he conveyed the important despatch to
the Prince's headquarters are available in the Byng narrative—
for Aylmer arranged that Lieutenant Byng and Captain Hastings
should accompany him on the journey. In order to avoid suspicion in case of interception, the trio provided themselves
with pretended letters to Mr Secretary Pepys.[3] Then, so the
story says,[4]

"fearing the garrison of Portsmouth should stop them", they "went
up in their boats to Chichester; where, being furnished with horses,
they proceeded on. But when they came to Midhurst, it being at
the time all the nation was alarmed with the apprehension of the wild
Irish, they were seized and (carried to a house where they were)
strictly examined; and tho' they were of the Prince of Orange's
party, yet it was not proper for them to declare their message; so
they were thought to be of the King's (side), especially when Aylmer
(being asked of what country he was, answered an Irishman; and one
of them declared positively that Mr. Byng was an Irish priest, and
that he had heard him often say mass in the Queen's chappell). So
they wrote to the Duke of Somerset at Petworth, not far from
thence; and tho' he writ the town a letter, to satisfye them they were
coming to him, yet they were attended thither by many people on
horseback (and even went up with them into the Duke's bedchamber
to be convinced they were his friends)".

The narrative shows that, freed at last of these unwelcome
attentions, "they continued their journey and came to the

---

[1] "Journal of Captain Grenville Collins", Dartmouth MSS, xv, 1, p. 58.
[2] Dartmouth MSS, xi, 5, p. 238.
[3] Ibid. p. 231 (for text).
[4] Memoirs...Torrington, p. 35.

Prince at Windsor, the day he arrived there" which was Friday, December 14th. They "delivered my Lord Dartmouth's letter, which was very acceptable to the Prince".

To round off this account of the surrender of the royal fleet, it is necessary to observe that, after the Admiral had summoned the council of war to concur with the message to the Prince and to witness the surrender of the commissions of the Papist officers, that is to say, upon Thursday the 13th or just before, he had received from Mr Secretary Pepys an Order, dated Tuesday the 11th instant[1] which, the Secretary explained[2], proceeded from "a councell of Peers Spirituall and Temporall that upon advice of his Majesty withdrawing, did meet", on the morning of the desertion, at the Guildhall, to issue various emergency instructions (including an instruction to Lord Feversham and a commission to Lord Lucas to displace Skelton now commanding the Tower) and to send ambassadors to the Prince. The place of that emergency committee in the history of the interregnum crisis is, of course, well known. The order in question required Dartmouth to desist from further action against the Dutch and to dismiss the Catholic officers in the royal fleet; but, beyond the fact that it gave Dartmouth a certain satisfaction to learn, after the critical step had been taken, that a body of twenty-three lords, presided over by the Primate,[3] had given such an order and also applied to the Prince, the paper had no practical value. It arrived too late to influence the Admiral's action either in respect of the Prince or with regard to the dismissal of the Catholic officers.[4] The same council, however, had issued, at the same time, an order to the Secretary of Admiralty which, probably, much operated to hamper would-be fugitives. No person, it provided, could be permitted to go by water below Greenwich unless he could

---

[1] Dartmouth MSS, XI, 5, p. 229.
[2] *Ibid.* p. 228.
[3] Berkeley's signature is among them.
[4] Dartmouth MSS, XI, 5, p. 279. "I had deliberated with myselfe (upon the surprisall and unfortunate newes of His Majestie's withdrawing himselfe) before the receipt of your Lordships' and was putting it in execution and it is now actually done, and have likewise (with the unanimous concurrence of the fleet) addressed myselfe (as I see your Lordships have done) to the Prince of Orange".

produce a warrant signed by five peers or by the Lord Mayor of London.[1]

Not much can be said about the Dutch fleet from December 1st to the 14th; but a questionnaire[2] which, on the 8th, passed from Lieutenant-Admiral-General Herbert to the Prince to be answered by marginal comments on the 10th, from Newbury, is worth notice. Its first enquiry and answer are best to be understood on the assumption that Herbert had received warning reports that war between France and the United Provinces could not be avoided.[3] Herbert desired to know whether it would not be reasonable to be instructed concerning the French. To that William replied, "attaque tous les armateurs francois. Et prendre tous les vaisseaus marchands et les mainer en Flandre". The rest of the questions and answers cohere but loosely. Conciliatory intentions governed William's order that a month's pay in advance should be given no less to seamen than to land deserters. Ships, forts, etc. coming over to his side were to seize French ships if opportunity arose. English ships were not to be required to change their flag. "Il n'ont qu'a se servir du Pavillon Angleterre". The Dutch fleet and whatever transports it had taken with it to Plymouth continued to lie in that harbour. Provisioning proceeded. By land all went well. The Prince realised that the disaster that had shattered the cause at Salisbury could not fail to react and smash the last fibres of the moral of the royal fleet. Better than ever William could afford to pursue a waiting policy. He could be morally certain that either a reply to his invitation would come quickly to hand or that there would reach him soon by some other channel appropriate signal of the surrender of Admiral Dartmouth's fleet. The transport return question lost all urgency. How the signal of surrender did reach the Prince on Friday December 14th, has just been told.

*   *   *   *   *   *   *

The attempt of James to induce his Admiral to give facilities to the scheme for conveying the baby Prince from Portsmouth

---

[1] Admiralty Papers in P.R.O. Orders in Council, Ad. 1, 5139.
[2] B.M. MSS, Egerton 2621.
[3] Actually declared November 26th (N.S.).

into France neither hastened nor retarded the surrender of the royal fleet. The attitude of the nation had made the submission inevitable. When it occurred, it was rightly regarded by all concerned as much less a noteworthy than a necessary event. With the capitulation, the part played by the English Navy in the Revolution of 1688 may be considered ended; though subsequent events—those following the surrender and preceding the proclamation of William and Mary as King and Queen—form a necessary supplement or epilogue.

CHAPTER VII

From December 14th, 1688
to February 13th, 1688/9

ON Friday, December 14th, Dartmouth suitably acknowledged the Order of the Lords who had met in council at the Guildhall; and he simultaneously reported to the Secretary the state of the fleet. When the packet left on the 15th instant, it bore a postscript to Pepys which indicated that the Admiral, whose informants at this time were numerous, had been made aware that the King had been stopped in flight. Such news not unnaturally led Dartmouth to express a hope that James would be able somehow to come to "a happy agreement with the P[rince] of Orange".[1] Letters awaiting despatch to the Lords Feversham[2] and Rochester[3] also received additions voicing the same sentiment. But the unexpected news of James's interception in no way shook the Admiral's newly pledged fidelity to the Prince.

Dartmouth received, on the 14th, overdue and through the common post, a paper which the King, at his "departure from Whitehall in the night" (that is to say, in the early morning of Tuesday the 11th) had sent to the Admiralty, with instructions to the Secretary to forward it to the flagship. Pepys had straightway committed it to "another express"; but that gentleman, it must be supposed, had found an impediment to his duty. In this paper, the King strove, with a shallow reason, to justify his miserable conduct; and, in lieu, no doubt, of those orders which he had intended to confide to the Duke of Berwick for transmission to the Admiral, suggested that any commanders anxious to continue active allegiance to their lawful King should head their ships for Ireland and obtain instructions from the Lord Deputy, the Earl of Tyrconnel.[4] Though quite useless,

---

[1] Dartmouth MSS, XV, 1, p. 69.
[2] *Ibid.* XI, 5, p. 279; see also p. 232.
[3] *Ibid.* p. 280; see also p. 232.   [4] *Ibid.* pp. 226, 228.

such a letter had ample power to distress the Admiral. It provoked, on the 17th[1] (by which date the Admiral knew that the King had been prevailed on to leave Rochester and come to town), a reply as outspoken as the Admiral's earlier protest against conveying the infant Prince from Portsmouth to the continent. The Admiral professed a complete inability to make allowance for the action which his Majesty had taken in sending away the infant Prince and Queen; and the King's own flight, whether to be regarded as the outcome of "pernicious and destructive council" or of personal desperation, he could no more readily understand. At the very least, Dartmouth contended, the "desperate" and "morally impossible" decision to "absent" himself should have caused James to wonder whether he could not best have found "honour and safety" and immunity from "violence" and "unhallowed hands" on the decks of his "owne fleet". That he, James, had not sought asylum aboard the 'Resolution' suggested to the Admiral a lack of confidence which, as "many could witness", had "almost broke (his) heart". Then Dartmouth briefly stated that he, like all the nation, had applied to the Prince of Orange, that he could only hope that all would work towards his Majesty's "happy reestablishment". Dartmouth sent this rebuke under cover to his Secretary, Phillip Musgrave, at the Cockpit.

Opportunity to serve the common good and the Prince's cause fell to the Admiral while he waited the coming back of Captain Aylmer. For the better part of a week after the departure of Dover to London with the baby Prince, Sir Edward Scott, the Lieutenant-Governor, attempted to blackguard the Corporation and townsfolk into making preparations for resistance to the daily expected forces of the Prince. The mayor, Thomas Hancock, appealed to Dartmouth (who, as it happened, had formerly filled the office of Governor of the town); and only the Admiral's determined intervention prevented arson at the docks and the loosing of Irish soldiery upon the inhabitants. In the end, Dartmouth induced Scott, that "uneasy man", to take up quarters aboard the 'Resolution' while naval officers assumed control of James and Charles Forts and, particularly,

---

[1] Dartmouth MSS, XI, 5, p. 282.

of Southsea Castle. Berwick, the Governor, whose "sayings and orders" had been "little valued" and who, like his fellow Catholic, Dover, had behaved with duplicity to Dartmouth, was simply left to make the best of the impending necessity to surrender to the oncoming troops of the Prince and to hope for a safe conduct from Portsmouth.[1]

Captain Aylmer and his companions returned to the fleet on Wednesday, December 19th, and brought the Admiral a suitable acknowledgment of his surrender to the Prince. It was dated the 16th December from Windsor and ran:

My Lord, I receaved your letter of the 12th of this instant December, and am glad to finde you continue firme to the Protestant Religion and Liberties of England, and that you resolve to dispose the fleet under your command to those ends; to which not only the fleet, but the army and the nation in generall have so frankly concurr'd. Neither shall my care of the honour and dignity of this nation be wanting in matters of disputes between the two fleets as you seeme to apprehend; I therefore send you such orders as are necessary to prevent that, and usefull to this Kingdome. As to the methods you have taken to purge the fleet from papist officers, I aprove very much of it, and, as to all other matters in general, I shall referr them to the ensuing parliament. I expect your speedy compliance with the orders I send you here inclosed, and when you have brought the fleet to the Boy in the North (*sic*) I desire to see you that I may have your advice, not onely relating to the fleet, but to the publique in generall.

I am

Your affectionate Friend

Prince D'Orange.[2]

As the orders enclosed with the letter required that 13 men-of-war, the 'Elizabeth', 'St Albans', 'Dover', 'St David', 'Tiger', 'Mary', 'Deptford', 'Swallow', 'Portsmouth', 'Bristol', 'Defiance', 'Constant Warwick', 'Woolwich' and two fireships, the 'Richmond' and 'Pearl' should remain in the Spithead under Sir John Berry, it is plain that William intended that not by any means all the fleet should work round

---

[1] Dartmouth MSS, XI, 5, pp. 230 *et seq.* and 281 *et seq.*; many references; also XV, 1, p. 70.

[2] Dartmouth MSS, XI, 5, p. 235.

to the Nore under the Admiral's flag. Dartmouth was also bidden straightway to stop all local enlisting and impressment; instruct Sir Richard Beach to cease the further fitting out of ships; empty the departing vessels of surplus supplies for the benefit of Berry; and enjoin on Berry both the need to guard against any "affront" by the French and to prevent the sailing from Portsmouth of vessels carrying suspected persons.[1]

This reply and the enclosed orders from the Prince, reflecting in all probability considerations which the Admiral had asked Captain Aylmer to put to his Highness, suited well with Dartmouth's anticipations and, in particular, with his desire to be near the capital during the forthcoming deliberations on the future of the State.[2] Dartmouth at once held a council of war and made ready to weigh anchor.[3] But, in his reply to the Prince, sent upon Thursday, December 20th, under cover to Lord Rochester, he necessarily pointed out that he would be unable to sail at once if the winds continued to "hang easterly", and that, in such a case, since he could get no more provisions from the so recently disturbed port off which he lay, new consignments would have to be sent to him. The Admiral mentioned, with some satisfaction, his work on the Prince's behalf in Portsmouth; he remarked that, had it not been for the need to perform that duty, his ships would, sometime before the date on which he wrote, have put back to the Nore, if only because of the difficulty of provisioning. He strongly advised the Prince to send ships immediately to cruise off the Guernsey banks and urged him to "put good garrisons in Jersey and Guernsey", the latter of which, he said, "if it should be possessed by the French (would be) a thorne in England's sides for ever". Affairs of the Ordnance Office were touched on and the Admiral said he would send Mr Bowles, his Secretary, to the Prince as soon as the fleet could be got under sail.[4]

The favouring gale seemed disinclined to blow. In the enforced delay, officers canvassed for the commands left vacant

[1] Dartmouth MSS, XI, 5, p. 283; the order was slightly amended.
[2] Ibid. (Admiral to Col. Norton.)
[3] "Journal of Captain Grenville Collins", Dartmouth MSS, XV, 1, p. 59.
[4] Devon's pamphlet previously cited.

by the papist purge. Lieutenant Byng secured the 'Constant Warwick'.[1] Vice-Admiral Berry recommended Captain Clements for the 'St Albans'.[2] Captains Matthew Aylmer, Botham and Thos. Leighton were all candidates for the place of Captain Laton of the 'Mary'. Their presumption greatly annoyed Captain (afterwards Sir George) Rooke who argued against them on the grounds of seniority.[3] As a result, the 'Warspite' was offered to Rooke in consolation; but he refused her on the grounds that she was ill-manned and likely to be paid off.[4] The 'Warspite' was last spoken of as William Jennens's vessel. Jennens had not been dismissed for professing Romish views. It had so happened that he had had aboard as his prisoner a certain Marquis de Querian, whom he had been accused of starving. In rebutting the charge, Jennens had lost his temper and been guilty of "very unmannerly conduct" towards his Admiral. An apology had been tendered; but Dartmouth, unfavourably disposed towards Jennens for his earlier liberty of speech, had not seen fit to accept a "seeming submission". So Jennens's supercession had followed as a matter of course. These changes of command have only small interest; and the case of Jennens is only worth mention because one of its "exhibits" startlingly reveals how lax could be the

---

[1] *Memoirs...Torrington*, p. 34.

[2] Dartmouth MSS, XI, 5, p. 233.

[3] *Ibid.* p. 237. The seniorities of the officers concerned were:

G. Rooke	13 Nov. 1673		remained in the *Deptford*, 4th r.
Wm Botham	12 Apr. 1678	Appointed by	*Warspite*, 3rd r.
Mat. Aylmer	9 Jan. 1678/9	Dartmouth	*Mary*, 3rd r.
Thos. Leighton	11 Jy 1682	on 22 Dec. 88	*St David*, 4th r.
Jno. Laton	15 June 1688	to	*St Albans*, 4th r.

The incident is interesting, as seniority lists were still in an elementary stage.

The incident arose out of the dismissal of Strickland on December 13th. Apparently Berry, his successor, hoisted his flag in the 'Elizabeth'. Laton, no doubt, was moved out of the 'Mary' because she had ceased to be a flagship. A very junior Captain was regularly appointed to a flagship as 2nd Captain, the Admiral being his own 1st Captain, except in the case of the Commander-in-Chief, who in a large fleet had two Captains, a 1st, who was very senior and ranked as a Rear-Admiral; and a 2nd, very junior, corresponding to the modern Flag-Captain. In this case the Admiral had only one Captain, but he, Wm Davies, was of seniority of 1665, and was given his flag by Dartmouth on December 13th, 1688. It is clear that he was a 1st Captain.

[4] Dartmouth MSS, XI, 5, p. 239.

discipline on board a badly managed vessel in the Navy of that time.[1]

One remarkable thing, however, happened in the period of wind-bound waiting. Preserved among Dartmouth's papers is the following letter, signed James R, and dated from Rochester on Friday, December 21st.

At eight at night I send this bearer Mun Eliott[2] to the Downs to see if you be there, and to know if you designe to stay there, or are obliged for want of victuals to come up to the Nore; 'tis of concerne to me to be informed of it as you will find by what this bearer has to say to you from me, to whom you may giue intire credit, which is all I shall say, till I have an answer to this.

The cryptic letter bears an equally tantalising endorsement.

Brought to me by Captain Floyd at Spitthead, but Captain Elliot came not with it nor was it answered but by worde of mouth, by Captain Floyd; and I sayled immediatly, but the King went away the same night he write this letter so both my hast and Captain Floyde's were in vayne.[3]

There are two hypotheses to account for such a communication; one that, influenced by the recent rebuke from his Admiral's pen and determined a second time on flight, the King desired to escape to the decks of his fleet; the other that he wished to evade naval vigilance in his intended passage from England to France. The balance of probability is against the former notion. On the night of the day on which he wrote this mysterious message to the Admiral, James, attended by Berwick and one or two more, slipped from his prison to the Medway, took a skiff to the open stream and entered a ready vessel. In a night and a morning he crossed the wintry sea to Ambleteuse. It is impossible to believe that James could not have coasted down Channel to his fleet, had he seriously purposed to do so. Dartmouth says that he himself "sayled immediatly" In what

---

[1] Dartmouth MSS, XI, 5, pp. 238, 239, 245; Jennens complained to Pepys and got small satisfaction (p. 242).

[2] Mun Elliot, Edmund Elliot, was the Captain of 'Rose Sally Prize', a fireship which had not rejoined the flag after the westward sailing (see p. 121). He was given permission by Pepys to refit at Sheerness (Dartmouth MSS, XI, 5, p. 213). At about this time Elliot was recommended by Pepys to Dartmouth as a man whom the King desired to see advanced (op. cit. p. 209).

[3] Dartmouth MSS, XI, 5, p. 238.

single ship or with what few selected frigates he put out, what ostensible errand he alleged to his officers, whither, how, and how far he fared in the teeth of the opposing breeze or gale, are questions of interest which none of the known circumstances assist in the slightest degree to answer. This much, however, may be soundly asserted. Dartmouth, whatever the terms of the message he received from Captain Floyd, did not sail to help James's passage to a foreign strand; he tacked towards the eastward, either in the hope of intercepting a King who, he believed, waited to be carried to the shelter of the royal fleet, or in order, by the last pleas of impassioned loyalty and reason, to dissuade him from some newly suspected folly.

Christmas came and passed. The winds still held in an adverse quarter. Pepys, who had been silent since he had sent down the order from the Council of Lords and who had shown Dartmouth's reply to James during the monarch's brief return, broke his silence upon Christmas Day.[1] Speaking as the mouthpiece of the new master, he was greatly concerned, in view of the known shortage of their provisions, at the long detention of the ships; he promised orders to give effect to Dartmouth's recent suggestion to the Prince concerning cruising off the Guernsey banks and instructions for checking the annoyance which French privateers had begun to cause the packet service to and from Holland. Thereafter, till Pepys had reason to believe the Admiral had weighed anchor, communications flowed from the Admiralty to the Spithead. There is, however, no call to consider in detail their contents. They were mainly slight modifications of orders already given and new advices concerning yachts, special services in the St George's Channel, the reconversion of a few fireships to their original rates and the too great plentifulness of officers on leave in town. Sad to tell, the Admiral and the Secretary were not, just before the year's end, on quite good terms. Pepys, in spite of his own ten days' silence towards Dartmouth, thought himself neglected and probably resented that the Admiral (according to an intention expressed in his last letter to the Prince) had chosen to send his Secretary, Mr Bowles, direct from the fleet to report to his

---

[1] Dartmouth MSS, XI, 5. p. 239.

Highness. Happily, Dartmouth was too wise, once he had gathered Pepys's difficulty, to allow the great Secretary, whom he regarded with a warm esteem, to rest under the apprehension of a slight; and, equally fortunately, Pepys, on his part was something more than a dull precisian. So the breach was readily healed.[1] Mr Bowles's journey was not unconnected with the Admiral's concern to remain in state employ.[2]

[3]At 11 a.m. on the morning of Sunday, December 30th, Dartmouth weighed; and, at the sound of the gun signalling the Admiral's departure, those ships left with Sir John Berry drew closer to his flag.[4] By midnight, Dartmouth's vessels were off Beachy. At dusk, on Monday the 31st, they came to anchor four miles west of Dover. At 2 o'clock on the morning of Tuesday, January 1st, they sailed on the flood tide but, making little headway, brought up in 16 fathoms water with Dover bearing three miles due north. "A great fog all the afternoon with frost and snow" baffled progress; but at 2 in the afternoon the ships got under way on the flood and plied[5] for the Downs where they came to anchor about 7 o'clock. Upon Wednesday, January 2nd, once more the ships weighed. They sailed a little further to the southward, 'Resolution' anchoring in the "Admiral's berth". There, at 2 o'clock night, Captain Hoskins came off from the shore with letters and brought word that the frigate 'Sedgemore' was ashore "under the Foreland".[6] For some days no headway could be made; and Dartmouth attempted unsuccessfully to secure permission to go overland. Rear-Admiral Lord Berkeley, who had once more returned to the fleet, put back to Portsmouth "with some men-of-war and

---

[1] Dartmouth MSS, XI, 5, p. 239 *et seq.* and pp. 284, 285. See also XV, 1, p. 70 *et seq.*

[2] *Ibid.* XI, 5, p. 242. (Bowles to Admiral.)

[3] "Journal of Captain Grenville Collins", Dartmouth MSS, XV, 1, p. 59 for the rest of the paragraph except as (4) and (2) on the next page show.

[4] Admiralty Papers in P.R.O. Masters' Logs 63, 'Mary'. This Log of the 'Mary', Strickland's old ship, was begun by a new 1st Lieutenant on Dec. 24th, and is one of the few extant Logs of this time.

[5] "plied" = beat to windward (in this case making use of the flood).

[6] A court martial was held Ap. 6th, 1689, by order of the Lords Commissioners of Admiralty on board the 'Mary' yacht, Capt Wm. Davis President, Henry Croome Judge Advocate. Result—adjourned, no conviction (Admiralty Papers in P.R.O. Courts Martial, Ad. 1, 5253.)

fireships" on Monday, January 7th. Next day at half past nine, Dartmouth's remaining ships "went out to the Gulf Stream",[1] at eleven, steered N.E. and held that course till one on the afternoon....Anchor was cast off the Buoy of Nore upon Friday, January 11th. Exactly when Dartmouth hauled down his flag is not known; and with whom he left the command cannot be decided. He probably made use of the 'Katharine' yacht for conveyance up River to London.[2] On what day the Prince gave him audience is not clear; nor is it possible to say anything of the interview.[3]

From the dozen or so ships left under Berry at Portsmouth, those required for duties off the Channel Islands and in the St George's Channel were provided. On Tuesday, January 15th, Berry split his squadron and the 'Elizabeth', 'Deptford', 'St Albans', 'St David' and 'Woolwich' went out under orders for the Downs. The 'Dover', 'Swallow', 'Tiger' and 'Mary' at once "shifted their pendants to the main-top-mast-head while Captain Ashby, presumably still in the 'Defiance', became 'Commodore'.[4] The move of the 5th was probably part of a great re-shuffling which, about the middle of January, on orders issued by Pepys to the "Principal Officers and Commissioners of the Navy" (the Navy Board), took place. They were instructed to fit and victual three squadrons out of the fleet for service for the Straits, in Ireland, and in the Channel; while the residue were to be left in sea pay with the least possible complement of men.[5] It must be supposed that William, finding the international outlook menacing, changed the notions of retrenchment which Pepys had previously credited him with[6] and resolved to omit no precaution. At that time, a Declaration was

---

[1] Gulf Stream = Gull Stream? The Gull Stream, the water immediately inside the Goodwins, has long been the usual passage from the Channel to the Thames. Curiously enough, Collins's *Great Britain's Coasting Pilot* does not mark it; but it may be found mentioned in John Seller's *The Coasting Pilot*, which is a little earlier in date.

[2] Dartmouth MSS, XI, 5, p. 252.

[3] He voted in the House of Lords for the establishment of a regency. (Oldmixon, p. 770.)

[4] Log of 'Mary' previously cited. This use of the term is probably the earliest instance.

[5] House of Lords MSS, Hist. MSS, Comm. XII, 6, p. 185.

[6] Dartmouth MSS, XI, 5, p. 241.

published to the effect that, as the ships came in, the wages of the seamen were to be made payable retrospectively and a pardon offered to all deserters reporting in 15 days.[1]

Some few facts concerning the Dutch fleet and transports from December 15th onwards remain to be stated. Upon December 26/16, from Windsor, as soon as he himself became aware of the fact, the Prince informed Lieutenant-Admiral-General Herbert at Plymouth of the submission of the English fleet. Therefore Herbert's project of blockading Dartmouth's forces in order that the transport vessels might be safely convoyed into Holland, a plan which the Prince had approved as far back as November 22/12, as a necessary and reasonable modification of Section 4 of the Instructions issued to his Admiral before sailing, but which, for reasons already shown, the Admiral had never attempted to put into operations, died, at last, a natural death. Section 5 of the Instructions, which pictured diversions to assist the land operations after the return of the transports to Holland, never, of course, came to possess the slightest practical significance.

Together with the news of Dartmouth's surrender, certain fresh orders for disposing of the fleet and transports were, it appears, forwarded to Herbert. But the winds which detained the English squadron at Spithead rendered the new Instruction inapplicable and still further orders had to be sent upon December 26th from William, then at St James's, to Herbert, still at Plymouth, requiring (1) that "douze vaisseaux de guerre" according to list and three "Bruhlers" under Vice-Admiral Almonde (his vessel making the 13th) should go to "l'embouchure de mer nommée 't veersche Gat" thereupon to be employed as the States General might declare necessary for the conduct of the Mediterranean convoy; (2) that five or six others should sail with Van der Putten "à Spit Head" to cruise in the Channel ("dans le Canal") to stop the ravages of "Corsaires Francois dans cette mer"; (3) that Lieutenant-Admiral Evertsen, with the rest of the said fleet, should come about "dans cette Riviere"; (4) that Lieutenant-Admiral Bastiaensze

---

[1] Luttrell's *Relation* puts the date after Jan. 16th.

should be instructed "d'y renvoyez des vaisseaux de Transport autant qu'il en faudra pour passer en Hollande 1000 Chevaux et 6000 Fantassins et qu'avec le reste il s'en retourne en Hollande suivant mes ordres precedents". William stated that he hoped to see Herbert in London soon.[1]

It remains only, so far as the movements of ships are concerned, to observe that Herbert[2] went out with a squadron and several yachts to meet d'Almonde, who left Holland soon after February 18/8, bringing over Mary, Princess of Orange, to these shores.[3] Her Highness's vessel came off the Foreland upon Monday the 11th instant. Next day, she landed at Greenwich; and, on the morrow, Wednesday, February 13th, 1688/9, stood side by side with her husband at the historic gathering in the Banqueting House at Whitehall. There jointly, by virtue of their assent to the Declaration of Right, they began their reign as "King and Queen of England, France and Ireland and the dominions thereunto belonging";[4] and that day, presumably, the ships of their Majesties' Royal Navy, and such vessels of the Admiralties of the United Provinces as had not then cleared our coasts, boomed, in their rejoicings, much good gunpowder into the winter air.

[1] B.M. MSS, Egerton 2621, "Ordres precedents", probably refers to permission of Nov. 22/12.
[2] *London Gazette*, Feb. 11–14.
[3] Macaulay II, p. 659 *et seq.*
[4] Bill of Rights.

The English Navy—Administration, Matériel and Personnel; a brief survey of the Dutch Naval Organisation; remarks upon the Navy of Louis XIV

IT becomes necessary, at this stage, to discuss first, the method of administering the English navy at this date, October 1st, 1688, devoting, in so doing, a special attention to the *matériel* and *personnel* which the administration controlled; secondly, to add a brief similar survey of Dutch naval organisation; and lastly, to comment, in few and general remarks, on the navy of Louis XIV.

I[1]

It was following a spell of five years of disordered governance in naval affairs that James, Duke of York, a little before his brother's death, was virtually restored to the control of the service he so well knew; and Samuel Pepys, who had fallen under official displeasure at James's downfall, came back to act as James's Secretary. Pepys was no less anxious than his master that the service he too knew and loved should prosper; and it was he who was chiefly responsible for pushing on a scheme which, just before the death of Charles II, had received the preliminary assurances of success. By this scheme a special commission of properly qualified persons, endowed with adequate funds (some £400,000 annually, to be paid in quarterly instalments) was instructed to clear up, in three years, all the legacy of past disorder and to refurbish the great weapon of national and trade defence. Actually the Commission was appointed by warrant on March 6th, 1685/6[2], and the principle

---

[1] The facts concerning the administration, *matériel* and *personnel* of the navy, prior to, and after, October 1688, are dependent on the Pepysian materials in the Navy Records Society's publications, which Dr Tanner, of Cambridge, has so ably compiled; on lists in Jackson's *Naval Commissioners*; on original official materials examined at the P.R.O. and elsewhere; on an entertaining section of *Angliae Notitia* for 1687: and on *Samuel Pepys and the Royal Navy*, an excellent, indeed invaluable, compendium of naval administrative history for the Restoration period, from Dr Tanner's pen.

[2] Jackson, *Naval Commissioners*.

of staffing obviously was to associate with the Treasurer of the Navy—Lord Falkland—Sir Anthony Deane, Sir John Narbrough, Sir John Berry, Sir John Godwin, Wm Hewer, Balthazar St. Michell (in charge at Deptford) Sir Phineas Pett (at Chatham) Sir Richard Beach (at Portsmouth) as "Principal Officers and Commissioners of the Navy", while retaining for the purpose of "bringing up of the old accounts" Sir Richard Haddock, the Controller, Sir John Tippets, the Surveyor, and James Sotherne, the Clerk of the Acts.[1] The Commission was really an enlarged Navy Board with special means and powers, a Navy Board being (as will shortly be explained) the main instrument in the Lord High Admiral's hands for the purpose of maintaining his fleets. The ordinary routine of administration was therefore little altered by what was a mere *ad hoc* modification of the usual plan. James, at his accession, in the month before the warrant was issued, retaining control of the Navy in his own hands, had become his Lord High Admiral. So the Commission may be regarded as having worked from the outset under the King's view which, in practice, meant under the supervision of Mr Secretary Pepys.

At the moment when Lord Dartmouth received his Instructions, this Commission still sat; a fortnight later (October 13th, 1688) the Commission had ceased to exist and the "ancient constitution",[2] as far as it had been temporarily dislocated, had been restored. The Commission had ceased to exist because its work was finished and, possibly, because it was held unadapted to war-time necessities. If one is to credit Pepys (and one may with fair confidence do so), the two and a half years had sufficed for the Commission to produce substantially all the results expected of it. A sum of just over £1,000,000 had been drawn; but a balance of a third of it remained unspent. If names are to be singled out, those of the ship-designer Sir Anthony Deane, whose services Pepys had laboured with amusing Machiavellianism to obtain, and Sir John Narbrough perhaps deserve that special honour; but the professional advice of such a widely experienced officer as Sir John Berry must also have been very useful. Sir John Narbrough had dropped from the Commission in 1687[3] as also had Sir John Godwin; Sir Wm Booth had been added in that year.[4]

It is pretty certain that the intention to dispense with the

[1] Jackson, *Naval Commissioners*.   [2] *Ibid.*
[3] Narbrough sailed to command a small squadron in the W. Indies in September 1687 (see p. 10).
[4] Booth apparently replaced Godwin from December 25th.

special Commission and to restore carefully the old administrative system was present in the mind of James and Pepys appreciably earlier than October 13th, on which date the restoration was actually completed; and for all practical purposes it may be assumed that the "ancient constitution" about to be described functioned in entirety, and with the staffing about to be given, from the outset of these hostilities—that is to say, from October 1st when Dartmouth's Instructions were issued.

At the head of the service stood the Lord High Admiral (lineal successor to the Lord Admiral of mediaeval days). King James acted as his own Lord High Admiral and scarcely differentiated the latter aspect and rôle from the office of Kingship. As Lord High Admiral he was much more than the controller of the naval service. He necessarily assumed and maintained all the King's legal and customary authority over the English seas and their users, as well as the King's pretensions to, and duties of, admiralty upon wider waters. Shouldering heavy responsibility, he enjoyed special legal facilities for the performance of his duties; and to the performance attached considerable rights and perquisites. But those aspects of the office may be put outside present discussion; and certainly outside present discussion any consideration of the place of the Lord High Admiral's proper court, the High Court of Admiralty, in the judicial system of England. Even where only the great naval service was concerned, the duties and powers of the Lord High Admiral had long been quite indefinable in any thoroughgoing way; and while James, a King, in person exercised the office, the powers and duties attached to it were indeed just what he, acting in the dual capacity, caused them to be. For one thing, the encroaching authority of the Privy Council trenched upon the exercise of the office, though to a less degree than before 1685 and to a much less extent than when, after the Revolution, the Tudor system of government by Council and Council Committees was markedly revived, and the Privy Council seemingly took the narrowest views of the powers of the Commission on which devolved the exercise of the Lord High Admiral's duties. For working purposes, however, James's duties as Lord High Admiral may be summed up as consisting (i) of the maintenance, both in peace and in war, of a fighting force of King's ships; and (ii) of the direction of the force in peace time and when hostilities actually began.

(i) By maintenance is implied the ordinary care of existing ships, the building of new units, the fitting out, officering, manning and keeping at sea of the necessary fleets or squadrons. For the purpose of maintenance the Lord High Admiral possessed yards, depôts, hospitals, etc. Such maintenance was no small matter—even for James, working through an efficient Secretary such as Pepys. The task was, in practice, lightened to the extent to which the Principal Officers and Commissioners of the Navy —the Navy Board (which had a definite continuity traceable from Henry VIII's reign)—rendered assistance. How far that might be may be gathered from a consideration of the functions of the Board. The officers and names were as follows:

Treasurer	Viscount Falkland.
Comptroller	Sir Richd. Haddock.
Surveyor	Sir Jno. Tippets.
Clerk of the Acts	Jas. Sotherne, Esq.
Comptroller of the Victualling	Sir John Berry.
Comptroller of the Stores	Sir Wm. Booth.
Deptford—in charge at	Balthasar St. Michell, Esq.
Chatham ditto	Sir Phineas Pett.
Portsmouth ditto	Sir Richard Beach.

The first four were the Principal Officers, the rest the Commissioners of the Navy. All were appointed upon October 13th by letters patent.[1] It is interesting to note that when this change had been completed, the four most important officers in the Navy Board of the new régime (the "Principal Officers" of the new régime) had not been moved from the posts they held in the old; three others in the new Navy Board (three of the "Commissioners", of the new régime) had not changed their former duties; and the remaining two members of the new Navy Board (the two remaining "Commissioners" of the new order) had come to it also from the old. The title of Treasurer calls for no explanation; on the warrant of the Principal Officers, the Treasurer of the Navy drew money from the Treasury of England to meet all charges due. The office was no sinecure; but it was one of much dignity and many times better paid than those of the remaining three confrères of the Treasurer. The Comptroller also was a financial official whose business it was to have a less aloof, a much more practical knowledge of naval finance. The Surveyor's work, of a nature suggested by his title, was both general and particular; the yards and the units of the fleet were his care; but so, not less, were the stores handed out to every commissioning ship. The Commissioners—the Comptroller of the Stores, the Comptroller

[1] Jackson, *Naval Commissioners*. See also Chamberlayne who gives rates of salary.

of the Victualling, the Commissioners at Deptford, Chatham and Portsmouth—discharged duties closely connecting them with those two Principal Officers, the Comptroller and Surveyor. The Clerk of the Acts was the Secretary of the whole Board. The Board was responsible for effecting building programmes and also for repairs.

In close concert with these above-named Principal Officers and Commissioners of the Navy worked other officials of importance.[1] A "Victualling Office" attended to the task of victualling. At this time it was again buying its sanctioned supplies of the merchants "on account" rather than by the sometime method of "contract".[2] At the yards, Deptford, Chatham and Portsmouth,[3] there were of course responsible technical and other posts which needed to be filled; and at subsidiary yards and stations a few officials were assisted by the necessary supplementary staffs.[4]

The Navy Office was at this time in Seething Lane by the Tower, the Victualling Office not far distant.

It is plain, therefore, that the Navy Board considerably lightened the work of the Lord High Admiral.

But other duties of maintenance remained. At the instance of the Lord High Admiral and his Secretary, the guns and arms of a ship were, like the arms and artillery of land regiments, provided by the Officers of the Ordnance at the Tower. On the Lord High Admiral, through the Surgeon-General, fell the duty of caring for the sick and hurt, at sea and in hospital. The Lord High Admiral was the originator of all ordinary commissions and warrants to officers and the proximate authority at least for the impressment of men.[5] He provided chaplains. He was the custodian of many records, including the records of officers' services. He was the appropriate person with whom to lodge request for any special compassion or favour. All said and done,

[1] For 1687 the names may be gathered from Chamberlayne.
[2] Chamberlayne gives the names, for 1687, as Sir Richd. Haddock, Alderman Sturt, John Parsons and Nicholas Fenn. They were Commissioners of Victualling as early as 1684 (Dartmouth MSS, XI, 5, p. 107). Associated with Sir Richard, Mr Fenn and Parsons (then Sir John) were still, in October 1688, at that Office (Dartmouth MSS, XI, 5, p. 159).
[3] Chamberlayne gives also Sheerness, Woolwich and Deptford with Harwich as a minor yard. Deal had a Storekeeper (p. 109). It seems quite clear that Sheerness and Harwich were very small yards, possibly with little more than Storekeepers (Dartmouth MSS, XI, 5, pp. 182, 200; XV, 1, p. 63). The fact that Chamberlayne gives a full staff for Sheerness should make one chary of accepting this "Whitaker" as up to date.
[4] See Chamberlayne.
[5] See p. 25. The Privy Council would be concerned initially.

the responsibility for actual maintenance, which, in spite of the assistance rendered by the Navy Board, rested with the King and Pepys, was onerous; and on Pepys the burden chiefly lay. No more important civil servant had then existence, or perhaps has since been known, than that great model for all civil servants, he who was so noted for "indefatigable care and pains...that most expert gentleman Mr Samuel Pepys, Secretary of the Admiralty".[1]

(ii) Direction of the fleets in peace and in war rested with the Lord High Admiral. He weighed experience; he took advice; he issued general Fighting Instructions to govern the main tactics of all engagements. And such particular supplementary directions as he deemed called for he sent out from his office.

The Admiralty at this time was in Whitehall.

The *matériel* under the Lord High Admiral's care was considerable. In that *matériel* a great change had occurred between 1660 and 1688, the era of the Second and Third Dutch Wars and the development of the French menace. The change may be followed in Samuel Pepys's "Register of Ships", where, for a period of 28 years, the detailed record of every ship in the Royal Navy is made available. Pepys's register proves clearly that, so far as what we should now call "capital ships" were concerned, late in that period larger models definitely found favour. The reason is not far to seek. The First Dutch War had shown the mere agglomerating movements into which, up to that time, all great maritime battles had resolved themselves, giving way, on both sides, to three-squadronal formations striving to operate in line ahead, a plan which naturally led straight to the desire to eliminate all small and doubtful vessels from the line, and so reacted strongly on subsequent building programmes. Thus, at this time, there were 59 ships of about 1000 tons, classed as first, second and third rates, whereas, in 1660, not five 1000 ton ships were to be found in all the Navy.

Most of the first and largest second rates were essentially of the same design. A really big ship of 13 or 14 hundred tons might measure 140 feet along the keel, something over 170 feet over the gun deck (just above the water line) with a beam width of 45 feet, a depth of 18 or 19 feet and a draught of about a foot more. Most had three decks distinct from their upper works; their rig consisted, apart from the bowsprit, which carried the spritsails, of fore and main masts, with the customary

---

[1] Chamberlayne, p. 137.

three sails, and a mizzen with a lateen sail and at least a topsail
For armament a hundred guns might be carried; a score of
light guns on the upper works and about equal numbers of
sakers, whole culverins and cannon of seven respectively on
the upper, middle and lower decks. Apparently the saker
threw a six-pound and the whole culverin an eighteen-pound
shot, while the cannon of seven was a forty-two pounder.
Powder was expended in the ratio of half the weight of the
shot. The range of the largest cannon was really considerable;
but relative accuracy was not expected at more than a few
hundred yards; and, for action, the alongside position was
certainly preferred. The third rates resembled the first and
second rates but had no middle deck; consequently their armaments and crews were somewhat less. Below the approximately
1000 ton ships ranked 41 fourth rates, 500 ton two-deckers throwing a broadside a quarter the weight of that of a first rate. Two
fifth rates of about 250 tons, but dissimilar in build to the fourth
rates in that they boasted only a partial lower deck of guns, as
well as 6 sixth rates, with one gun deck only, were in existence.[1]

Ships of less than three complete decks were often called
frigates and these good sailors were sometimes employed on
duties which belong to ships of the modern 'cruiser—destroyer'
class. But 14 yachts, deemed sufficient for all advice-work
contingent on warfare in the narrow seas, were more properly
the counterpart of that category.

Intermediate between the two main types are to be grouped
the 3 bombers, 26 fireships, 6 hoys, 7 hulks, 3 ketches, 1 pontoon,
4 smacks and 1 towboat. Of these the fireships were the most
important, and the precursors of the torpedo boat as such.[2]

It must not, however, be supposed that all these 173 vessels
were intended to be employed at the same time, or that, in spite
of what has been said as to the Commission's completed work,

[1] From a schedule in the "Register" it may be gathered that at the time
of making the list one of the first rates, the 'Sovereign', was 51 years old;
two of the second rates, the 'George' and 'Victory' were 66 and 68 years old
respectively; nine of the third rates had an average age of 36·2 years; 24
fourth rates had an average age of 37·1 years; 7 fifth rates had an average
age of 34·6 years; 1 sixth rate was 36 years old (p. 305). But some of these
ships had been rebuilt. Pepys's "Register" does not always show re-
buildings.

[2] These figures are from the "Register".
Pepys has an abstract in his *Memoires* for December 18th, 1688: "...that
signal day that puts a natural Bound to the subject of these Notes, I
mean the Day of my late Royal (but most unhappy) Master's retiring in
December..." which records very slightly different class totals. See also
next page note (2). For monetary value of vessels see *Memoires*, p. 104.

they were all, in this first fortnight of October, as far ready for sea service as was customary and desirable, in that day, to hold the King's ships. Strictly speaking, the figures given are for mid-December of this year; none at all are available, or exactly calculable for October 1st. True, the total number of vessels in the Royal Navy did not vary between the two dates; Pepys in his *Memoires* says that on December 18th, 1688, only 11 ships remained unrepaired.[1] At this date the number unrepaired was doubtless somewhat, if only slightly, greater.

Of the state of the personnel at the disposal of the Lord High Admiral for service afloat, in October 1688, the following observations may be made.[2]

When a ship was put into commission, the men who could be detained in naval pay or induced or cajoled into service were, unless it were known that a popular captain were about to hoist his pennant, usually far too few to make up a complement. The rest were secured by impressment of sailors out of the mercantile service, or from the shore, through press-gangs operating on specific warrants emanating (after higher authority

[1] *Memoires*, p. 127.
[2] The following tables (on this and the next page) are from Pepys's "Register". They relate *matériel* and *personnel* and may be found of value. There is very slight discrepancy between Table I and the Table in the *Memoires*, p. 127.

Table I (p. 306 "Register")

Ships and Vessels	Rate	No.	Tons	Men	Guns
Ships of the	1	9	12,756	6,705	878
	2	11	15,302	7,010	974
	3	39	37,832	16,525	2,640
	4	41	21,945	9,440	1,914
	5	2	562	260	60
	6	6	839	420	90
Bombers	—	3	457	115	20 and 4 mortars
Fireships	—	26	4,762	925	224
Hoys	—	6	266	15	—
Hulks	—	7	4,467	59	18
Ketches	—	3	230	115	24
Pinks	—	—	—	—	—
Pontoons	—	1	80	—	—
Sloops	—	—	—	—	—
Smacks	—	4	92	8	—
Tow-boats	—	1	—	—	—
Yachts	—	14	1442	343	104
		173	101,032	41,940	6,950 and 4 mortars

obtained) from the Office of the Navy Board. Expediency dictated that the warrants should apply most frequently to seaport towns, or affect the crews of trading ships; but, wherever, or through whatever persons, the warrants ran, the number of men obtained and the quality of the victims almost invariably left much to be desired.

On board, the common hands found their level at or below the rating of able seamen. A first rate carried about 700 men. Presumably, a simple petty-officer system was interposing itself between the seamen and such officers as the gunner, the carpenter, the purser, the boatswain and the chirurgeon. The captain and his lieutenants exercised a full commissioned authority. The master was the navigating officer. Of course, the lesser rates carried proportionately less men and the smaller ships far fewer officers. If a master were not to be borne, then a captain who had passed his examination at Trinity House, according to an Admiralty Order of 1674, would be appointed. Many of the officers were of a class which regarded the sea life as a chosen profession; they were "tarpaulins" rather than mere gentlemen adventurers.

The sea-pay of the "A.B." was somewhat over £1 per month (lunar); the gunner and his class got between £2 and £4. The captain of a first rate received a remuneration of £21 per month and other considerable allowances, equal roughly to his pay, and intended to render him proof against all undignified ways of making money. Captains of other rates got less in proportion. The lieutenant's pay was equal to the highest gunner's pay. There were, as occasion will arise to show, Admirals of the fleets,

Table II ("Register", Introduction to, p. 239)

'Royal Charles'		Guns	Men
Cannon of 7—to each	7 men	26	182
Whole Culverin—to each	4 men	28	112
Saker—to each	3 men	28	84
Minion—to each	3 men	14	42
3 pounders—to each	2 men	4	8
To carry powder to all the guns		—	34
To fill and hand powder for all the guns		—	15
Chirurgion and crew in hold		—	10
Carpenter and crew		—	8
Purser and crew in hold		—	5
Men for small shot		—	110
Men to stand by sails		—	120
Men for the boats and tops		—	50
		100	780

with Vice-Admirals and Rear-Admirals of the fleet. And, when the fleets were large and the squadrons of the three Admirals were subdivided into three smaller squadrons, there were Vice-Admirals and Rear-Admirals to each subdivision—or nine Admirals in all in a single fleet. An Admiral of the fleet received as regular pay, apart from allowances, £4, a Vice-Admiral £2. 10s., and the Rear-Admiral £2 per day. The Vice-Admiral of a squadron got only £1. 10s., and the Rear-Admiral £1 per day. Admiral's pay had been increased much more recently than the other officers' remuneration. Reduced harbour pay varied the constancy of the sea money. Actual payment was far from satisfactorily made. The men received, from their ships, tickets which were really bills payable on demand at the Navy Office in Seething Lane. In practice the men did not present the tickets in London; they availed themselves of the proffered services of brokers, frequently unscrupulous, to discount them at the port of paying off. If, as had all too frequently been the case, the Navy Office failed to honour the ship tickets, evil effects had followed the delay. Prize money grants always entered into the prospects of the sailor, whether man or officer.

The life afloat was a hard one, which, except in the day of battle, the men detested.[1] Under the "Rules" of 1652 and 1661 (from them the present day "Articles of War" have developed) discipline could be severely enforced.[2] But punishments were not, for that age, severely meted out. Considerable licence was, on occasion, allowed—women were quite commonly aboard when vessels were in harbour.[3] The sailors of one ship did not necessarily show the respect of a salute to the officers of another vessel. The men were tolerably well fed and thought much of their beer. There was no common uniform. The health of the sailor cannot have been good, for his ship was, at best, a foul-smelling prison house. The presence of the chirurgeons in the larger ships argued some care of the sick, some recognition of the duty of attention to those wounded in action. There were also ports at which some hospital provision was made; but all that provision was of a very rudimentary kind. For the disabled man there existed the uncertain charity of the Chatham Chest.[4]

---

[1] How bad it must have been can be inferred from the later *Roderick Random*, Smollett.

[2] A few Admiralty Court Martial Records are extant from this time. Admiralty Papers in P.R.O. Ad. 1, 5253.

[3] The *Diary* of Henry Teonge (1675–9) gives a very readable picture of the conditions afloat at the time.

[4] The Chatham Chest was a box of iron with five locks. In it compulsory

Officers, even if they were not sure of any continuation in service as a prescriptive right, had at least begun to think of their rank as permanent. Permanent rank began with half-pay, which existed before the Revolution for flag officers, for many Captains, and some Masters. The warrants had long been 'standing officers'. Officers had not, of right, retiring pensions.[1]

The true place of James's October counter-preparations in the total naval economy of England needs to be ascertained—the extent to which the counter-preparations against the Dutch, actual and on paper, drew on the King's reserve. No one, turning the page on the foregoing survey, and contrasting the figures there given with those to be found on p. 29, can fail to notice the low ratio of Lord Dartmouth's actual and paper strength to the total fighting strength of the English Navy. Third and fourth rates were the largest vessels mentioned in the paper accompanying Dartmouth's Instructions. But when it is realised that the oncoming winter season made the use of the larger ships most undesirable, and that no English sailor of that day would expect the Dutch to use, in winter seas, larger vessels than the English third and fourth rates, this fact will cause no surprise. Nor will the smallness of the number of the vessels commissioned or commissioning on October 1st (25 of the total 41 fourths and 12 only of the 39 thirds) be regarded as strange, if it is borne in mind that the Lord High Admiral, counting ships against ships, had no grounds at all, up to October 1st, to suppose that his fleet, at sea, was not being maintained at an adequate strength, a strength increasing quite as fast as the Dutch preparations could be augmented. It follows that more than half the naval forces of England lay, on October 1st, in unused reserve behind Lord Dartmouth. The fact is extremely interesting.

II[2]

The task of describing comprehensively, for a given date, the administration of the naval forces of the Dutch, coupled with the requirement to treat fully of the *matériel* and *personnel*

---

donations from the pay of men and boys were placed, together with fines, etc., derived from various sources, in order that a benevolent fund for needy seamen might be created. The Chatham Chest was instituted in 1590. The funds were not always well administered.

[1] By Order in Council, Captain Thomas Smith (Sheerness Attendant) received a pension to be settled by necessary order from Pepys, November 17th, 1688. (Admiralty Papers in P.R.O., Orders in Council, Ad. 1, 5139.)

[2] de Jonge, and numerous scattered sources.

comprised, would be difficult. It is true that, on October 1st, 1688, a Stadholder, backed by a States General sympathetic to his policy, but, of course, not without a faction opposed to his aim, swayed, with popular approval, and with a firm hand (which as much resembled the rule of a king as the guidance of the president of a union) the destiny of the sovereign Provinces. But a more cumbersome arrangement than that which still existed for the regulation of the Provinces' affairs of admiralty it would have been hard to find.

The Stadholder, in his capacity of Admiral-General, held, as did the Lord High Admiral of England, complete operative control; but five different Boards of Admiralty-authorities, of widely different importance in respect of areas of control and the wealth of their resources, bodies different in deliberative *personnel* and executive staffing, as inevitably also in methods of management and routine, carried on the administration. They were the Admiralties of Amsterdam, the Maas (with headquarters at Rotterdam), Zeeland, Friesland and North Holland; and their areas of authority were not altogether co-terminous with the sovereign provincial boundaries. The really important criticism of Dutch naval administration lies on the surface in the inherent difficulty of controlling five Boards under a central authority and the divided responsibility of the five Boards to the same. From the point of view of the central authority, it was a system which, of course, placed a premium on confidential negotiations and on the service of those of the staffs and permanent officials of the various Boards who could best be trusted; it was a system which, in an emergency, one would expect to find worked in spite of, rather than through, its elaborate machinery. That the system had worked even as, in history, other strange devices of government have, from time to time, operated to produce tolerable results, was, doubtless, due to the fact that, after all, it had, however clumsily, a real relation to business facts and needs.

While the Dutch administration can, for present purposes, be left at these few remarks, so a special consideration of the *matériel* and *personnel* controlled by the Boards need not be handled further than in two short comments concerning *matériel* and in a few general remarks on Dutch officers and men.

Because the two Admiralties of Amsterdam and the Maas were by far the most important of the five authorities, deriving their normal revenue from the import and export duties levied at the ports within their areas, so, though they were always in difficulties and were compelled to raise loans, they were expected to yield, on requisition, the highest naval quotas. As to the effectively available ship and gun strength of the five Boards of Admiralty, it may be observed that the shipping and gun strength which they put forth and maintained, from time to time, through the thirty years' era of the three Dutch Wars, suggests the conclusion that, since the fighting strength of the Boards, both exerted or held in reserve, throughout the three decades, often rivalled our own, at this time, even after the great English overhaul, it must have been no mean counterpart to King James's total ship strength. More exact balancing is impossible for want of fact and figure. Moreover, in quality and build there were certain differences between Dutch and English ships. The Dutch ships, though conforming to the common sea-going design of the period, were sometimes slighter of build and less in draught than the English vessels. Certainly Dutch third rates were not well built. Those which served at Beachy Head were unsatisfactory and no more were built.

Of the officering and manning of the Dutch ships, it will be enough to say that so maritime a people were natur-ally well served. The Dutch officer was a competent seaman and fighter. Faction and Province and Admiralty and a lack of the complete trust of the directive authorities often spoilt him; but, that much said, he must be pronounced a worthy foe. The ranking of the Dutch officers did not quite correspond with our own. The seaman, knowing his job, did it well. He does not seem to have been worse treated than his English enemy.

These very brief remarks on the Dutch administration and the *matériel* and *personnel* of the forces available under it will throw a useful light on the little (it is unfortunately little) that has been, or can be told, in complement to the main theme of this work, concerning the Dutch aspect of these hosti-lities. One observation, parallel to that concerning the English reserve, is, however, rendered immediately possible. It has been shown that there is every reason to think that the mobilised Dutch strength at the opening of October stood at 25 sail— which was about the strength of English ships actually in com-mission at that time. So, though on the Dutch side, as on the English, more ships than those then at sea were fast fitting out, it remains likely enough that on October 1st, as not half the English Navy was in commission or commissioning, so not more than half the total Dutch ships were requisitioned for service.

It should be noted that this observation applies only to fighting ships and that the question of transport has not, so far, been raised.

III[1]

The French navy was essentially the work of Louis XIV. What Richelieu had achieved Mazarin had neglected; but Colbert's proverbial energy had, as part of his commercial policy and in promotion of the grander aims of Louis, multiplied tenfold, in a few years, the visible fighting ship strength of France. Viewed administratively it was a highly centralised marine which Colbert had created and which, for and on behalf of the Admiral of France, his son Colbert de Seignelay and a Council at this time controlled. In this marine all things were governed through voluminous and meticulous regulations. But if the multitude of ordinances sharply distinguished the duties of maintenance and executive, the aspects of 'la plume' and 'l'épée', as they were called in the code into which at this time they were rapidly being reduced, the orders did not achieve, for all the precision of their language, the harmonious working of the civil and executive sides which their logic set up. The *matériel* afloat in 1688 was certainly considerable. As the ports of France had been repaired and supplemented, Brest, Rochefort and Toulon becoming chief, so naval construction had grown. Some 270 fighting ships of different sorts was Colbert's estimate for 1677.[2] The vessels were organised in two squadrons; that called 'du Ponant' the western ocean-going fleet based on Brest, that called 'du Levant' the eastern Mediterranean squadron based on Toulon. A lot of the ships included in the imposing total were of the type peculiar to the calm Mediterranean waters—the galley; and there seems no reason to hold that the ships that could be used in western waters were numerically more than those of England or the Provinces taken separately. Many were, without doubt, finely designed. It is well known that the 'Superbe', which was in English waters during the Third Dutch War, had been thought worth imitation by the English designer, Sir Anthony Deane, and that his copy the 'Harwich' was a type to which many English third rates were laid down after 1677. The officering of the French fleets was dissimilar in some ways, to the English, not least in enjoining on certain officers of what would now be called 'paymaster' or 'purser' class (the servants of 'la plume' at sea) duties which must have worked out in downright espionage on the behaviour of the fighting officers. As a class the executive or military officers

[1] Authorities scattered. See latter half of note 5, p. 23 of this work. Hannay, *A Short History of the Royal Navy*, II, p. 11, gives an excellent summary.
[2] *Camb. Mod. Hist.* v, p. 14.

were drawn far too exclusively from the French 'noblesse'.
Perhaps it is permissible to say they were not essentially seamen.
In any case there were far too few of them; for there existed no
real war-time reserve. Crews to man the vessels were less easily
obtained than in England or the Provinces; and the operation
of the hateful system of the 'classes' was commonly invoked.
Even this conscriptive device failed to supply men in sufficient
numbers. For the detested rowing banks of the galley slaves
were employed; and to supplement them the judiciary of
France was called on to condemn its hundreds—Huguenots and
prisoners—to the living death of a bondage which, until the
Revolution, blotted indelibly the name of France.

The French navy was, in fine, a forced growth, in administration and in the *matériel* controlled, a brand-new, outwardly
imposing, considerable thing. So far as its ships, its officers
and men had, in the Third Dutch War, been tested outside
Mediterranean waters, they had been sadly wanting—wanting
in efficiency and, some would also say, with all due allowance
to the apologists pleading political causes, in courage also.
Yet if, under conditions of equal, or even unequal conflict, the
French navy would not be likely to inspire fear, it would scarce
be an object for quite contemptuous neglect in the calculations
of William. He might (it has been said) dismiss from mind all
thought of the possibility of an unsupported naval attack by
the ships of Louis upon his Provinces; but, even then, and no
matter whether or no his agents had made him conversant with
the circumstances preventing Louis from providing a squadron
to unite with the English fleet, he could not, on October 1st,
quite neglect the common-sense precaution of keeping a wary
eye on the port of Brest.

As events actually fell out, France took no part in the hostilities of the English Revolution of 1688; but because, on October
1st, the French navy in part constituted, at least on paper, this
potential, if unwanted, reserve to James, and a just conceivably
separate menace to the Provinces, it has been thought well to
add this concluding observation.

LIST OF AUTHORITIES

CONTEMPORARY

(A) *Manuscript.*

At British Museum:

(*a*) Additional 31958. This was edited as Memoirs relating to the Lord Torrington, by Sir J.K. Laughton, for the Camden Society, London, 1891. See note attached to this list of Authorities.

(*b*) Egerton 2621. Correspondence—Prince of Orange and Admiral Herbert, etc.

(*c*) Sloane 3560. Though this MS is entitled "Lord Dartmouth's Instructions", it contains later materials and was not compiled before 1689; its squadron lists and signal drawings are valuable.

At Public Record Office:

(*a*) Admiralty Records.

(i) Relevant portions of the very considerable and main mass of papers catalogued in 1904. See Lists and Indexes No. XVIII.

(ii) The relevant portions of papers since catalogued—Ships-books, Dockyard records.

For the year 1688, these, especially on the executive side, are disappointing. Much of the Admiralty records for Pepys's régime have found their way to the Pepysian Library at Magdalene College, Cambridge. An article, Naval Preparations of James II in 1688, by Dr J. R. Tanner, English Hist. Review, 1893, is based on, and adequately quotes, the Pepysian Library materials, at least to the place at which the Dartmouth MSS (q.v. *infra*) completely fill the gap.

(*b*) State Papers Domestic (King William's Chest) uncalendared.

At Watermen's Hall, London:

Correspondence with Admiralty. Not important.

(B) *Printed.*

Avaux, J. A. de Mesmes. Négociations du Comte d'Avaux en Hollande 1679(-88). Ed. E. Mallett. 6 vols. Paris, 1752-3. English translation. 4 vols. London, 1754.

Burchett, Josiah. Memoirs of Transactions at Sea during the War with France, 1688-1697. London, 1703. See note referred to, (A) At British Museum. (*a*), *supra*.

*Bostaquet, I. A., Dumont de. Mémoires inédits de Dumont de Bosta-
quet gentilhomme Normand, sur les temps qui ont précédé et
suivi la révocation de l'Edit de Nantes....Publiés par MM. C.
Read et F. Waddington. Paris, 1864.

*Burnet, Gilbert (Bishop of Salisbury). Bishop Burnet's History of
his Own Time. 2 vols. London, 1724. (For pagination). Edition
with notes by the Earls of Dartmouth and Hardwicke, etc. 6 vols.
(M. J. Routh.) Oxford, 1833.

Chamberlayne, Edward. Angliae Notitia. 1687 vol. London.

Clarke, J. S. Life of James II. (Memoirs of James II.) 2 vols. London,
1816.

Clément, Pierre. L'Italie en 1671: voyage du marquis de Seignelay,
lettres inédites, etc. Paris, 1867. Contains valuable despatches
from Versailles to London.

Collins, Grenville. Great Britain's Coasting Pilot. London, 1693.

Corbett, (Sir) Julian S. Fighting Instructions 1530–1816. Navy
Records Society. London, 1905.

†Dalrymple, (Sir) John. Memoirs of Great Britain and Ireland. 3
vols. Edinburgh, 1771. A valuable appendix reprints original
diplomatic papers.

Dalton, Charles. English Army Lists 1661–1714. 6 vols. London,
1892.

Dartmouth, Manuscripts of the Earl of. Historical MSS. Comm. XIth
report, appendix 5, and XVth report, appendix 1. Correspondence,
mainly despatches to and from the English fleet. These are of
primary importance. The Journal of Captain Grenville Collins.
An important and private (?) log, is included in the latter
report.

Devon, F. Vindication of the first Lord Dartmouth from the charge
of conspiracy or high treason, brought against him, 1691, and
revived by Macaulay in his History of England, 1855. London,
1856. This reprints letters of highest importance missing from
the Dartmouth MSS and now undiscoverable. See note, p. 143.

*Huygens, Konstantijn (the younger). Journaal gedurende de veld-
tochten 1673, 1676, 1677 en 1688. Utrecht, 1881. The entries for
the expedition period are useful.

†Jonge, T. C. de. Geschiedenis van het Nederlandsche Zeewesen.
3 vols. Hague and Amsterdam, 1833–4. Official materials for
this standard work badly damaged by fire at the Hague Archives.
The appendices, which reprint many documents, are particularly
valuable.

Kennet, White (Bishop of Peterborough). Compleat History of
England. London, 1706.

Lords, Manuscripts of House of, 1689–1690. Historical MSS. Comm.
XIIth report, appendix 6.

Luttrell, Narcissus. A brief historical relation of State Affairs from
September 1678 to April 1714. 6 vols. Oxford, 1857.

Markham, (Sir) C. R. Life of Captain Stephen Martin 1666–1740. Navy Records Society. London, 1895.

Müller, P. L. Wilhelm III von Oranien und Georg Friedrich von Waldeck. 2 vols. 1873. Contains letters from William on landing at Torbay.

Pepys, Samuel. (a) "Register" of Ships and Officers. In A descriptive Catalogue of the Naval Manuscripts in the Pepysian Library at Magdalene College, Cambridge. Vol. 1. Navy Records Society. London, 1903.

—— (b) Memoires relating to the State of the Royal Navy of England, for ten years determined December 1688. London, 1690.

(a) is reprinted from a considerable mass of Admiralty papers which should have found a place, with similar materials, in the P.R.O.; (b) reprints official documents. Both are valuable for administration, *matériel* and *personnel*.

*Rapin-Thoyras, Paul de. The History of England.... Translated by N. Tindal. 2 vols. London, 1732–3.

Seller, John. The English Pilot. London, 1671.

Smith, John, Captain (of Virginia). Sea-grammar..., etc. London, 1626. (1691–2 edition used.)

Teonge, Henry. The Diary of Henry Teonge, Chaplain on board his Majesty's Ships 'Assistance', 'Bristol' and 'Royal Oak', anno 1673 to 1679. London, 1825.

Whittle, John. Diary of the late Expedition..., etc. Licensed Ap. 23, 1689.

Pamphlets.

Address of thanks, for calling Parliament, from royal fleet, Dec. 1, 1688. Bodley 1688/179.

A declaration, 1688. Somers Tracts, IX, p. 269.

Admiral Herbert's letter to the English fleet. Bodley 1688/1, 2433.

Expedition of the Prince of Orange to England 1688. Signed "NN" (= Burnet). Harleian Miscellany, I, p. 449; Somers Tracts, IX, p. 276.

The Prince of Orange's appeal to the English fleet. Bodley 1688/1, 2435.

Newspapers.

Gazette. Useful for sea news.

Prints and Engravings.

Sutherland Collection, in Bodley.

SECONDARY

Blok, P. J. Prins Willem III naar Torbay. Article in Bijdragen voor Vaderlandsche Geschiedenis en Oudheidkunde. Hague, 1924.

Charnock, John. (a) Biographia Navalis. 6 vols. London, 1794.

—— (b) History of Marine Architecture. 3 vols. London, 1801–2.

Clark, G. N. The Dutch Alliance and the War against French Trade 1688–1697. Manchester, 1923.

Clowes, (Sir) W. Laird. The Royal Navy. 7 vols. London, 1897.

Corbett, (Sir) Julian S. Some Principles of Maritime Strategy. London, 1911.

Echard, Laurence. History of England. 3 vols. London, 1707.

Hallam, Henry. Constitutional History of England. 3 vols. London, 1854.

Hannay. A Short History of the Royal Navy. 2 vols. London, 1898.

Jackson, (Sir) G. Navy Commissioners. 12 Chas. II–Geo. III. Ed. Sir G. Duckett. London, 1889.

Lingard, J. History of England. 10 vols. London, 1849.

Macaulay, T. B. (Baron). History of England. 5 vols. London, 1858. Footnote quotations from original documents useful.

Mackintosh. History of the Revolution in England in 1688. London, 1834.

Maitland, William (and others). The History and Survey of London from its Foundation to the Present Time. 2 vols. 1756.

Mazure, F. A. J. Histoire de la Révolution de 1688 en Angleterre. 3 vols. Paris, 1848. Useful, with d'Avaux (q.v. *ante*), in absence of any special naval history of the period on the French side. C. de la Roncière, Histoire de la Marine Française, and G. Lacour Gayet, La Marine Militaire de la France sous les Règnes de Louis XIII et XIV, have not reached this period. L. Guérin, Histoire Maritime de France, III, does not mention the English Revolution.

Oldmixon, John. History of England during the reigns of the Royal House of Stuart. London, 1730.

Oppenheim, M. A History of the Administration of the Royal Navy 1509–1660. London, 1896.

Ralph, James. History of England during the reigns of King William, Queen Anne and King George I with an introductory review of the reigns of the Royal Brothers Charles and James, etc. 2 vols. London, 1744.

Ranke, L. von. History of England principally in the Seventeenth Century. English translation. Oxford, 1875.

Seeley, Sir J. R. The Growth of British Policy. 2 vols. Cambridge, 1895.

Tanner, J. R. (*a*) Naval Preparations of James II in 1688. Article in English Historical Review, 1893. See entry under P.R.O. (*ante*).

—— (*b*) Introduction to A descriptive Catalogue of the Naval Manuscripts in the Pepysian Library at Magdalene College, Cambridge. (Navy Records Society's Publications, vol. xxvi, 1903.)

—— (*c*) Samuel Pepys and the Royal Navy. Cambridge, 1920.

Dictionary of National Biography. Lives of sea officers (by Sir J. K. Laughton) especially useful.

Note on the relation of *Memoirs relating to the Lord Torrington* to Burchett's *Transactions at Sea.*

In 1889 the late Sir John Knox Laughton edited, for the Camden Society, the manuscript British Museum, Additional 31958, entitled *Memoirs relating to the Lord Torrington.* It must, as he says, have been a task of considerable difficulty to reduce this manuscript to order. Penmanship, spelling and grammar all are bad; interlineations, erasures and transpositions abound. The manuscript deals with part of the career of George Byng, Viscount Torrington. Its author is unknown. Laughton worked in vain at the only clue the work itself affords, which suggests that a permanent official of the Admiralty wrote the document. The present writer, who has pursued the same lines, can offer no solution. It is certain that, whoever the unknown author was, he had access to the private papers of his hero. Laughton's preface refers to the manuscript as "an unique contribution to the naval history of the period. Nowhere else is there a satisfactory account of the intrigues by which the navy was won to the cause of the Prince of Orange; and though the more purely naval relation is often overlapped by Burchett's *Transactions at Sea,* many of the details here given are interesting and novel". It is surprising that, in making such a reference to Burchett, Laughton did not remark more precisely upon what is really a close verbal dependence of large parts of the *Memoirs* upon the *Transactions.*

In 1703, Josiah Burchett published his *Memoirs of Transactions at Sea during the War with France, beginning in 1688 and ending in 1697.*

Burchett, before 1688, had had experience of the naval service and accompanied Dartmouth (not for the first time) in October of that year (*vide Transactions*, p. 12); he was Secretary to the Admiralty at the time he wrote. Eighteen crown octavo pages in all are devoted to the account of the 1688 episode—fifteen to events up to the point at which Dartmouth, in October, took command and only three to what took place after he did so. Half of those fifteen pages are direct quotations of the two Admirals' Instructions and of ship lists; also, the remarks connecting the quotations are apparently based on official data. For the last three pages Burchett's experience afloat would serve. Most of Burchett might therefore be assumed as duplicating or summarising official documents and the small remaining portions as the evidence of an eye witness. The fact that the *Memoirs* were written after the elevation of Byng to the peerage, i.e. in 1721, prove clearly that Burchett did not have the *Memoirs* before him. Of the *Memoirs,* eighteen pages in the Camden edition are taken up with the affairs of the fleet in 1688. Somewhat over a third of the narrative, practically continuous, represents the compiler's greatest debt to Burchett and nearly all Burchett's first fifteen pages are utilised to form the staple of this compiler's pre-October story. The remaining two-thirds is obviously from the privileged sources. One might go further in tracing the dependence of the writer of the *Memoirs* upon Burchett, for the debt extends beyond the 1688 story; but that enquiry, for the present purposes, would not be to the point. Without doubt, the writer of the *Memoirs* relied on the 1703 or later edition of Burchett, in places where his materials wore thin or where he sought to avoid the troubles of composition or to better the sincerest form of flattery.

The portion demonstrably dependent on Burchett, being second hand, has, of course, no special evidential value. The great worth of this work is the unique revelation of intrigue to which Laughton refers. One can only hope that, in giving so important sole evidence, the unknown author has used his privileged sources honestly. Judging from the way he has handled Burchett, one would expect to discover, should the privileged sources ever come to light, that he has employed them neither with meticulous care nor conscious dishonesty, in order to present the unvarnished tale which is now quite invaluable.

INDEX

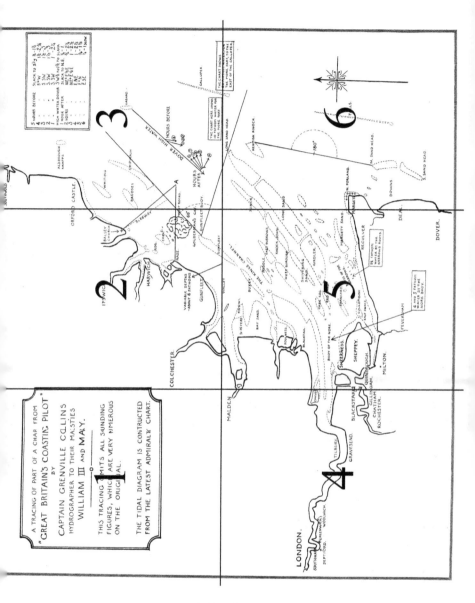

Key to following pages

A TRACING OF PART OF A CHART FROM

"GREAT BRITAIN'S COASTING PILOT

BY

CAPTAIN GRENVILLE COLLINS

HYDROGRAPHER TO THEIR MAJESTIES

WILLIAM III AND MARY.

———o———

THIS TRACING OMITS ALL SOUNDING
FIGURES, WHICH ARE VERY NUMEROUS
ON THE ORIGINAL.

THE TIDAL DIAGRAM IS CONSTRUCTED
FROM THE LATEST ADMIRALTY CHART.

1

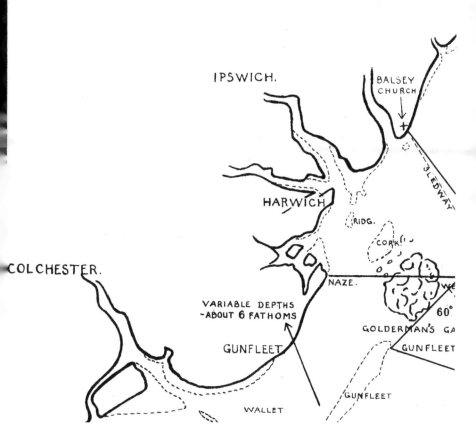

ORFOR

IPSWICH.

BALSEY
CHURCH
+

3 LEDWAY

HARWICH

RIDG.

CORK!

COLCHESTER.

NAZE.

WE

VARIABLE DEPTHS
-ABOUT 6 FATHOMS

60°

GOLDERMAN'S GA

GUNFLEET

GUNFLEET

GUNFLEET

WALLET

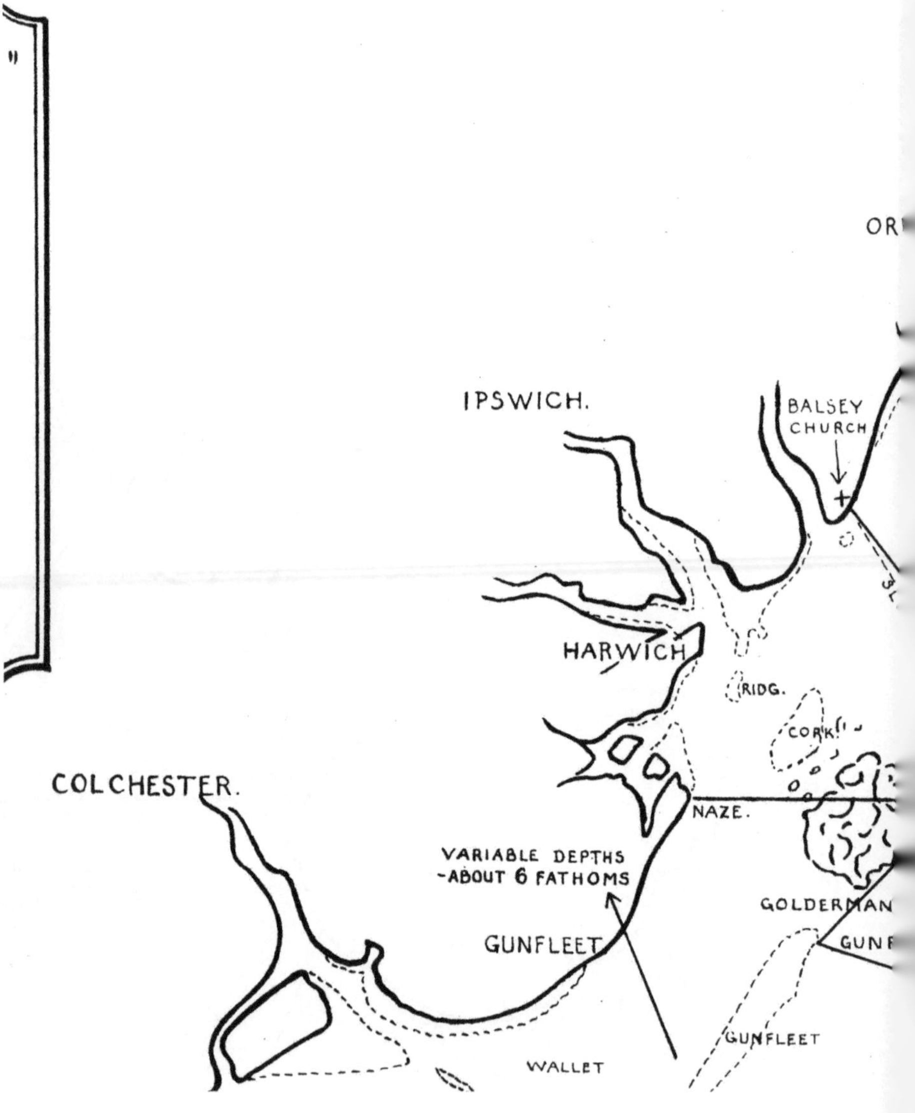

OR

IPSWICH.

BALSEY
CHURCH

HARWICH

RIDG.

CORK

COLCHESTER.

NAZE.

VARIABLE DEPTHS
-ABOUT 6 FATHOMS

GOLDERMAN

GUNFLEET

GUNF

GUNFLEET

WALLET

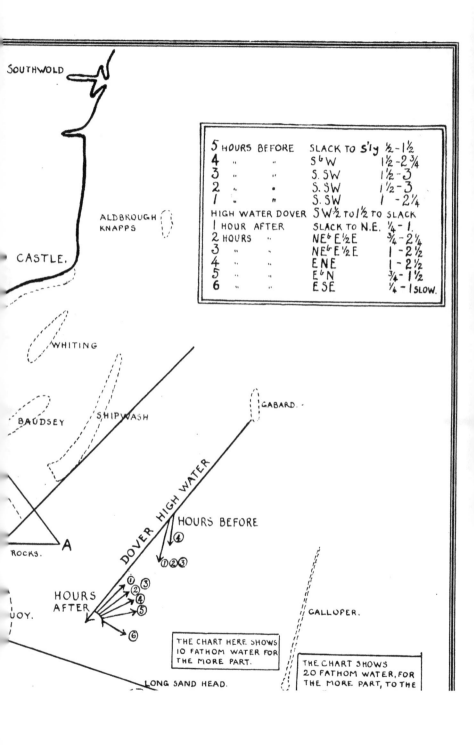

SOUTHWOLD

5 HOURS BEFORE	SLACK TO S'ly	½ - 1½
4 " "	S ᵇ W	1½ - 2¾
3 " "	S. SW	1½ - 3
2 " "	S. SW	1½ - 3
1 " "	S. SW	1 - 2¼
HIGH WATER DOVER	S W ½ to 1 ½	TO SLACK
1 HOUR AFTER	SLACK TO N.E.	¼ - 1.
2 HOURS "	NE ᵇ E ½ E	¾ - 2¼
3 " "	NE ᵇ E ½ E	1 - 2½
4 " "	E N E	1 - 2½
5 " "	E ᵇ N	¾ - 1½
6 " "	E SE	¼ - 1 SLOW.

ALDBROUGH
KNAPPS

CASTLE.

WHITING

GABARD.

BAUDSEY   SHIPWASH

DOVER HIGH WATER

HOURS BEFORE
④
①②③

ROCKS.   A

HOURS
AFTER
① ③
②
④
⑤
⑥

BUOY.

GALLOPER.

THE CHART HERE SHOWS
10 FATHOM WATER FOR
THE MORE PART.

THE CHART SHOWS
20 FATHOM WATER, FOR
THE MORE PART, TO THE

LONG SAND HEAD.

MALDE

LONDON.

SOUTHWARK

GREENWICH.

DEPTFORD.   WOOLWICH.

TILBURY.

GRAVESEND.

BLACK

CHAT
ROCHEST

4

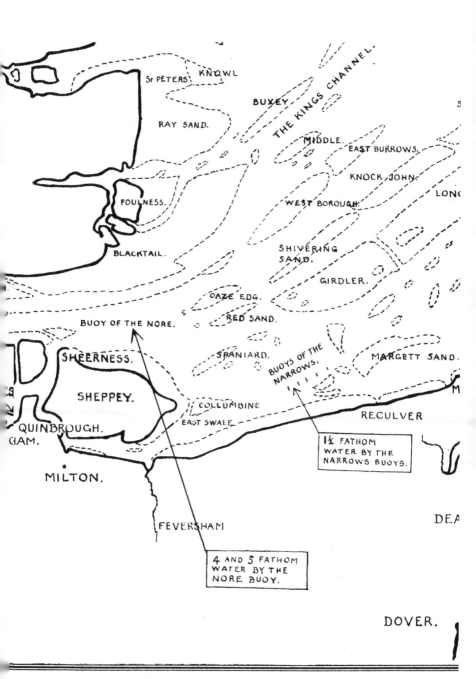

Sr PETERS

KNOWL

BUXEY

THE KINGS CHANNEL.

RAY SAND.

MIDDLE.

EAST BURROWS.

KNOCK JOHN.

WEST BOROUGH.

LONG

FOULNESS.

BLACKTAIL.

SHIVERING SAND.

GIRDLER.

OAZE EDG.

RED SAND.

BUOY OF THE NORE.

SPANIARD.

BUOYS OF THE NARROWS.

MARGETT SAND.

SHEERNESS.

M

SHEPPEY.

COLLUMBINE

RECULVER

EAST SWALE

QUINBROUGH.

GAM.

1½ FATHOM WATER BY THE NARROWS BUOYS.

MILTON.

FEVERSHAM

DEA

4 AND 5 FATHOM WATER BY THE NORE BUOY.

DOVER.

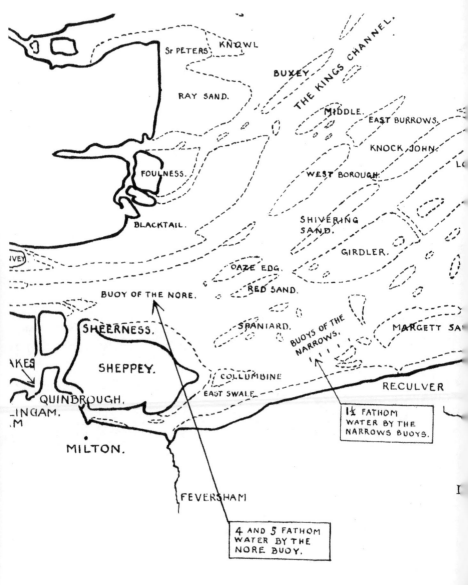

Sr PETERS KNOWL

BUXEY

THE KINGS CHANNEL.

RAY SAND.

MIDDLE.

EAST BURROWS.

KNOCK JOHN.

FOULNESS.

WEST BOROUGH.

BLACKTAIL.

SHIVERING SAND.

GIRDLER.

OAZE EDG.

RED SAND.

BUOY OF THE NORE.

SHEERNESS.

SPANIARD.

BUOYS OF THE NARROWS.

MARGETT SA

SHEPPEY.

COLLUMBINE

RECULVER

EAST SWALE

1½ FATHOM WATER BY THE NARROWS BUOYS.

QUINBROUGH.

LINGAM.

M

MILTON.

FEVERSHAM

4 AND 5 FATHOM WATER BY THE NORE BUOY.

DOVER.

EAST OF THE GALLOPER.

NCK.

KENTISH KNOCK.

SAND

180°

N. PORLAND.

RGETT

FALLS.

N. SAND HEAD.

DOWNS.

S. SAND HEAD.

For EU product safety concerns, contact us at Calle de José Abascal, 56–1°, 28003 Madrid, Spain or eugpsr@cambridge.org.

www.ingramcontent.com/pod-product-compliance
Ingram Content Group UK Ltd.
Pitfield, Milton Keynes, MK11 3LW, UK
UKHW012347130625
459647UK00009B/587